China

Higher Education Reform

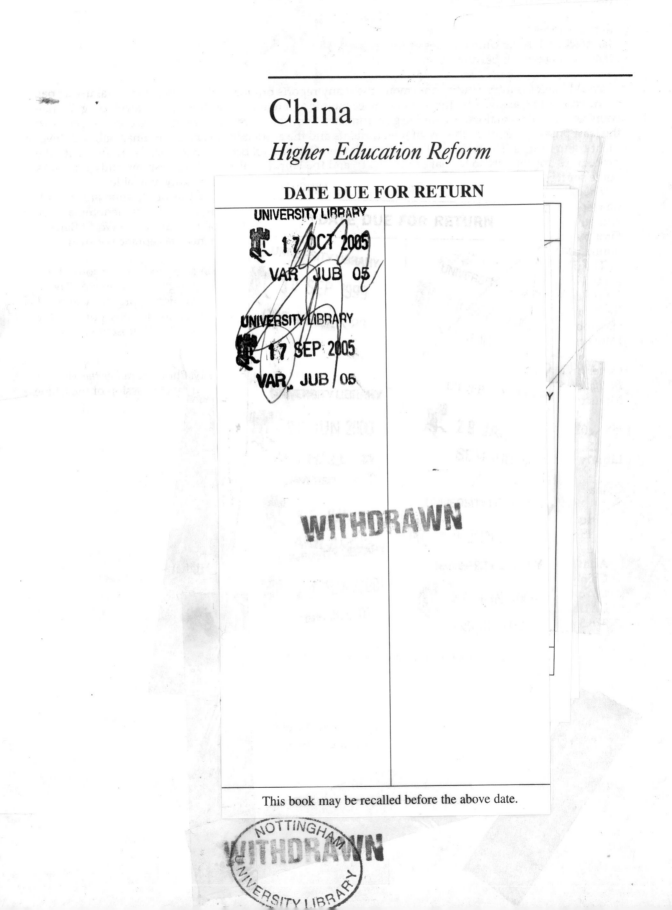

World Bank Country Studies are among the many reports originally prepared for internal use as part of the continuing analysis by the Bank of the economic and related conditions of its developing member countries and of its dialogues with the governments. Some of the reports are published in this series with the least possible delay for the use of governments and the academic, business and financial, and development communities. The typescript of this paper therefore has not been prepared in accordance with the procedures appropriate to formal printed texts, and the World Bank accepts no responsibility for errors. Some sources cited in this paper may be informal documents that are not readily available.

The World Bank does not guarantee the accuracy of the data included in this publication and accepts no responsibility whatsoever for any consequence of their use. The boundaries, colors, denominations, and other information shown on any map in this volume do not imply on the part of the World Bank Group any judgment on the legal status of any territory or the endorsement or acceptance of such boundaries.

The material in this publication is copyrighted. Requests for permission to reproduce portions of it should be sent to the Office of the Publisher at the address shown in the copyright notice above. The World Bank encourages dissemination of its work and will normally give permission promptly and, when the reproduction is for noncommercial purposes, without asking a fee. Permission to copy portions for classroom use is granted through the Copyright Clearance Center, Inc., Suite 910, 222 Rosewood Drive, Danvers, Massachusetts 01923, U.S.A.

Cover photo: Doctors' and masters' degree laureates at Tsinghau University. Photo from *For the Most Brilliant Cause Under the Sun: Education of China & the World Bank,* 1996. Used by permission of the Chinese Ministry of Finance and the Chinese State Education Commission.

ISSN: 0253-2123

Library of Congress Cataloging-in-Publication Data

China : higher education reform.
       p.   cm. — (A World Bank country study)
    Includes bibliographical references.
    ISBN 0-8213-4022-0
    1. Education, Higher—China. 2. Universities and colleges—China—
Administration. 3. Higher education and state—China. 4. Education, Higher—
China—Finance.
I. World Bank. II. Series.
LA1133.C443 1997
378.51—dc21
                                               97-30029
                                               CIP

CONTENTS

TABLES

FIGURES

FOREWORD

With one of the fastest-growing economies in the world, China continues to face many challenges as it implements reforms simultaneously in several sectors. Educating and training young Chinese to lead, manage and develop the diverse areas of growth are formidable tasks for the higher education sector. As with other sectors such as labor markets, reform efforts in education are working toward a market economy and greater decentralization.

As this Report points out, China records a range of successes. However, the reform agenda shows much still to be done. The State Education Commission (SEdC) and the Bank's task team had jointly identified the major clusters of policy and practice measures that require attention: relationships between universities and the State, changing requirements of university management, financing of higher education, and quality improvement in instructional programs. With policy directions increasing in clarity, SEdC made the request that the study avoid advice that is couched in terms of general principles: rather it should focus on specific ways in which reform could be managed or implemented. The international task team worked closely with Chinese counterparts to provide concrete responses to the request and has presented detailed activities in the four areas for the consideration of policymakers and practitioners.

In the 1993 *Guidelines for Development and Reform of China's Education System*, China has rightly pointed out that the strategic initiative in international competition in the 21st century will be gained by those whose education looks forward to the new millennium. *What* students learn will be as important as *how* they learn. The nation will require flexibly-trained graduates whose strong, broad-based education and problem-solving skills permit creative combinations of the elements of knowledge, facilitating adaptation to a constantly changing and evolving economic and social environment.

In order to sustain economic growth, a critical mass of highly-trained personnel is essential. But public expenditure on higher education confronts many constraints. Escalating costs of higher education have forced governments everywhere to seek new sources of funding while preserving academic standards and principles of equity. China's recently-introduced tuition fee system is a step toward the diversification of institutional financial resources that will require further development. In parallel to the step toward efficient use of resources, equity will have to be served in terms of increasing access to higher education for appropriately qualified young people from poor rural homes. Relative to most rapidly-growing economies in the East Asia region, China's higher education participation rates are low and the low number of graduates has serious implications for sustainable economic development. This Report is timely in drawing relevant and critical national and international data to the attention of policymakers.

China's important leadership role in the Pacific Rim countries and beyond is undisputed. National bilateral agencies and institutions, and multilateral organizations and financial institutions can contribute to that role and its attendant responsibilities through well-formulated partnership activities. This Report, therefore, is intended for policymakers and practitioners, as well as a broad range of stakeholders in the education sector, both in China and internationally. This will include academic and nongovernmental organizations as well as domestic and private sector business concerns: in short, all those who are interested in facilitating China's long-term economic and social development.

Nicholas C. Hope
Director
China and Mongolia Department
East Asia and Pacific Region

ABSTRACT

China's fast economic growth and social development have increased the demand for more highly skilled personnel and technological advancement in the country. The tasks of educating the leadership and generating and utilizing knowledge for her continuing development effort present major challenges to the nation's higher education institutions. Although many reform initiatives and improvements have been made within the system in the past decade, except for the "key" universities, the majority of higher education institutions in China still do not have the managerial, financial, academic and technical expertise to contribute to economic stabilization and long-term growth, nor to the development of an open and civic society. They are the main concern of the study presented in this report.

This report takes a historical and comparative approach to examine the higher education development in China at both systemic and institutional levels in the context of broad social and economic changes in its society. The investigation focuses on four areas: relationships between universities and the State, impact of changes on university management, financing higher education, and quality improvement in instructional programs. By reviewing literature and drawing evidence from field visits and experiences from other countries, the report provides a fair picture of strengths and weaknesses of Chinese higher education institutions in relation to their histories, current conditions, and potentials as well as recommendations for their future development.

ACKNOWLEDGMENTS

This report is based on work done by a team of World Bank staff and consultants who visited China during 1993-94. The team comprised Hena Mukherjee (Task Manager), Chung Yue Ping, John Fielden, Ruth Hayhoe, He Jin, Marjorie Lenn, Min Weifang and Kin Bing Wu. Zhang Yanhong managed the institutional data, Cao Xiaonan assisted with the updating of supporting research, and Ibrahim Dione assisted with data entry. Insightful comments from Thomas O. Eisemon, Josephine Douek-Hykin and William Saint were appreciated.

The study could not have been completed without the close cooperation of the Finance Department of the State Education Commission, Beijing, the Academic Degrees Committee of the State Council, Education Commissions at provincial and municipal levels of Anhui, Guangdong, Sichuan, and Shanghai, and the higher education institutions the team was privileged to visit. Their support is gratefully acknowledged. Thanks are also due to senior government officials and the Chinese academic community for their comments and contributions at the Report Dissemination Seminar held in Beijing in April 1995. The seminar was jointly organized by the Finance Department of the State Education Commission and the World Bank.

The earlier version was prepared by Sandra Erb and Cao Xiaonan. This report was edited by Cao Xiaonan and Shobhana Sosale. Meredith J. Dearborn worked on the desktop publication of the report. The study was carried out under the supervision of Vinay K. Bhargava and completed under the general direction of Joseph Goldberg. The Director is Nicholas C. Hope and the Lead Economist is Richard S. Newfarmer.

ABBREVIATIONS AND ACRONYMS

ADC	-	Academic Degrees Committee
ADCSC	-	Academic Degrees Committee of the State Council
CD	-	Curriculum Division
CP	-	Communist Party
GDP	-	Gross Domestic Product
GNP	-	Gross National Product
GOC	-	Government of China
HEI	-	Higher Education Institution
HEMC	-	Higher Education Management Center
MIS	-	Management Information System
MOF	-	Ministry of Finance
NAEA	-	National Academy of Education Administration
PEdC	-	Provincial Education Commission
SEdC	-	State Education Commission
SO	-	Special Office
SPC	-	State Planning Commission

CURRENCY EQUIVALENTS
(1994)

Currency Unit: Yuan (Y)

$1.00 = Y 8.62

FISCAL YEAR

January 1 - December 31

WEIGHTS AND MEASURES

Metric System

EXECUTIVE SUMMARY

The Macro Context

The economy of China is one of the fastest growing in the world, with an annual average Gross Domestic Product (GDP) growth rate of 9.8 percent in real terms between 1978 and 1994. According to the Ninth Five-Year Plan (1995-2000), the Government's target for GDP in 2000 is to quadruple that in 1980, and that for GDP in 2010 is to double that in 2000. This entails an average annual growth rate of 8 percent between 1995 and 2000, and over 7 percent between 2000 and 2010. Given the momentum of China's historical growth rate, it is realistic to expect the GDP to continue to grow at an annual average rate of 7-9 percent in real terms over the next 25 years. If the population growth rates are held down, its GDP per capita would be $600-$700 (as in 1996 constant terms) by 2000; $1,100-$1,600 by 2010; and $2,100-$3,500 by 2020, according to this study's projection. In other words, in five years' time, China would be on its way to becoming a lower-middle-income country, and in 25 years' time, it would be poised to join the league of upper-middle-income countries. To sustain these economic growth rates, the demand for well-educated personnel is likely to be high.

Chinese higher education institutions play two key roles in sustaining economic growth rates and in facilitating socially and environmentally responsible development in the country. First, they prepare citizens to fill high-level scientific, technical, professional and managerial positions in the public and private sectors. Second, in their capacities as repositories, generators, and communicators of knowledge, they underpin internal technological advancement, particularly in transforming research and development results for industrial productivity, and provide access to and adaptation of ideas from elsewhere in the world.

These tasks of educating the leadership and generating/utilizing knowledge for China's development effort present major challenges. Destroyed by the Cultural Revolution (1966-76), China's higher education system was rebuilt only in the late 1970s as one element of a strategy to modernize the country. The 1978-94 period witnessed remarkable proliferation of public regular higher education institutions from 598 to 1,080, and extension of enrollment from 0.86 million to 2.8 million full-time students in undergraduate and short-cycle courses, at an annual growth rate of 7.7 percent. Graduate enrollment rose from zero to 0.13 million. While this achievement was impressive, the proportion of the appropriate age cohort enrolled in regular higher education institutions was only 2.4 percent in 1994, barely above that in 1960. When enrollment in all adult tertiary institutions is considered, it amounts to just over 4 percent of gross enrollment in higher education. This ratio is low in comparison not only with other fast-growing East Asian countries [for example, 10 percent in Indonesia, 19 percent in Thailand, 20 percent in Hong Kong, 39 percent in Taiwan (China), and 51 percent in Republic of Korea], but also with India, which had a per capita GNP of $300 in 1993, lower than China's $490, and yet had an enrollment rate of 8 percent in higher education.

According to the UNESCO Statistical Yearbook (1995), only about 2 percent of the Chinese population over the age of 25 have had postsecondary education, compared to 11 percent in Hong Kong, 14 percent in Republic of Korea, 21 percent in Japan, 14 percent in the former USSR, and 45 percent in the United States.) The US National Science Foundation estimated that in 1990, only 5.6 scientists and engineers engaged in research and development per 10,000 persons in the work force in China, compared to 30 in Singapore, 38 in Taiwan (China), 37 in Republic of Korea, 75 in Japan, and 75 in the United States. Emerging evidence of growing economic returns to higher education and increased wage inequality in Hong Kong, Taiwan (China), Malaysia, Indonesia, and Chile indicates that fast-growing economies can face skill scarcity if supply of well-educated people is unable to keep pace with demand. Given China's small stock of highly educated people, skill scarcity would reduce China's attractiveness to foreign investment, particularly in the medium-to-high technology areas, limit the options for industrial upgrading, undermine the institutional capacity in all sectors, and exacerbate income inequality in a more liberalized labor market.)

The Chinese government invested heavily in universities and research laboratories prior to 1980. Significant technological achievements have been made by the sector, but transforming research and development results into increased productivity has been limited. In 1991, only 6.2 percent of domestic technology trade originated in universities and colleges (World Bank, 1995g). (As world trade expands, China will face increasingly competitive pressure from lower-wage economies (such as Vietnam and Bangladesh). The increasing integration of the world economy and the global acceleration of technological change would make the reliance on low-skilled labor-intensive production a nonviable option for future development.)For China to speed up its development and to raise her living standards in the 21st century, it is imperative that the manufacturing of medium-skilled products be mastered and a move toward production of high-technology goods and services be fostered.)

Since 1978, the Chinese Government has placed priority within the education sector upon rapid expansion and improvement of higher education to help reduce the serious human resource constraints on the country's economic and social development. In 1985, the Government adopted the document *Decision on Education Reform*, which aimed at providing the mix of skills of a rapidly changing society; to improve efficiency, quality and equity; and releasing resources required to develop and enhance education at lower levels. More recently, in order to speed up nationwide transformation from a planned economy to a market economy, the Government in its *Guidelines of China's Educational Reform and Development* (GOC, February 1993) advocates changes at two levels: chiefly, governmental policy and institutional practice. The major strategic approach is that of decentralization in institutional management and administration while maintaining managerial oversight at the macro level. Devolution of power and responsibilities to institutions has brought new challenges to the higher education sector. **The purpose of this report is to review China's higher education reform efforts over the last 10 years in relation to goals delineated in the 1985 document, with the objective of providing advice for continuation of reforms over the next 25 years.**

The Higher Education System

The Chinese higher education system is dominated by 1,080 regular public universities and colleges that are under the jurisdiction of and obtain their funding from one of three administrative authorities: (a) State Education Commission (SEdC) in the central government, (b) central ministries, and (c) provinces and municipalities. In 1994, there were 1,080 such institutions. The distribution of their enrollment was: 11 percent in 36 national key universities funded by SEdC, 34 percent in 331 ministry-funded institutions, and 55 percent in 713 provincial and municipal institutions. Of the total student body in these public institutions, 52 percent enrolled in degree-earning undergraduate studies, 44 percent in short-cycle, nondegree programs, and 4 percent in postgraduate studies. These institutions employed 1.04 million staff, of whom 38 percent had teaching responsibilities, 44 percent were administrative and support staff, and 18 percent were employed in organizations affiliated with universities (such as factories, enterprises, and research institutes). Of the total staff, only 2 percent held a doctorate degree, 19 percent with a master's degree, 49 percent with a bachelor's degree, and 30 percent with short-cycle diplomas or without a degree but finished degree course work. How to expand the capacity of these regular public institutions, in quantitative and qualitative terms, is the focus of this study.

There are, in addition, 1,172 public adult education institutions at postsecondary levels, including radio and television universities, schools for workers, peasants, and cadres, pedagogical colleges, independent correspondence colleges, and correspondence or evening courses run by regular higher education institutions. In 1994, these institutions enrolled 2.35 million students on a part-time basis and employed 0.21 million full-time staff (of which 45 percent were teachers) and 0.03 million part-time teachers. About 90 percent of enrollees were in short-cycle programs, and only 10 percent in regular undergraduate studies. Although these adult education institutions are not the focus of this study, they are taken into consideration in some of the recommendations for improving cost-effectiveness, quality and equity of the higher education system in this report.

Furthermore, over 800 private postsecondary institutions have been in operation (enrolling about 1 to 5 percent students in addition to those in the regular public institutions). However, only 16 of these institutions have been accredited by the government. Since no official data have been collected systematically on them, these private institutions are beyond the scope of this study, but the recommendations in this report take their potential contribution into account.

Since 1981, eight Bank projects totaling $910.4 million have been undertaken in China in such fields as science and engineering, economics and finance, agriculture, medicine and education in support of the government's aim to increase the quantity and quality of high-level skilled manpower. The Bank's first sector report (1986) looked at key issues in management and financing of higher education, which became significant components in subsequent projects. The overall impact of the higher education projects has been on enrollment expansion, improved quality of instruction, strengthened research capacity, improved management and curricular reform. Important lessons were learned from these projects with respect to faculty and curriculum development, as well as managing and developing university-based research. Beginning with the prestigious key universities, assistance was spread to provincial normal (teacher training) universities, universities under line ministries—agriculture and forestry, public health—and short-cycle vocational universities. A significant tier that has not been included in any of the projects is a range of nonspecialized universities under provincial jurisdictions, which are the main concern of this study.

Challenges Confronting Institutions

The fundamental challenge of current economic and educational reform is to orient institutions to a more open labor market as well as to a more open society. Regular higher education institutions were established with the aim of meeting the skill requirements of a centrally planned economy and funded according to State planning. The operating environment in the recent past and the next two decades might be characterized in the following way: from a command economy to a socialist market economy; from the practice of job assignments and lifelong employment in one institution to increasing choice and mobility of the labor market responsive to changes in skill requirements; from a system that derives all directives for policy and action from the center to a more managerially and financially decentralized one, characterized by increasing autonomy; from a situation that isolates the subsector to one that sees higher education as fundamentally linked with government, business, and the local community, and with national and international institutions. Overall, the entire system in the country might shift from an input- and supply-driven model to an output- and demand-driven one, effecting wide-ranging changes in management, faculty, students, and academic programs.

The key issues confronting institutions are: (a) lack of clarity regarding respective roles and powers of SEdC, central ministries, and provincial and municipal governments; (b) ineffective management and administrative structures and processes; (c) inefficiency in the use of scarce resources for qualitative improvement and quantitative expansion; (d) inappropriate resource allocation system for improving operational efficiency and institutional quality; (e) difficulties relating to a balance between market-oriented programs of study and basic disciplines; and (f) uneven distribution of managerial, financial, academic, and technical capabilities and capacities among regions, provinces and institutions.

In the context of this operating environment and these challenges, the report's recommendations are organized around four core themes crucial to reform goals: (a) the changing role of government in relation to higher education institutions; (b) the implications of reforms for institutional management; (c) the diversification of structure and sources of financial support and its utilization; and (d) quality improvement in higher education with particular emphasis on staffing and curricular issues. Identification of core themes and subthemes of the report was guided by SEdC's verification of the issues posed by the reform goals to the system as a whole, to institutions in particular, and to their prioritized problem areas.

Recommendations

Education is a key element of China's strategic initiative to reach international competitive standards in economic and social terms by the 21st century. In order to achieve this goal, this report recommends that the following overarching *principles* be observed and reinforced in the implementation of reforms:

(a)   the role of the State be clearly that of policy and standard-setting, monitoring and regulating;

(b)   the State creates an "enabling environment" in which institutions can have greater financial and managerial autonomy; and

(c)   the State provides leadership for increasing institutional capability to handle such autonomy by establishing a national body to give advice to individual universities and provinces or municipalities.

This report finds an uneven picture of the impact of reforms on higher education institutions across the country. Except for those institutions that are well-funded by the government, have a well-developed tradition of scholarship and research, and are located in or close to areas of socioeconomic change, the majority of higher education institutions do not have the managerial, financial, academic and technical expertise to contribute to economic stabilization and long-term growth nor to the development of an open and civic society. These disparities may in themselves become the seeds of destabilization. To meet the developmental needs of the higher education system and to address its internal disparities, this report *recommends* that:

(a)   the role of the State be defined unambiguously vis-à-vis universities within the framework of the new Higher Education Law, which should provide definitions of the respective roles, responsibilities and powers of the national, provincial and municipal authorities and the universities themselves;

(b)   effective funding and policy-making bodies be established with defined functions within post-reform structures; the principle of autonomy be strengthened in the devolution of new managerial, administrative and academic responsibilities and powers to institutions;

(c)   universities be empowered through training and exposure, nationally and internationally, to prepare and implement their own strategies for development and to strengthen their managerial capacity. A National Higher Education Management Center should be established to assist individual institutions, provinces and municipalities;

(d)   a sound information base be established by designating an agency to be responsible for collection, processing and publishing data that emphasize indicators of performance and achievement;

(e)   nongovernmental or private institutions be encouraged and accreditation procedures and support facilities be expedited to maintain national standards;

(f)   critical assistance be provided to provincial institutions in poor areas that are resource-starved and have little access to professional and technological support;

(g)   funding methodologies for both recurrent and capital funding be reviewed so as to reward efficiency and encourage expansion at below cost;

(h)   policies and programs be developed that encourage universities to generate further income from the provision of short-term training, professionally-managed enterprises and donations or endowments from all sources;

(i)   policies of cost sharing through tuition fees be continued and student loan schemes (initiated by financial capital from government sources) along with other financial assistance programs be put in place to protect poor, minority and female students;

(j)   funding policies for research and training be refined in order to rectify the balance among institutions, among discipline areas, while observing gender and ethnic priorities;

(k)   financial and nonfinancial incentives be established and clearly spelled out in order to move institutional practices such as better research and publication outputs toward qualitative goals;

(l)   accreditation procedures and structures be extended and accelerated, accompanied by training using both local and international expertise, spearheaded at provincial level by the establishment of "quality centers" whose sole task would be to institutionalize accreditation procedures, working with national and provincial bodies; and

(m)   "centers of excellence" be established serving provinces or regions, building on institutional excellence in specified cognate areas. Their function would be to provide and coordinate degree-level and nondegree training for ongoing professional development of faculty; and to stimulate and coordinate research and publication activities.

This report suggests five approaches that may assist the government in its gradualist and selective path of reform in the subsector. First, there should be wide participation in the planning of change to win support and to provide legitimacy. Second, the outcomes of participatory planning should become visible as concrete and realizable targets for action. The development of appropriate monitoring indicators should be included in the exercise. Third, the government needs to orchestrate efficient information flows without which planning becomes a futile exercise. Fourth, while national standards are set by the center, specific provincial and institutional targets should vary according to capacity and capability. National standard setting does not imply uniformity. Finally, reform targets should be based on carefully focused reward and incentive mechanisms that will induce institutions to move toward local and national goals.

Relationships Between Universities and the State

Context

Since the early 1980s the government has been gradually moving away from a centralist model in which it controlled the detailed operations of higher education institutions. This was originally applied by central control of five key functions: provision of core funding, setting student enrollments for each institution, approving senior staff appointments, authorizing all new academic programs and managing the student assignment process. As the numbers of institutions and students grew, it became increasingly difficult for State bodies to exercise this control in a way that was compatible with the needs of the rapidly growing socialist market economy. As a result, the government began consultations on the legal framework that will designate universities as independent legal entities and establish the mechanism on which the university's managerial autonomy will rest. The legal framework will allow universities to set their own strategic goals, define their own academic focuses ("specialties") in order to respond to local and provincial needs, and control their resources.

Although the State will still continue to provide core funding, it recognizes that it can no longer provide all the funds itself. As a result, it has set up the China Education and Scientific Trust Investment Corporation, which acts as a commercial banker specializing in the education sector. It provides short-term loans to institutions, secured on their assets, for their buildings and equipment. It has been unclear, however, whether poorer institutions will have the necessary collateral to access such financing. Some initial steps have been taken to encourage the development of nongovernment (or "minban") institutions of higher education. The minban universities usually use staff from nearby State-financed universities. Although it is clear that there are significant economies of scale and relatively few risks of poor-quality teaching in the early stages, the advantages could disappear as the nongovernment sector grows, requiring quality-control procedures to be set up by government. National accreditation activities which could expedite these procedures are moving slowly.

Issues

The gradualist approach to introducing change is pragmatic and careful, but involves a judgment by a central authority as to whether a level of management is considered "ready" to acquire new responsibilities. As a result, there is sometimes resentment among some universities at the slowness with which freedoms are accorded or power delegated. Another predictable consequence of the pragmatic, selective introduction of new freedoms is that because of the variation within the system, different decisions about provinces by SEdC and about universities' capabilities by provinces are resulting in a sometimes confused, uneven picture.

A direct consequence of the change in the national funding flows appears to be an increase in the influence of the provincial governments in higher education compared to SEdC. It is still a fluid situation that also varies according to the wealth of the province and the importance it places on higher education. Moreover, economic pressures are threatening to distort the balance of courses offered. Universities are finding it increasingly hard to maintain some core academic disciplines for which students do not enroll. The number applying for the basic sciences and humanities subjects are far below what is considered efficient for comprehensive universities.

China is in the midst of moving from a "state-control model" to a "state-supervising model" (in current terms from "macrocontrol" to "macromanagement") as regards the relationship between universities and government. There are difficult questions to answer about the respective roles and powers of SEdC, central ministries and provincial/ municipal governments. What could be the split of powers and control that would still allow the State to fulfill its "macromanagement" function and yet at the same time unleash the latent energy and enthusiasm within institutions?

Recommendations

A program of action has been suggested as a possible response to the above issues. In order to achieve the program's objectives, the capacity of the center needs to be greatly enhanced. The operative principles underlying the proposed program are: (a) that the role of the State should be to monitor and regulate, rather than exercise detailed control; (b) that the State should create an "enabling environment" in which universities can plan their own destiny within State-set policy frameworks or efficiency targets; and (c) that universities should be encouraged to develop individual strategic plans showing how they aim to serve their specific province or community.

Impact of Changes on University Management

Context

Universities are presently operating in a policy environment in which the management role of university presidents should be strengthened. However, there is continuing evidence that presidents are still subject to the direction of the Party Secretary although university presidents do appear to maintain academic autonomy. Moreover, many universities have established Boards of Trustees in order to develop links with society and local enterprises. The roles of these Boards vary tremendously. Some Boards provide contacts with a wide range of commercial enterprises and their funds, some stress involvement of provincial or municipal government officials in university activities while others are actively involved in the actual internal management of the institutions. University organizations' structures are changing but most new structures seem to be very flat with a relatively large number of people reporting directly to the president.

Issues

As Boards of Trustees and Councils become a more integral part of the university, there will be a need to define precisely the respective roles of SEdC, the Governing Council/Board of Trustees and the President. Many presidents are also experiencing a conflict between their roles as manager/fund-raiser and academic leader. Senior academic staff have not been trained to take on management tasks and they have had difficulty reconciling the two disparate functions.

The management of university enterprises is assuming growing importance as financial pressures increase and enterprises are seen as one of the principal sources of additional finance. This raises two management issues: (a) whether they can continue to serve dual academic and financial objectives given the basic conflict between using a company as a research test bed and teaching forum and using it to generate profits; and (b) whether it is right that teachers who are appointed on essentially academic criteria should be expected to manage industrial holding companies in an increasingly competitive environment.

One main task of university presidents is to improve institutional efficiency. However, presidents feel constrained in their freedom to make major changes in the staff structure of their universities. They do not have the power to dismiss unproductive or ineffectual teachers. As long as society expects them to provide a total package of care for their employees, regardless of the level of the individual's contribution to the university, the universities will not become fully efficient.

University presidents are also unable to obtain adequate information support. The present management information systems (MIS) are unable to meet the needs and demands for appropriate information in relation to decision-making. There is a massive task of training ahead in all aspects of designing and implementing integrated management information systems.

Recommendations: Government Actions

A professionally enhanced center can assist in strengthening the internal management of institutions by the following government actions: (a) including guidance about the role and composition of the university Governing Body or Council in its legal framework; (b) clarifying the position of universities with regard to their tax free status; (c) modifying its encouragement of the expansion of university enterprises so as to make clear the options for managing or holding investments in them; (d) encouraging universities to prepare strategic plans that are linked to the annual funding process; and (e) encouraging universities to collaborate in the costs of developing computerized management information systems.

Recommendations: Universities

For their part, universities need to: (a) develop strategic plans of action that assess their options in the context of their history, academic strengths and potential local and regional markets; (b) develop action plans for improving management efficiency as an important element of strategic plans; (c) request university councils to review current practices of managing their enterprises; and (d) formulate a strategy for computerizing their administrative systems.

Financing Higher Education: Diversification of Resources

Context

Since China embarked on economic reform in 1978, the GDP has grown by an impressive 9.8 percent per year in real terms, from Y 1,006 billion to Y 4,501 billion in 1994 (in constant 1994 prices). However, the growth rate of government revenue fell far behind that of GDP, increasing at an annual average of only 2.6 percent over the period. This resulted from decentralization and from permitting production units to retain much of their earnings without simultaneously putting in place a national tax administration until 1994. The revenue-to-GDP ratio declined from 34 percent in 1978 to 13 percent in 1994. Government expenditures, nevertheless, increased at 3.3 percent per year and were higher than its revenue, resulting in budget deficit in all but one year. Between 1987 and 1993, the public sector deficit hovered around 11-12 percent of GDP and was a key factor underlying inflationary pressures in the economy. In 1994, the public sector deficit declined to 9.9 percent.

Public expenditure on education increased from Y 21 to 98 billion (in constant 1994 prices), by an annual average of 10 percent between 1978 and 1994, far exceeding the respective growth rates of the total government revenue and expenditure. As the overall public spending shrank over the years, public expenditure on education as a percentage of total government expenditure rose from 6.2 percent in 1978 to 17 percent in 1994. However, public expenditure on education as a percentage of GDP rose from 2.1 percent in 1978 to the height of 3.1 percent in 1989, and then fell back to 2.2 percent in 1994. This level of public spending on education is low in comparison with least-developed countries' average of 2.8 percent, developing countries' average of 4.1 percent, and developed countries' average of 5.3 percent.

Total public allocation to higher education grew from Y 4.2 to 18.6 billion (in constant 1994 prices), by an annual average of 9.7 percent between 1978 and 1994. Public spending on higher education increased from 20 percent of total public expenditure on education in 1978 to the peak of 29 percent in 1984, then declined to around 17 percent between 1989 and 1992, and climbed back to 19 percent in 1994. Since under 2 percent of the age cohort were enrolled in higher education in much of the 1980s, the high share of public spending devoted to them reflected the effort to rebuild the higher education system.

At the same time, given the very low enrollment ratio in China, public spending on higher education was high by international comparison. For example, Indonesia, Malaysia, Thailand, Taiwan (China), Republic of Korea, and Japan, which had a much higher enrollment ratio in higher education, spent only 11 to 17 percent of their respective total public education expenditure on higher education, and mobilized the rest of the resources from private resources; the rest of their public expenditure was spent on lower levels of education. In 1980, China spent 27 percent of its public education expenditure on the primary level, 34 percent on the secondary level, 0.5 percent on preprimary education, and 18 percent on others. By 1993, the share of primary education went up to 34 percent and that of secondary education to 38 percent, while preprimary and other types of education claimed 1.3 and 9 percent, respectively. Since the lower levels of education are where the poor have access to, whereas middle- and upper-class students tend to be overrepresented in universities, allocating more public resources to lower levels of education is more equitable. In China, in 1990, public spending per-student in higher education was 193 percent of GDP per capita, that in secondary education was 15 percent, and that in primary education was 5 percent. In 1994, this was 175 percent. While improvement has been made, this percentage is still considerably higher than the 1990 average of 98 percent in East Asian countries. The relatively low per-student spending at the tertiary level in East Asia was made possible by the relatively large enrollment in higher education and efficient use of resources, resulting in reduced unit cost.

The public allocation per student in real terms peaked in 1984, and then went on a decline with year-on-year fluctuations. The increasing share of university-generated income and student fees made up for the shortfall. In 1994, the total allocation per student amounted to Y 8,168 of which Y 6,645 were public allocation and Y 1,515 were allocated from university-generated resources. In other words, in spite of rapid enrollment expansion, the total public and institutional allocation per student maintained the average unit allocation at a relatively stable level for higher education.

Issues

The central government and line ministries have delegated financial responsibilities to provincial governments for higher education. However, the financial capacity varies from province to province. Regional disparities in funding of higher education have serious implications for the ability of poorer provinces to attract and retain capable faculty members and to provide quality education. Even within a province, disparity is evident in the resources available for provincial universities and national universities.

In conjunction with financial decentralization, the nonfungible line-item budget was replaced with a block grant allocation from the State to the university. In addition, the incremental approach to allocating recurrent funds was replaced with a formula approach, with the major allocation parameter being the number of full-time equivalent students enrolled. Although this has improved the transparency in resource allocation, it does not provide incentives to improve efficiency or quality. This is due in large part to the fact that the national norms for allocating public funds are extremely generous.

The reforms have also given higher education institutions more autonomy to generate their own revenues. In 1992, public allocation accounted for 81.8 percent of total revenue in public higher education institutions, income generated by universities themselves for the rest. The main independent sources of income (1992 figures) are from: (a) university enterprises that provide approximately 3.7 percent of higher education revenue. However, not all institutions have the relevant management expertise and not all investments produce positive returns; (b) commissioned training for enterprises that constitutes the second largest (2.3 percent) independent share of revenue. Commissioned training has potential to generate further income; but the potential for rural universities may be limited; (c) income from other educational services was 1.1 percent; (d) research and consultancy that accounts for approximately 1.3 percent. This also has limited potential for provincial colleges and teacher colleges , where the research budget is very small and research and consultancy is limited; (e) income from logistic services (dining halls, etc.) was 0.7 percent; (f) income from other funded activities was 3.7 percent; (g) donations that contribute 0.8 percent of income. Once again, small provincial universities in the interior are rarely the recipients of donations, which heightens the disparity between national universities and the others; and (h) student tuition fees contribute 4.6 percent. The total amounts to 18.2 percent of universities' funding for 1992.

The former student stipends system, which distributed funds equally to all students, was changed into a new system of merit scholarship and loans for needy students in 1988. Currently, these scholarships cover between 50 and 80 percent of students. The sums awarded are very small, ranging from Y 60 to 300 per year, which was equivalent to 1.2 to 6.1 percent of state allocation per student in 1992, and was hardly adequate support.

The report's analysis of the reforms for diversifying sources of funding and changing patterns of expenditure has found that part of the financial difficulties experienced by institutions stems from disparities in their natural endowment and location, part is due to the funding mechanism that does not provide incentives for efficiency improvement, and part stems from the welfare burden that the socialist system requires institutions to bear. Since most provincial universities are much more disadvantaged than national universities (and yet enroll over 50 percent of students), their financial plight has serious implications for the higher education system as a whole. Changing the funding mechanisms may improve efficiency and reduce some disparity in natural endowment, but systemic change is required to reduce the welfare burden.

Recommendations

To enable higher education institutions to expand enrollment under conditions of public resource constraints, three policies need to be pursued simultaneously. First, the **operating efficiency of the system needs to be improved** by: (a) containing staff growth; (b) encouraging the growth of existing public institutions in size through expansion or merger, and the expansion of private universities; (c) devising funding mechanisms that encourage efficiency and reward cost-effective provision; (d) reviewing the norms and space formulae for allocating capital funding; (e) allowing for flexible duration of study as long as course requirements are fulfilled; and (f) making better use of educational technology to reduce cost and assure minimum quality. Second, institutions can **enhance their capacity for resource generation** by: (a) conducting short-term training for industries, governmental agencies, and communities using new technology in management/administration; (b) increasing income from research development-related research, and consulting activities; (c) ensuring that university enterprises are managed professionally; and (d) effectively mobilizing donations from enterprises, Chinese citizens and overseas Chinese. Third, **cost-recovery policies** should be continued and monitored, complemented by strong provision of a **financial assistance** system.

Quality Improvement in Instructional Programs

Context

Striking changes have taken place during the 1980s in China's higher education curriculum with adjustments in enrollment that reflect both personal needs and rising social demand, relaxation of central control over content, movement toward more broad-based structures of knowledge and experimentation with course organization and delivery methods. Moreover, university based research has been recognized as a necessary foundation for curriculum development in new fields, good graduate study and teacher preparation in all subject areas. These changes have put considerable demands on the faculty in Chinese universities. The demands are different by field, region and level of institution. However, the most important differences exist between faculty in terms of their geographical location, in the center of economic growth or at the periphery, and of the level of their institutions, i.e., at the national, provincial or local level of institution.

There have been solid achievements in faculty development since 1980. During the 1980s, the promotion processes changed from being based on age and seniority to evaluation of teaching quality and research. Significant investment has been made in training, both domestic and overseas. China recognizes the long-term benefits contributed by overseas research and study experience to updating and revitalizing the higher education curriculum; and to research and publication advances in many specialist areas. Current policies to improve the quality of teachers are aimed at raising the formal qualifications of faculty under 40 to graduate level and new promotion requirements are based on these qualifications. Considerable efforts have also been made to attract and retain young teachers within the system.

China also began a step toward quality assurance in 1985. Common to all quality assurance practices are: (a) the development of standards; (b) the application of those standards to a program or institution by third parties for the purposes of assessment and enhancement; and (c) the subsequent improvement of the education entity. However, accrediting activities in Chinese higher education are still very modest.

Issues

In the curricular change process over the decade, universities and their faculty have had increasing freedom to shape their own programs. As institutions take on greater managerial, professional and academic responsibilities, they are called upon to make decisions for which they have little training and experience. An appropriate balance needs to be found between (a) consideration of maintaining academic standards and the constant upgrading of the knowledge content; (b) concerns about the macroregulation of emphasis on various fields in relation to national needs; and (c) concerns about providing a foundation of knowledge and nurturing a professional attitude, which fosters abilities for an ongoing self-development process that goes beyond immediate market demands.

Despite the fact that absolute levels of research have increased, more appropriate balance is required (a) between institutes; (b) between discipline areas; and (c) between basic and applied research. Research findings need to be fed into curriculum, faculty development, and industrial innovations. Increasing investment in higher education and national research and development has become an important element in economic growth strategies. Recent studies indicate that the social rate of return from investments in new industrial technology in developed countries seems to be high. Technological change in many industries and increased output of society have been based on recent academic research.

The key to curricular change is the people who make it happen—the teachers. While changes have taken place in the character and definition of instructional programs and is making them more flexible, broad-based and overtly market-oriented in terms of content/knowledge, there has been less change in teaching methods and fundamental pedagogical approaches. This opens up questions of effective change. There is great variation across provinces and their institutions according to available human, financial and material resources. Priority policies for institutions, particularly those in the interior provinces, would include the creation and implementation of favorable working conditions; insisting on high academic qualifications; investing in inservice graduate study; and implementation of national policies on better living conditions.

Recommendations

While priorities in quality improvement would depend on each institution's unique needs and be expressed in its strategic plan, the recommendations in this section focus on four key aspects in the quality improvement strategy: curriculum, teaching and research, quality assurance, and educational inputs and facilities. In order to maintain systemic and institutional quality in both government and nongovernment institutions, a nationwide system of accreditation should be supported, building on achievements made in this area and strengthening existing training providers. It will entail the setting up of a National Steering Committee and Secretariat; identification, training and organization of accreditation bodies; and establishment of staff development and support mechanisms in the form of "quality assurance centers" and "centers of excellence."

1. THE REFORM AGENDA

Introduction

Since 1978, the Chinese Government has placed priority within the education sector upon rapid expansion and improvement of higher education to help reduce the serious human resource constraints on the country's economic and social development. In 1985, the Government adopted the document *Decision on Education Reform* that, inter alia, aimed at providing the mix of skills of a rapidly changing society; to improve efficiency, quality and equity; and to release resources required to develop and enhance education at lower levels.

In order to speed up nationwide transformation from a planned economy to a market economy, the State Council and the Communist Party jointly issued the *Guidelines for Development and the Reform of China's Education System* in February 1993 to outline the strategy for further reform of the Chinese higher education system. The document identified higher education as being linked to China's competitive position in the world: "Whoever receives education that is oriented toward the 21st century will gain the strategic initiative in international competition during the 21st century." The document called for reforms to (a) provide the required specialists for China's modernization and for establishment of a socialist market economy; (b) improve the social status, work and living conditions of teachers; and (c) build up 100 key universities and establish several key courses of study. To attain these goals, among the reform measures introduced are decentralization with educational institutions gaining more autonomy; restructuring the system of college enrollment and job placement for graduates, diversifying channels of funding; and improving the quality of the subsector.

Within this context of reform and the sectoral priorities of efficiency and quality, this report examines the implementation of reform goals in terms of four core themes: (a) changing role of government in relation to higher education institutions; (b) implications of reforms for institutional management; (c) diversification of structure and sources of financial support and its utilization; and (d) quality improvement in higher education with particular emphasis on staffing and curricular issues. Identification of core themes and subthemes of the report were guided by the State Education Commission's (SEdC's) identification of the challenges posed by the reform goals to the system as a whole, to institutions in particular, and by the Commission's prioritization of problem areas to be examined. This chapter reviews the implementation of reforms to date, and assesses progress by examining a number of system indicators.

Higher Education and Economic Reform

Background

China's present higher education system was created in the early 1950s with the goal of training high-level personnel according to perceived manpower needs of the central plan. Between 1949 and 1959, higher education expanded sixfold in order to meet the skill requirements for industrialization, agricultural modernization, and political mobilization. During the Cultural Revolution (1966-76), enrollment was reduced to below the 1949 level, examinations were abolished, and admission and graduation were based on political criteria. In short, teaching and research came to a halt. After the fall of the radicals in 1976, economic reform was initiated in 1978. The thrust of the reform devolved decision-making authority to lower levels of government, replaced the collective system with individual responsibility in agriculture, allowed the provinces and state-owned enterprises to retain much of their earnings for their own development, recognized the role of private enterprises in economic development, opened China to foreign investment, and encouraged foreign trade. These policies resulted in rapid growth of the Gross Domestic Product (GDP) at an annual average of 9.8 percent between 1978 and 1994 in real terms, making the Chinese economy one of the fastest growing in the world.

Higher education was rebuilt as a key element to modernize the country. The national university entrance examination was reinstituted in 1979 to establish a merit-based system, and enrollment was expanded. Faculty members were supported to upgrade their skills and academic qualifications through domestic or overseas training. In 1991, 17 out of 36 presidents of national key universities had overseas study experience (Cao, 1996). Overseas training in general increased from 860 students going abroad in 1978 to 19,000 in 1994 (China Statistics Bureau, 1995), except that after 1985 overseas study was for short-term stints. Its long-term benefits continue as evidenced by the contribution of academic links and exchanges to curriculum revitalization, research, and publication. These reforms gradually rehabilitated the higher education system. The turbulent history of Chinese higher education development is reflected in the enrollment trends (Figure 1.1). Annex 1 provides brief historical information on the subsector.

FIGURE 1.1: ENROLLMENT IN REGULAR HIGHER EDUCATION INSTITUTIONS, 1952-94

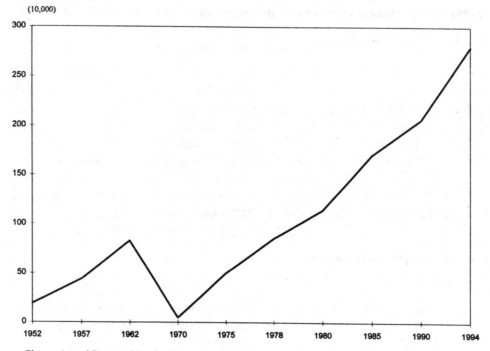

Source: China: Annual Statistical Yearbooks.

The First Wave of Higher Education Reform

In order to speed up the transformation from a planned economy to a socialist market economy, the Government published the document *Decision on Education Reform* (CPC, 1985), which aimed at reforming the higher education system in order to provide the appropriate mix of skills to meet the developmental needs of the changing society. The reform emphasized the implementation of a three-level management system—at the central, provincial, and major municipal levels. It gave universities new powers, particularly with regard to content and methods of teaching, as well as freedom to admit students outside the state plan if they are financed by enterprises or are self-financing, and to develop new programs, including postgraduate programs, and even new local institutions at the short-cycle level and in adult education.

Another major change was focus on quality and the integration of teaching with research. Prior to 1985, the main function of higher education was teaching, with a separate system for research established under the Chinese Academy of Sciences and various national line ministries (see Annex 4 for a brief account of research and development in science and technology in China). A large number of research institutes developed, with research topics and funding assigned by the state plan, which had very little connection with the higher education system, except for the fact that research staff were drawn from its graduates. A few institutes undertook programs in graduate education. In the 1985 reform, universities were given new functions as centers of teaching and research. With quality improvement as a goal of teaching, one of the most important changes in higher education over the last decade has been the development of a research function, which made it possible for universities to conduct basic and applied research. The intention was to revitalize both curricular content and teaching, taking advantage of the impact of research results.

The Higher Education System

Between 1978 and 1994, higher education provision in China grew from 598 to 1,080 regular public universities and colleges.[1] These regular institutions are the focus of this study. Enrollment in undergraduate studies and short-cycle courses in these regular institutions increased from 0.86 to 2.8 million, and that in postgraduate studies moved from zero to 0.13 million. Over this period, staff also increased from 0.5 to 1.04 million persons. These public institutions obtain their principal funding from three sources: (a) SEdC; (b) central ministries; and (c) provinces and municipalities. About 11 percent of students were enrolled in 36 national key universities funded by SEdC, 34 percent were in 331 ministry-funded institutions, while 55 percent of them were in 713 provincial and municipal universities (Table 1.1). Of the total, state-sponsored students constituted 71 percent, enterprise-financed students, 17 percent, and self-financed students, 12 percent. The policy of charging tuition fees was adopted after 1989, and has resulted in each student having to pay for his own education, although the fee level of the state-sponsored students was much lower than those of the other two categories. In 1994, the fee levels for students financed by the state, enterprises or themselves were unified, and fees were raised across the board. (See Chapter 4 for discussion on cost-recovery.)

---

[1]   The figures of institutions, staff, and enrollment in regular higher education institutions and adult tertiary education institutions are drawn from *China Statistical Yearbook 1995*, and *Educational Statistics Yearbook of China 1994*, pp. 18-21, 24. The sources and page numbers of most of the figures cited in the text are reported in the tables and annexes. Percentages are rounded to facilitate readability.

TABLE 1.1: ENROLLMENT IN REGULAR HIGHER EDUCATION INSTITUTIONS, 1994

	Insti-tutions	Undergraduate enrollment ('000 persons)	Short-cycle enrollment ('000 persons)	Total enrollment ('000 persons)	Total undergraduate enrollment (%)	Total enrollment (%)
Under the Jurisdiction of:						
SEdC	36	223	47	269	15	11
Central ministries	331	629	328	956	41	34
Provincial or municipal authorities	713	666	907	1,573	44	55
Total	**1,080**	**1,518**	**1,282**	**2,799**	**100**	**100**
Enrollment Arrangement:						
Enrolled according to State Plan		1,370	623	1,993	90	71
Enrolled by contract with enterprises		71	412	482	5	17
Self-financed students		74	245	319	5	12
Inservice teacher training courses		2	2	5	0	0
Total		**1,517**	**1,282**	**2,799**	**100**	**100**

Source: SEdC, *Educational Statistics Yearbook of China*, 1994, pp. 20-21.

In addition, there exists an adult postsecondary education system which comprised 1,172 public institutions in 1994, including radio and television universities, schools for workers, peasants, and cadres, pedagogical colleges, independent correspondence colleges, and evening or correspondence courses run by regular higher education institutions. These institutions enrolled 2.35 million students on a part-time basis in 1994, and employed 0.21 million full-time staff (of whom 45 percent were teachers) with an additional 0.03 million part-time teachers (Annexes 7A and 7B). The adult higher education institutions admit enterprise-sponsored students as well as self-financing students. These adult education institutions are not the focus of this study, but some of the recommendations do take these into consideration.

Nongovernment or private institutions have proliferated, with more than 800 institutions approved by various levels of government (representing 1 to 5 percent of additional enrollment, according to SEdC), of which only 16 have been approved by SEdC to issue diplomas or certificates recognized by the government. Because official information about these institutions is not available, they are beyond the scope of this study. The recommendations, however, do take private providers into account.

Deepening of the Reform

The *Guidelines for China's Educational Reform and Development* (GOC, 1993) advocates changes at two levels, chiefly (a) government policy; and (b) institutional practice. The major strategic approach is that of decentralization in institutional management and administration while maintaining managerial and supervisory oversight at the macro level. Continuing the theme of decentralization, efforts to devolve more responsibility for financial provision marks a sea-change in the higher education system: this is evidenced by current efforts to diversify the funding basis of institutions in expectation of declining shares in government allocations. The goal was to recover 20 percent of the cost through charging tuition fees by 1997.

A policy that is at the heart of the relationship between economic reform and higher education is the two-way job selection policy. To ensure that each graduate was trained to fill a position as a state cadre, in 1956, a unified national job assignment system was established. The system was managed jointly by the State Planning Commission, the sectoral or line ministries, and the then ministry of higher education. The high degree of predictability in personnel planning was linked to an economic situation where the priorities were to build an economy based on heavy industry. Students enrolled free of charge and were provided with stipends; after graduation, they were obliged to accept job assignments from the state in whatever the position and wherever the location. Since 1978, the move from such a planned system to a market system has signaled that a supply-driven approach must give way to more demand-driven practices. With the success of economic reforms, there are pressing needs for professional personnel with skill profiles different from those the system was designed to serve. The emphasis has moved from traditional industries and governmental services to new industries serving a rapidly growing internal consumer market reaching out to international markets, paralleled by a burgeoning service sector. With the introduction of the two-way job selection system, employment decisions are reached through consultation among employers/hiring units, students, and universities, implying an element of choice and competition. Nonetheless, the labor market has not been fully liberalized. When state-sponsored students cannot find employment after graduation, the state still has the responsibility to provide jobs, mostly in the government service or in state-owned enterprises.

Having come such a long way, where does Chinese higher education stand now? Has it expanded too fast or not fast enough? How is quality identified and maintained? Have scarce resources been used efficiently? How do women and students of workers and peasants fare under the new system? Are development efforts regionally balanced? To answer these questions, measures of progress such as working with commonly-used indicators of quantity, quality, efficiency, and equity, and comparing with benchmarks achieved in other countries in order to identify the areas that require improvement are required. Available data from **Asia-Pacific Economic Cooperation** (APEC) countries (which include East and Southeast Asian countries, Australia, New Zealand, the United States, Canada, Mexico and Chile) as well as major Western European countries and a few large countries (such as India, Russia, and Brazil) are included for comparison purposes. The sources of these data are cited in the tables and the annexes.

System Indicators

Over- or Undersupply?

This is a key policy question in countries all over the world. In China, the speed of enrollment expansion has led to concern about its impact on quality and financing. This concern has given rise to suggestions by policymakers to limit the number of degrees granted, irrespective of enrollment. However, an examination of a number of indicators found that the stock of well-educated persons is still very low in China, and supply may not have met demand yet.

While China has achieved substantial growth in higher education enrollment, the proportion of 18-22 age cohort in regular, public higher education institutions was only 2.4 percent in 1994, barely above that in 1960. Even when enrollment in adult education institutions is taken into account, which adds another 2 percent, this gross ratio is still low, in comparison not only with other fast-growing East Asian countries [for example, 10 percent in Indonesia, 19 percent in Thailand, 20 percent in Hong Kong, 39 percent in Taiwan (China), and 51 percent in Republic of Korea], but also with India, which had a per capita GNP of $300 in 1993, lower than China's $490, and yet an enrollment rate of 8 percent in higher education (Table 1.2).

TABLE 1.2: GROSS ENROLLMENT RATIOS IN AND PUBLIC EXPENDITURE ON HIGHER EDUCATION IN SELECTED COUNTRIES

Country	GNP per capita 1993 dollars	GNP per capita Annual growth 1980-93 (%)	Gross enrollment ratio on higher education 1980	Gross enrollment ratio on higher education 1993	Public spending on higher education (% of all levels) 1980	Public spending on higher education (% of all levels) 1993	Total public spending on education as % of GNP, 1992
China							
Regular System	490	8.2	1	2	25	19	2.1
Adult System	-	-	-	2	-	-	-
Asia							
India	300	3.0	4	8+	13	14+++	3.7
Indonesia	740	4.2	4	10+++	22	15	2.2
Philippines	850	-0.6	28	26	22	15+	2.3
Thailand	2,110	6.4	13	19+++	13	16++	4.0
Malaysia	3,140	3.5	4	7+	12	15	5.5
Republic of Korea	7,660	8.2	16	51++++	9	7+++	4.2
Taiwan (China)	10,215	7.8	18	39+++	-	17+++	5.5
Hong Kong	18,060	5.4	5	20++	25	30++	2.9
Singapore	19,850	6.1	8	19+	17	31+	4.4
Japan	31,490	3.4	29	32	11	23	4.7
Oceania							
New Zealand	12,600	0.7	27	58	28	37+++	-
Australia	17,500	1.6	25	42	23	29	4.5
Latin America							
Brazil	2,930	0.3	12	12	19	26	4.6
Chile	3,170	3.6	13	27	24	21	2.8
Mexico	3,610	-0.5	14	14	12	14	6.0
Argentina	7,200	-0.5	22	41	23	18	4.7
North America							
Canada	19,970	1.4	41	71+	27	29+++	7.6
United States	24,740	1.7	56	72+	39	24+	5.7
Western Europe							
Britain	18,060	2.3	19	37	22	21	4.1
France	22,490	1.6	35	40	13	14	5.1
Germany	23,560	2.1	26	36	15	24+	3.7
Former USSR	2,340	-1.0	22	45	14	12+	8.2

Key:+ = Data of 1990; ++ = Data of 1991; +++ = Data of 1992; ++++ = Data of 1994.

Notes: (1) Gross enrollment ratio is calculated by dividing the number of pupils enrolled in all postsecondary institutions by the population in the university-going age group. Countries differ in the age group they adopt; the cohort aged 20-24 is commonly used, but OECD indicators use several age cohorts such as 18-21, 22-25, and 26-29. The very high enrollment ratios in Canada and the United States are attributable to a large number of learners over age 24 enrolling in higher education; in fact, the net enrollment ratio of the 18-21 age group in 1992 was 27 percent of Canada and 42 percent for the United States. See OECD, *Education At a Glance*, p. 153-155.
   (2) The percentages are rounded.
   (3) Germany refers to West Germany before 1990.

Sources: World Bank, *World Development Report 1995*, Washington, DC, pp. 162-3 and pp. 216-7 for GNP and GNP growth rates; UNESCO, *Statistical Yearbook 1995*, pp. 3.35-3.75 for enrollment data and pp. 4.4-4.18, 4.49-4.50 for public expenditure data in most countries, and UNESCO, *World Education Report 1993*, pp. 144-145 and pp. 156-157 for supplementary information; United States National Science Foundation, *Human Resources for Science and Technology: The Asian Region*, NSF93-303, 1993, Washington, DC, p. 62 for enrollment ratios in Singapore; OECD, *Education At a Glance: OECD Indicators*, Paris, 1995, pp. 73, 98 & 153 for public expenditure data; World Bank, *University Research for Graduate Education Project*, Staff Appraisal Report 12841-IND, 1994, p. 2 for Indonesian spending on higher education; *Taiwan Statistical Data Book 1993*, Taipei, p. 1 for economic information on Taiwan (China); and *Education Statistics of the Republic of China*, 1993, p. 33 for enrollment ratio, and p. 40 for public expenditure on higher education in Taiwan (China); Chung & Wong (Eds.) *The Economics and Financing of Hong Kong Education*, 1992, p. 259 for estimates of public spending on education as percent of GDP in Hong Kong in 1991.

FIGURE 1.2: ENROLLMENT IN CHINA BY LEVEL OF EDUCATION, 1952-94

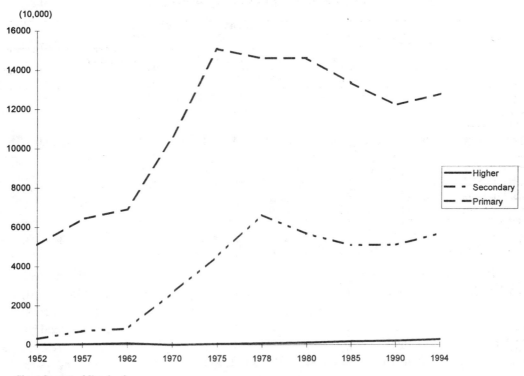

Source: China Statistical Yearbooks.

The Chinese education system is extremely selective, which is reflected by the sharply reduced entrant rates at higher levels of education (Figure 1.2). In 1993/94, while net enrollment of the school-age population in primary schools reached 98 percent, 86 percent of primary school graduates entered junior middle schools, 46 percent of junior middle school graduates made it to senior middle schools (including regular senior secondary, specialized secondary, and vocational secondary schools), and only 4.5 percent of senior middle school graduates were admitted to regular higher education institutions (see Table 1.3 for sources). By contrast, in Taiwan (China) and Republic of Korea, 88 and 94 percent of graduates from junior secondary schools enrolled in various types of senior secondary schools, and 60 and 57 percent of graduates from senior secondary schools were admitted to higher education, respectively (Table 1.3).

Repetition and dropout rates for all grades are unavailable in China. If dropout rates in the pre-university levels are assumed to be zero, based on the above-mentioned entrant rates, only 1.8 percent of a given cohort eventually would make it to universities. The only advantage of such a selective system is that, after many rounds of screening at lower levels, dropouts from regular universities are rare. In 1994, for example, out of 2.8 million enrollees, only 5,635 students quitted their programs, 4,249 were suspended, and 594 were expelled (*Educational Statistical Yearbook 1994*, p. 29).

TABLE 1.3: PERCENTAGE OF GRADUATES ENROLLED IN THE NEXT LEVEL OF EDUCATION

	China 1993/94	Taiwan (China) 1991/92	Republic of Korea 1990/91
% of School-age Children in Primary Schools	98.4	99.6	99.9
% of Primary School Graduates Entering Junior Middle Schools	86.6	99.5	99.5
% of Junior Middle Graduates Entering Senior Middle Schools	46.4	88.3	94.0
% of Senior Middle School Graduates Entering Regular Higher Education	4.5	60.0	57.0

Sources: *China Statistical Yearbook 1995*, Tables 18-6 and 18-7, p. 588, Table 18-21 on p. 595, and Table 18-25, p. 598; *Education Statistics of the Republic of China*, 1993, p. 28 and p. 29; *Educational Indicators in Korea*, 1991, p. 51.

In China, only 2 percent of the population aged 25 and over have had postsecondary education (See Table 1.4 for sources). This compares poorly with the higher education attainment of the population in Hong Kong (11 percent), Republic of Korea (14 percent), Japan (21 percent), and the United States (45 percent) (Table 1.4). The US National Science Foundation estimated that in 1990, only 5.6 scientists and engineers engaged in research and development per 10,000 persons in the work force in China, compared to 30 in Singapore, 38 in Taiwan (China), 37 in Republic of Korea, 75 in Japan, and 75 in the United States (Table 1.9b).[2] With such a small stock of well-educated people, China's major comparative advantage in the world economy is the abundance of low-cost labor.

However, the increasing integration of world economy and the global acceleration of technological change (mostly in the form of computer and labor-saving technologies) would reduce the viability of relying on labor-intensive production as an option for future development. As world trade expands, China will face increasing competitive pressure from lower-wage economies (such as Vietnam and Bangladesh). For China to raise living standards of the people in the 21st century, it is imperative to master the manufacturing of medium-skilled products and to move into the production of high-technology goods.

Currently, the economy of China is one of the fastest-growing in the world. According to the Ninth Five-Year Plan (1995-2000), the Government's target for GDP in 2000 is to quadruple that in 1980, and that for GDP in 2010 is to double that in 2000.[3] This entails an average annual growth rate of 8 percent between 1995 and 2000, and over 7 percent between 2000 and 2010. Given the momentum of China's historical growth rate, it is realistic to expect the GDP to continue to grow at an annual average of 7-9 percent in real terms over the next 25 years. To sustain these growth rates, the demand for highly educated people is likely to be high.

---

[2] US National Science Foundation, *Human Resources for Science and Technology: The Asian Region*, Surveys of Science Resources Series, Special Report NSF 93-303, Washington, D. C., 1993, p. 123.

[3] The source is Premier Li Peng's "Explanation on the Suggestions about Formulating the National Economic and Social Development Goal for the Ninth Five-Year Plan and the Long-term Targets for 2010" (dated September 25, 1995, and published in the *People's Daily*, October 6, 1995).

TABLE 1.4: EDUCATIONAL ATTAINMENT OF POPULATION AGED 25 AND OVER IN SELECTED COUNTRIES

	% of Population Aged 25 and Over Who have			
	No Schooling	Primary Education	Secondary Education	Tertiary Education
China (1990)	29	35	34	2
Female	-	-	-	-
Asia				
Hong Kong (1991)	16	30	43	11
Female	23	29	40	8
Republic of Korea (1990)	11	21	54	14
Female	16	26	51	7
Japan (1990)	0	34	45	21
Female	0	36	47	17
Former USSR (1989)	8	15	63	14
Female	11	16	60	13
North America				
Canada (1991)	1	16	62	21
Female	1	15	64	20
United States (1990)	1	9	45	45
Female	-	-	-	-
Latin America				
Mexico (1990)	19	49	23	9
Female	21	49	23	7
Argentina (1991)	6	57	25	12
Female	6	57	25	12

Source: UNESCO, *Statistical Yearbook 1995*, pp. 1-30-1-51.

Emerging evidence of growing economic returns to higher education and increasing wage inequality in Hong Kong, Taiwan (China), Malaysia, Indonesia, and Chile indicate that fast-growing economies can face skill scarcity if the supply of well-educated people is unable to keep pace with the demand (see Annex 3 for details). At present in China, however, wage data cannot be relied upon to provide good indication of the changing skill requirements in the economy. This is because wages in the public sector are still set administratively, instead of being driven by the forces of supply and demand. Nonetheless, given China's very small stock of human capital, skill scarcity can be expected if the economy continues to grow at the historical rates. At present, the ease and speed with which graduates find jobs and the brain drain of capable people from the interior to the coastal provinces provide some indication of the potential magnitude of skill scarcity in the future. Skill scarcity would reduce China's attractiveness to foreign investment in the medium-to-high technology areas, limit the options for industrial upgrading, undermine the institutional capacity in all sectors, and exacerbate income inequality when the labor market becomes fully liberalized in the future.

To find out whether enrollment has expanded too fast and whether there is an oversupply of graduates requires tracing the employment patterns and wages of graduates by field of study. While wages of the public sector are not driven by the forces of supply and demand, those in the formal private sector tend to be more responsive. Policy decisions should be guided by monitoring the changing wage differentials over time between university and senior secondary school graduates in the formal private sector in the short run, and in the entire economy after the labor market becomes fully liberalized in the long run. A rising wage gap would indicate rising demand for skills and, hence, would justify further expansion as long as there is private demand for education. The implementation of cost-recovery has provided a mechanism to gauge the strength of private demand which has been manifested in the rapid increase of self-financed students and adult education enrollment. The issue of how to finance expansion will be discussed in full in Chapter 4.

What Levels of Quality have been Achieved, and have Resources been used Efficiently?

The quality of education is ultimately embodied in the skills of graduates and their ability to learn continuously and to adjust to changing needs of the time. At pre-university levels, tests are often used to assess cognitive skills. At the tertiary level, national professional examinations (such as in law, accountancy, and medicine) can provide indicators of professional competency. But in arts and science, national exit examinations are rare; more often, institutions administer their own examinations without any comparability in the instrument used across institutions. Hence, there is no national indicator of academic achievement at the tertiary level. Proxy indicators, however, are used to gauge the quality of education provided in the higher education system. These include enrollment by type of programs, the percentage of staff engaging in teaching, time of faculty members spent on research, the academic qualification and age distribution of faculty members, and research output as measured by the number of publications. The picture provided by these quality indicators of Chinese higher education is mixed.

In regular universities and colleges, only 52 percent of students were in undergraduate studies leading to a bachelor's degree, 44 percent in short-cycle, nondegree courses, and 4 percent in graduate studies in 1994 (see Table 1.5 for sources). In adult education institutions, 90 percent of enrollment was in short-cycle courses. In total, only 33 percent of students in tertiary education in China were in regular programs of undergraduate studies. This pattern of higher education enrollment by program type compares unfavorably with many countries where the majority of students enroll in degree programs (Table 1.5). Such a high percentage of students enrolled in short-cycle programs raises the question of the skill level of the graduates.

In terms of percentage of staff involved in teaching and research, there is room for improvement. Although regular universities and colleges in China had a staff of 1.04 million persons in 1994, only 38 percent of them have teaching responsibilities, 44 percent were administrative and support staff, and 18 percent were employed in organizations affiliated with universities (such as factories, enterprises, and research institutes) (see Table 1.6 and Annex 6 for sources). Of these full-time teachers, 52 percent engaged in research for over 10 percent of their time, and only 7 percent did so for more than 90 percent of their time (Annex 7B). By contrast, in Taiwan, faculty members with teaching responsibilities accounted for 75 percent of total staff and in the Republic of Korea, they accounted for 66 percent of total staff (Table 1.6).

A related issue is efficiency. With enrollment expanding faster than staff increase between 1978 and 1994, the student-to-teaching-staff ratio in regular higher education institutions in China rose from 4.3:1 to 7:1, while that of student-to-total-staff ratio increased from 1.7:1 to 2.7:1. Although efficiency gains have been made over the past 16 years, these ratios are still low by domestic or international comparison, as indicated in Table 1.6. This strongly suggests that the Chinese regular higher education institutions could triple or quadruple their ratios to make more efficient use of scarce resources.

TABLE 1.5: PERCENTAGE DISTRIBUTION OF HIGHER EDUCATION STUDENTS IN SELECTED COUNTRIES

| Country | Undergraduate Studies | | Postgraduate | Total No. of Students ('000 Persons) |
	Short-cycle Programs or Junior College (%)	Programs Leading to First Degree (%)	All postgraduate Programs (%)	
China (1994)				
Regular System	**44**	**52**	**4**	**2,798**
Adult System	**90**	**10**	**-**	**2,351**
Total	**65**	**33**	**2**	**5,149**
Asia				
India (1990)	-	-	-	4,425
Indonesia (1992)	56	44	-	178
Thailand (1991)	41	56	3	209
Malaysia (1990)	41	50	9	20
Republic of Korea (1990)	34	58	8	342
Taiwan (China) (1992)	53	42	5	653
Hong Kong (1992)	47	40	13	20
Singapore (1990)	-	-	-	51
Japan (1991)	33	62	5	697
Latin America				
Mexico (1993)	-	92	8	152
Chile (1993)	7	75	18	15
Brazil (1993)	-	100	-	240
Oceania				
New Zealand (1992)	20	57	23	17
Australia (1993)	6	68	26	132
North America				
Canada (1993)	74	22	4	671
United States (1990)	24	54	22	2,024
Western Europe				
Britain (1991)	36	45	19	400
France (1992)	57	31	12	389
Former W. Germany (1990)	33	60	7	256
Russia (1992)	56	41	3	1,038

Note: The percentages are rounded.

Source: *Educational Statistics Yearbook of China 1994*, p. 18, and p. 97; *UNESCO Statistical Yearbook 1995*, pp. 3.342-3.390; *Educational Statistics of the Republic of China*, 1993, pp. 111-113; and *USNSF, Human Resources for Science and Technology: The Asian Region*, 1993, p. 61, for statistics on India and Singapore.

TABLE 1.6: STUDENT-TO-TEACHER AND STUDENT-TO-TOTAL STAFF RATIOS

	Full-time teachers as % of total staff	Student-to-full-time teacher ratio	Student-to-total staff ratio
China (1994)			
Regular Higher Education	38	7:1	2.7:1
Adult Education	45	25:1	11:1
Comparative Data			
North American & European Universities	-	15-20:1	7:1
Taiwan (China) (1992)	75	21:1	16:1
Republic of Korea (1994)	66	33:1	21:1

Source: *China Statistical Yearbook 1995* for construction of the ratios in China; *Korea Educational Indicators*, 1994, pp. 164-166, 210-211, 212-213 for construction of the ratios in the Republic of Korea; *Educational Statistics of the Republic of China*, 1993 pp. 104-107, 144-155 for construction of the ratios in Taiwan; Personal Communication with Commonwealth Higher Education Management Services, Association of Commonwealth Universities, London, UK for ratios in North America and European Universities.

The support for staff development since 1978 has enabled an increasing number of full-time faculty members with teaching responsibilities to earn postgraduate degrees. This support has grown stronger by the year, as demonstrated by the increase from 860 students who were sent abroad to study by the State in 1978 to 19,000 in 1994.[4] In spite of these efforts, given the size of China, there is still a long way to go. Of the 390,000 full-time teachers in the regular higher education system in 1994, only 2 percent of academic staff held the doctorate degree, 19 percent the master's degree, 49 percent the bachelor's degree, and 30 percent short-cycle courses and some undergraduate training (Table 1.7). While more professors (5 percent) and associate professors (4 percent) obtained the doctorate degree, a much larger percentage of them (54 percent) than lecturers, assistants, and instructors had not even obtained the bachelor's degree. A large number of them (53 percent of professors and 54 percent of assistant professors) had completed undergraduate courses without obtaining the credentials. The fact that so many high-level academic staff had to upgrade themselves from a basic level is indicative of the quality issue in the Chinese higher education system. By contrast, in Korean and Taiwan (China) universities, 44 and 46 percent of the faculty members had doctorate degrees (Table 1.7). These indicators suggest that faculty development should command priority in the effort to improve quality.

TABLE 1.7: ACADEMIC QUALIFICATIONS OF FULL-TIME TEACHERS IN REGULAR HIGHER EDUCATION INSTITUTIONS, 1994

	Doctorate degrees (%)	Master's degrees (%)	Bachelor's degrees (%)[a]	Others (%)[b]	Total (no. of persons)
China (1994)	2.2	19.5	48.6	29.7	396,389
Of which females	0.7	14.9	58.2	26.2	127,060
Professors	5.4	8.5	32.5	53.6	28,281
Associate Professors	3.6	12.4	29.5	54.5	102,114
Lecturers	1.7	28.0	48.1	22.2	168,683
Assistants	0.4	15.7	74.5	9.4	76,573
Instructors	1.3	14.7	72.5	11.5	20,738
Comparative Data					
Taiwan (China) (1992)					
Universities	46.0	26.4	26.2	1.3	12,636
Colleges	28.5	35.8	32.0	3.5	5,155
Junior Colleges	3.7	56.2	31.9	0.0	13,639
Republic of Korea (1994)					
Universities	58.5	24.2	17.2	0.1	41,576
Junior Colleges	20.5	59.7	3.7	16.1	9,375

[a]   Bachelor's degrees include those who held it and those who had completed postgraduate studies without obtaining postgraduate degrees.

[b]   The "Others" category includes those who had completed undergraduate courses without obtaining the bachelor's degree, and those who had completed or attended short-cycle courses.

Sources: *Educational Statistics Yearbook of China 1994*, pp. 28-29; *Statistical Yearbook of Education (Republic of Korea)* 1994, pp. 594-595; *Educational Statistics of the Republic of China*, 1993, p. 104.

---

[4]   *China Statistical Yearbook 1995*, Table 18-8, p. 589.

The age distribution of faculty members also affects quality. In 1993, the largest groups (30 percent) were those in their 20s and 30s, while those in the 50s accounted for 24 percent of the total; however, those in the 40s were the smallest group, constituting only 14 percent of total faculty (see Table 1.8 for sources). By contrast, in Taiwan (China), faculty members in their 30s and 40s were the backbone of the university, each accounting for 30 percent or more of the total; the Republic of Korea exhibited a similar age distribution (Table 1.8). This pattern in China reflects the long-term effects of the Cultural Revolution (1966-76). First, those between the ages of 40 and 50 in the 1990s were born in the 1940s and 1950s, and came of age at the time of the Cultural Revolution. Their opportunities for higher education were severely curtailed, resulting in a much smaller share of the cohort becoming faculty members in higher education than any other age groups. This age distribution reflects a quality issue because young staff do not have the necessary experience to provide the academic leadership, while older teachers do not have the necessary academic training to guide university development. The fact that over 90 percent of professors were over 50 and yet 50 percent of professors had not even obtained the bachelor degree is indicative of an adverse impact on quality by basing promotion on seniority, rather than on academic qualifications (Tables 1.7 and 1.8).

TABLE 1.8: AGE STRUCTURE OF FULL-TIME TEACHERS IN REGULAR HIGHER EDUCATION INSTITUTIONS, 1994

	30 & < (%)	31-40 (%)	41-50 (%)	51-60 (%)	61+ (%)	Total Teachers
China (1994)	30.1	30.3	13.5	23.7	2.4	396,389
Of which female	39.2	30.6	12.5	16.8	0.9	127,060
Professors	0.1	2.5	6.2	63.0	28.2	28,281
Associate Professors	0.7	13.7	22.8	61.3	1.5	102,114
Lecturers	22.3	53.6	16.2	7.8	0.1	168,683
Assistants	81.0	17.7	1.1	0.2	0.0	76,573
Instructors	90.9	6.9	1.3	0.8	0.1	20,738
Comparative Data						
Taiwan (China): (1992)						
Universities	15.4	33.9	30.6	13.4	6.8	12,636
Colleges	14.8	41.4	29.6	11.0	3.2	5,155
Junior Colleges	22.5	46.5	20.8	7.2	3.0	13,696
Republic of Korea (1994)						
Universities	21.2	28.3	27.6	18.5	4.4	41,576
Junior Colleges	18.3	39.5	27.2	13.0	2.0	9,375

Note: In the case of Taiwan (China) and the Republic of Korea, the age grouping was under 30, 30-39, 40-49, 50-59, and 60 and over.

Sources: *Educational Statistics Yearbook of China 1994*, pp. 28-29; *Statistical Yearbook of Education (Republic of Korea)*, 1994, pp. 598-599; *Educational Statistics of the Republic of China*, 1993, pp. 104-107.

An international bibliometric-based assessment of research activity in Chinese higher education and research institutions, however, shows promising signs. Between 1988 and 1990, Chinese publications in international journals grew by 40 percent. This growth rate exceeded all other countries, including the United States and Japan, except Taiwan (China) and the Republic of Korea (see Table 1.9 for sources). The scope of research activities also expanded from covering only 21 percent of all fields to 26 percent (Table 1.9). Strengths were shown in physics, materials science, mathematics, and computer science, reflecting the emphasis on science and engineering in higher education[5] (see Annex 8 for sources). The research output from key universities such as Peking University (484), University of Science and Technology of China (420), and Fudan University (395) indicate that one of the goals of the 1985 higher education reform efforts, to restore the research function of universities, has been accomplished (Annex 8). The science policy of the government in fostering research and development is explained in Annex 4.

The fact that research has shown so much progress despite low academic qualifications of the total complement of faculty members demonstrates that China's existing policy of emphasizing key schools and centers of excellence at the tertiary level succeeds in preparing a very small cadre of world class academic elites. The success, however, is not broad based, and the volume is small. For example, of 345,000 papers cited in the Institute for Scientific Information Research Front Database, only 3,842 were Chinese, compared with 160,000 American, and some 5,800 Indian. Moreover, the output per researcher is low by international comparison. In 1990, the number of cited papers per researcher in the bibliometric database was 0.01 in China, compared with 0.06 in India, 0.05 in Taiwan (China), 0.06 in Japan, and 0.17 in the United States (Table 1.9A). The case of India is particularly noteworthy because India has a population size closely matching China's, its GNP per capita is lower than China's, its higher education enrollment rate is higher than China's, and its researchers' papers were cited six times more than China's in the bibliometric database (Table 1.2 and 1.9A). Although not all good articles are submitted to international journals and the English language is likely to be a high barrier, international bibliometric data still serve as a useful indicator of Chinese research having attained international standards. Thus, increasing publications in international refereed journals could provide the calibration needed to further improve quality (Table 1.9B).

In summary, most of the indicators for quality signal that there is room for improvement. The issue of the academic qualifications of faculty members is the most fundamental of all. When such a low percentage of them have had postgraduate training, the basis for expansion and improvement is weak. The policy options for providing high quality education will be discussed in Chapter 5.

Equal Opportunity for Women and Students of Worker and Peasant Background?

Since the founding of the People's Republic in 1949, the Chinese Government has officially promoted gender equity and the interest of workers and peasants. To what extent have these groups enjoyed equal opportunity in higher education in an increasingly market-oriented economy? Indicators on the participation rates of these groups provide clues.

Encouraging signs are shown in the increasing rate of female participation in higher education from 23 percent of total students in 1980 to 35 percent in 1994 (Table 1.10). This increase can be explained by the fact that female student enrollment as a percentage of total enrollment in lower levels of education has increased. For example, female students accounted for almost half of the enrollment in primary and secondary education, resulting in a "pipeline

---

[5]   "Science in China: A Great Leap Forward" in *Science*, Vol. 270, November 1995.

effect" by which more female students entered universities. Nonetheless, given the high rates of female participation at the lower levels, the same rate is not found in higher education. In this sense, opportunities for higher education are not equal for women, largely due to social factors that government policy should mitigate.

TABLE 1.9A: RESEARCH OUTPUT AS MEASURED BY CITED PAPERS IN THE INSTITUTE FOR SCIENTIFIC INFORMATION RESEARCH FRONT DATABASE

Country	Scope of research, 1988 (%)	Scope of research, 1990 (%)	Citing papers, 1988 (no. of papers)	Citing papers, 1990 (no. of papers)	Growth rates per year, 1988-90 (%)	1988 rank	1990 rank
China	21	26	2,746	3,842	40	18	17
World	100	100	345,080	375,346	9		
Top 7 countries							
United States	98	98	147,335	160,384	9	1	1
Britain	82	83	31,969	34,218	7	2	2
Japan	68	69	25,417	28,641	13	3	3
(West) Germany	73	37	22,170	24,743	12	4	4
France	68	70	19,076	20,820	9	5	5
Canada	73	74	18,208	20,017	10	6	6
USSR	47	46	13,686	13,609	-1	7	7
Asia							
India	34	36	5,489	5,873	7	12	13
Taiwan (China)	12	17	1,085	1,720	59	30	28
Republic of Korea	9	12	650	1,015	56	35	33
Latin America							
Brazil	16	21	1,499	1,942	30	27	25
Argentina	13	15	1,146	1,313	15	29	30
Mexico	10	12	721	884	23	34	34
Chile	8	8	581	686	9	38	36

Source: Roberts Coward, "Bibliometric Indicators of Research Activity and Infrastructure," World Bank, 1994, Table 2, pp. 18-22.

TABLE 1.9B: RESEARCH PAPERS CITED IN THE INSTITUTE FOR SCIENTIFIC INFORMATION RESEARCH FRONT DATABASE PER RESEARCHER, 1990

Country	Scientists & engineers in R&D ('000)	Scientists & engineers in R&D per 10,000 in the work force	No. of papers per researcher
China (1990)	391	5.6	0.01
Top Seven Countries			
United States (1989)	949	75.0	0.17
Britain (1992)	255	-	0.13
Japan (1990)	477	75.0	0.06
West Germany (1989)	176	-	0.14
France (1991)	129	-	0.16
Canada (1991)	65	-	0.31
USSR (1991)	878	-	0.02
Asia			
India (1990)	106	3.3	0.06
Taiwan (China) (1991)	32	38.0	0.05
Republic of Korea (1990)	69	37.0	0.02
Latin America			
Brazil (1985)	53	-	0.04
Argentina (1988)	11	-	0.12
Mexico (1984)	17	-	0.05
Chile (1988)	5	-	0.15

Sources: US National Science Foundation, *Human Resources for Science & Technology: The Asian Region*, 1990, p. 122; *UNESCO Statistical Yearbook 1995*, pp. 5-25-5-29.

TABLE 1.10: FEMALE PARTICIPATION IN ALL LEVELS OF EDUCATION

	1980	1994
A. Percentage of Female Students to Total Students		
Higher Education Institutions	23	35
Specialized Secondary Schools	32	48
Regular Secondary Schools	40	44
Vocational Middle Schools	33	48
Primary Schools	45	47
B. Percentage of Female Teachers to Total Teachers		
Higher Education Institutions	26	32
Specialized Secondary Schools	26	41
Regular Secondary Schools	25	35
Vocational Middle Schools	13	36
Primary Schools	37	46

Note: The percentages were rounded.

Source: *China Statistical Yearbook 1995*, Table 18-24, p. 597.

Female teachers as a percentage of total faculty members also increased from 26 percent to 32 percent over the same period (Table 1.10). To the extent that this share mirrored the share of female graduates from higher education, there is no evidence of discrimination against the employment of women in higher education. Moreover, that female teachers aged 30 or under accounted for 42 percent of total female teachers in 1993 showed that more women were hired in higher education in recent years than in the past. However, the disadvantages suffered by female teachers are reflected in their academic qualifications. Only 0.7 percent of them held the doctorate degree, and 15 percent the master's degree, significantly below the national average of 2.2 and 20 percent, respectively. But more female teachers (58 percent) had the bachelor's degree than the average of 49 percent, and fewer of them (26 percent) had below bachelor's degree (Table 1.7). Unfortunately, breakdown of qualification and rank by gender is not available to reveal the pattern of promotion. Nonetheless, the emerging question is that since female teachers had better undergraduate qualifications than men, why did a smaller share of them have postgraduate education? Do female faculty members enjoy equal support for staff development? If women with better basic qualifications than men are not given more opportunity for skill upgrading, what is the implication for the quality of education an institution provides? These issues will be discussed in depth in Chapter 5.

Institutional data from nine universities provide information on student social background in 1993 (Annex 10). On the whole, there was a sizable share of students from families of peasants (20-75 percent) and workers (20-40 percent), and the trend appeared to have increased participation for them between 1980 and 1993. However, the distribution of students from different family backgrounds differed across institutions. Students from families of intellectuals (6 to 22 percent) and government cadres (5-23 percent) have very high participation rates relative to their small share in the population. It was only in an agricultural college that the share of students from peasant background reached 75 percent, which closely mirrored the overall share of the rural population in the country. Students from peasant and worker background also had a much stronger presence than students from families of intellectual, managers, and government cadres in education and medical colleges. In other words, they tended to be tracked into fields that provided very important social services, but were not lucrative. The distribution of student background by field of study has important implications for the policy of cost recovery, which will be discussed in Chapter 4.

Regionally Balanced Development?

In 1957-58, with the Great Leap Forward, new comprehensive and normal institutions as well as various specialized institutions were established at the provincial level, designed to serve provincial needs. Unlike national universities, provincial institutions recruit students from within the province, at a somewhat lower level of marks in the national entrance examinations. Graduates are usually assigned to jobs at the provincial or prefectural level. As disparities in economic growth increase between the thriving coastal zones and the provinces, especially those in the interior, the contribution of the provincial universities to initiate and sustain growth at the regional level assumes great importance. They have a solid performance record in the past; they train most of the highly qualified manpower needed by the provinces in support of their economies; and they produce health and other professionals beyond what the national institutions can provide. They undertake research and make available technical services in areas important for local development. Their programs perform great social services, despite the fact they are funded on a per-student basis at a lower level than that provided to the national universities. Of special concern have been the low educational qualifications of many of their faculty, the lack of modern scientific and computing equipment, and deficiencies in their foreign-language library holdings. The decentralization of finance and planning has widened the gap between poor and more prosperous provinces. In 1994, there were 43.3 college students per 10,000 in China. For Beijing, the figure was 136, while geographically remote and economically backward Guizhou province had only 9. Strategies are required in order to make distribution of resources and educational opportunities more equitable and directed to poor provinces. (Annexes 11 and 12).

In summary, the above survey has found promises as well as challenges in Chinese higher education. To consolidate the gains in the past and expand the capacity of universities both quantitatively and qualitatively, and to meet the developmental needs of the future requires attending to several areas: (a) the relationship between the state and the universities; (b) financing; and (c) policies that foster improvement of quality, which the following chapters address.

World Bank Assistance

World Bank Investment for Higher Education in China

In 1980 the Chinese government approached the World Bank with a proposal assistance plan to strengthen its higher education. The goal of the Government of China was to build up high-level technical and managerial manpower required for national development. SEdC and the World Bank, working together, identified two manpower shortage problems: the low level of overall university enrollment and the imbalance of enrollment structure. In addition, SEdC reported that the university system was further constrained by the limited size of the university graduate programs that trained most of the country's researchers and specialized personnel. In order to eliminate these problems by the 21st century, the Government of China and the World Bank began designing a series of projects to assist the government in its efforts.

Since 1981, Bank assistance in higher education has supported China's economic priorities of alleviating manpower shortages in strategic areas mostly affected by the Cultural Revolution. Eight Bank projects totaling $910.4 million have been undertaken in Chinese higher education. These projects have dealt with science and engineering, economics and finance, agriculture, medicine and education in support of the government's aim to increase the quantity and quality of high-level skilled manpower. The overall impact of the higher education projects has been enrollment expansion, improved quality of instruction, strengthened research capacity, improved management and curricular reform. A complementary series of projects-directed interventions to 183 institutions across almost the entire subsector. Beginning with the prestigious key universities, assistance was spread to provincial normal (teacher training) universities, universities under line ministries—agriculture and forestry, public health—and short-cycle vocational universities. A significant tier that has not been included in any of the projects is a range of nonspecialized universities under provincial jurisdictions.

Lessons from World Bank Projects and Previous Sector Work

The first sector report relating to Chinese higher education looked at key issues in management and finance of higher education and at options for addressing them over the past 17 years. As a result, management and efficiency became significant components of each of the early Bank-supported university projects. Although much progress was achieved in improving management and efficiency through inputs such as training and equipment, there is still room for improvement. Evaluation of projects indicates that one of the most effective ways to improve both efficiency and academic quality is through sharing of scarce resources and cross-fertilization of ideas within and between universities as well as between universities and other organizations, including industry. In addition, if further improvements were to be achieved, universities would have to be given greater freedom to manage their financial and academic affairs under broad policies and directives established by the appropriate governing body.

Important lessons were learned with respect to faculty and curriculum development. Because of the skewed age distribution of staff, with about 40 percent due for retirement by the turn of the century, it became imperative for universities to seek effective ways to upgrade and promote sufficient numbers of young scholars while maintaining the quality of the higher education system. The rapidity with which institutions are mounting popular "market-oriented" programs indicates clearly the renewed urgency for training and retaining qualified staff. Among the chief conclusions relating to continued improvement were those of upgrading faculty qualifications and the establishment of an effective promotion system, both of which still need to be addressed.

Previous projects also addressed issues of fragmentation of teaching programs as evidenced by a proliferation of narrow specializations in almost all disciplines. There has been some progress in broadening curricula. Equally important was the conclusion that, in order to build curriculum revitalization into the system, long-term plans for cross-institutional curriculum reform and teaching materials development were necessary. In the quest for instructional quality, this report provides an opportunity for these long-term recommendations to be revisited.

The Nature and Structure of the Report

The Report summarizes the main findings of the two fact-finding missions. Chapters 2 to 5 review and analyze the three areas of investigation, incorporating diagnoses and suggested strategies for action in each of them. The content of this report and the extent of practical detail respond directly to guidance and requests from senior officials, policymakers and practitioners in China. The emphasis throughout is not so much on what needs to be done, as Chinese agencies and scholars have given this exhaustive scrutiny; rather the conclusions of this review stress how goals are to be achieved. To this end, Chapter 6—Achieving Reform Goals: Strategic Priorities—narrows down the range of strategies suggested in the earlier parts of the review to three major thrusts in the belief that incremental changes rather than a sweeping systemic overhaul is a pragmatic approach, beginning with those most pressing and responsive to the country's reform goals. Action Plan matrices are attached to the appropriate thematic sections and are seen as a launching pad for concrete discussion among the major stakeholders rather than a set of blueprints for action.

2. RELATIONSHIPS BETWEEN UNIVERSITIES AND THE STATE

Context

The State has recently developed a very different interpretation of its role vis-à-vis the universities. The principles behind this new approach were summarized in a recent publication of the Communist Party (CP) Central Committee and the State Council.[1] Paragraph 18 calls for deepening reform of the higher educational system "by gradually setting up a system under which the government exercises overall management while schools [universities] are run independently and geared to the needs of society." The document suggests that the areas where their managerial autonomy should be expanded are "enrolling students, adjusting specialties, appointing and removing cadres, spending funds, evaluating job titles, distributing wages, and conducting international cooperation and exchanges." It also proposes a gradual devolution of the state's overall management function from the center to autonomous regional and municipal authorities and suggests that, subject to various conditions, they should have the power to set enrollment levels and to decide on new academic specialties. Paragraph 19 outlines other changes in the enrollment system: for example, moving to a system in which all students pay fees with scholarship support where necessary, and to an employment system where "the majority of graduates should choose a job by themselves."

Changes have already been introduced to the direct relationship that SEdC has with universities. Consultations are under way within SEdC on the mechanics of designating universities as independent legal entities. This is the legal rock on which their managerial autonomy will rest, as it could allow them to set their own strategic goals, define their own specializations, and control their resources accordingly. In August 1992, SEdC made a formal directive which reduced central controls in 16 areas. The principal relaxations concerned the management of universities and the devolution of new responsibilities to university presidents. For example, universities were free to appoint or remove teaching staff below the level of vice president; they gained the right to choose academic specializations within the broad academic areas approved by SEdC; they could expand fee-paying and contract student numbers within a cap of 25 percent of their total enrollment; both capital and recurrent budgets were given as "global budgets," allowing spending flexibility within the total; they gained the freedom to approve travel and study overseas and they were free to pay bonuses, or rewards for good performance to individual academic staff. These liberties have since been acted upon energetically as Chapter 3 shows.

As a result of these changes, the current position in the five functions described at the beginning of this chapter is as follows:

---

[1] Program for China's Educational Reform and Development. Text issued by Xinhua News Agency. Beijing. February 26, 1993.

(a)   core funding is still provided by SEdC, a sponsoring ministry, province or municipality (or a combination of them), but universities have been strongly encouraged to widen the range of their sources of income;

(b)   the State sets student enrollment targets for those students funded by the State and usually attempts to set a limit on the numbers of self-financing or sponsored students; however, all students are expected to pay a fee of some kind and the fee level is increasing;

(c)   central control is usually only exercised over the appointments of the president, although some provinces still monitor the appointment of deans/heads of departments in some institutions;

(d)   major new programs still require the approval of the funding body; and

(e)   job assignment has virtually disappeared except for some specialist disciplines and has been replaced by "two-way selection" in which employers and graduates choose each other.

The State has changed its role in the provision of capital funding, since it can no longer provide all the funds itself. It has set up the China Education and Scientific Trust Investment Corporation, which acts as commercial banker specializing in the education sector. With initial funds from the Ministry of Finance (MOF), the State Planning Commission (SPC), SEdC and the China Trust and Investment Corporation, it provides short-term loans to institutions, secured on their assets, for their buildings and equipment. Institutions are encouraged to search elsewhere for capital finance: for example, a private university persuaded its sponsoring municipality to guarantee its loan from a bank, a provincial university on the basis of the president's guarantee obtained a large capital loan from a bank, and several universities visited by the mission persuaded overseas Chinese alumni to finance new academic buildings or libraries.

The government has recently taken steps to encourage the development of nongovernment institutions of higher education (or "minban"). To date, 15 institutions have been vetted and appraised prior to their formal approval by SEdC. Equally keen to encourage private investment in higher education, provinces have approved 800 institutions. Chapter 4 discusses the economic and financial implications of these policies. The institutions visited by the mission used teaching staff from nearby state-financed universities, and it is clear that, in these early stages, there are significant economies of scale and relatively little risk of poor-quality teaching. As the nongovernment sector grows in scale, these advantages could disappear. There is a need for quality control procedures to be set up by government.

In keeping with the overall, gradual approach to implementing change, several experiments are under way. For example, giving the provincial Bureaus of Higher Education a greater say in the management of SEdC's key universities in their provinces, local salary supplements to staff, and the enactment of Higher Education Administrative Decrees by provinces (Guangdong is a notable example). One province had also introduced a special 1 percent tax on goods and services, the proceeds of which were directed to higher education. Two institutions, Shanghai International Studies University and Southeast China University, were authorized to enroll all their students on a self-financing basis. In Hefei, two colleges of a university were operating with the bulk of their funding supplied by enterprises—an electronics company and a manufacturer of sporting goods.

Issues

This gradualist approach to introducing change is pragmatic and careful, but involves a judgment by a central authority as to whether a level of management (whether it be a province or a university) is thought "ready" to acquire new responsibilities. Inevitably, therefore, there is **resentment among some universities at the slowness** with which liberties are given or powers are delegated. Both SEdC and the provinces are sometimes resented by those they administer. There is a perceived gap between the rhetoric of policy and the actual pace of implementing change. The mission found many examples of university presidents who expressed a predictable wish for a more rapid acquisition of new powers. In particular, they were unhappy at the control on enrollment targets, especially where self-financing students were concerned, (one case was found where this control was no longer exercised) and at the State setting limits to fee levels in locations where enterprises and individuals could pay more. More autonomy in the decision to start new academic programs was also desired, particularly in those cases where there was strong, local, unmet demand.

Another predictable consequence of the pragmatic, selective introduction of the new freedoms is that **the system is very varied**; different decisions about provinces by SEdC and about universities' capabilities by provinces are resulting in a diverse, uneven picture that is difficult to summarize. Provinces are developing distinctive management styles and processes. This is not necessarily a weakness, but creates difficulties in getting an overall view of what is happening, and to establishing the standard national information collection and reporting systems.

As a direct consequence of the changes in national funding flows, there appears to be **an increase in the influence of provincial governments** in higher education compared to SEdC's influence. It is still a fluid situation that also varies according to the wealth of the province or the importance it places on higher education. Some of the poorer provinces such as Yunnan and Guizhou manage their universities well, despite their low incomes. Guangdong spoke of its plans for an age-participation ratio in higher education of 40 percent by the year 2010 and was preparing a plan to that effect. The province already coordinated higher education provision within its jurisdiction, including that offered by SEdC's key universities. In Sichuan, some universities that received funding from SEdC and central ministries told the mission that they wanted closer relationships with the province. The reasons were largely due to self-interest, in that they hoped to get funding from the province and wanted to know about provincial manpower needs and economic plans so that they could develop appropriate strategies. Provinces had developed innovative ideas: Guangdong awards an annual prize of Y 80,000 to the best university teacher; Anhui insists that each of its universities spends at least 5 percent of its recurrent grant on the purchase of library books and journals; and Sichuan encourages university libraries to collaborate in purchasing decisions, given the shortage of funds.

The pressures of the socialist market economy are threatening to distort the balance of courses offered. Universities are finding that it is **increasingly hard to maintain some core academic disciplines** when students do not enroll for them. The numbers applying for the basic sciences and humanities subjects were far below what is healthy for a "comprehensive university." Presidents were feeling isolated and threatened on this issue as they usually lacked any broadly based Advisory Council or Academic Board/Senate to offer them moral support in upholding the concept of a university. One provincial bureau claimed to have a policy of protecting some subjects, but also said that it would not interfere to stop a university from closing a key discipline (such as chemistry).

China is in the middle of the move from "a state-control model" to a "state-supervising model"[2] as regards the relationship between its universities and government. In this exercise **there are difficult questions to answer about the respective roles and powers of SEdC, central ministries and provincial/municipal governments.** What split of powers and controls will still allow the State to fulfill its "macromanagement" function and yet will also unleash the latent energy and enthusiasm within institutions? What kind of regulatory approach should be adopted? Should it be based on "command and control," on funding incentives to perform, or, on feedback from complaining customers?[3] How should this macromanagement role be exercised, and is it practical to split the strategic policy function from that of funding and operational management of the system?

The terms "macrocontrol" and "macromanagement" are widely used inside China to describe the role of government vis-à-vis universities. They still have to be fully defined in terms of the control and information mechanisms by which they are exercised.

Recommendations and Action Plan

A program of actions is suggested as a possible response to these issues. Figure 2.1 illustrates the objectives that the program seeks to achieve, together with the means and possible indicators for assessing the results. The basic principles behind the proposed program are:

(a)   that the State should move quicker toward adopting a monitoring, regulatory role and abandoning detailed control;

(b)   that the State should provide an "enabling environment" in which universities can plan their own destiny (but this still allows the State to set policy frameworks or efficiency targets within which institutions should plan); and

(c)   that universities should be encouraged to develop individual strategic plans showing how they aim to serve their specific province or community.

These principles are embodied in the Action Plan that suggests some possible initiatives for the government to consider. Each of the main action areas proposed in the plan is now discussed in turn.

Legislation

Once the Higher Education Law is promulgated, there will need to be four levels of legislation or control: the Law that sets out general principles; national, provincial or municipal regulations that would offer policy guidance; Higher Education Institutions' (HEIs') own Statutes, which are drafted by their Board, approved by the State, and set out the internal powers and responsibilities of the Board, the Council and the President; and, finally, HEIs' internal regulations, which are detailed rules approved by the University Council covering courses, fees,

---

[2]   Frans A. van Vucht (1991). "Autonomy and Accountability in Government/University Relationships." Paper prepared for the World Bank seminar. Kuala Lumpur, Malaysia. June.

[3]   David E. M. Sappington (1994). "Principles of Regulatory Policy Design." Background Paper for World Development Report. World Bank.

discipline, etc. Annex 2 describes the topics that are normally covered in such national Laws and in university Statutes.

FIGURE 2.1: ACTION PLAN: RELATIONSHIPS BETWEEN UNIVERSITIES AND THE STATE

OBJECTIVE	MEANS	INDICATOR	ACTION
Define the role of the State vis-à-vis the university	Enact a Higher Education Law setting out general principles. Confirm content and authorities of: • State regulations • University statutes • University regulations	Passage of the Act Publication of model statutes	State Council SEdC
Establish effective policy-making and funding bodies for higher education	Review roles of SEdC, ministries and provinces in setting higher education policy and funding individual institutions. Define who performs each role in a future structure.	 Confirmation of new policy and funding arrangements	 State Council
Provide enabling environment for universities to develop own strategies and strengthen their managerial capacity	Instruct universities to prepare strategic plans and issue comprehensive policy guidelines.	Publication of guidelines	SEdC and other sponsoring bodies
	Development of a national reporting system of key management information (and indicators of performance) in consultation with President and their staff.	Publication of standard information reports	SEdC
	Agreement on management staffing model for universities and development of a training strategy together with designation of training providers.	Completion of national training strategy for university managers	SEdC and sponsoring bodies
	Creation of a Higher Education Management Center to research best practice, publish guidance and sponsor training workshops.	Publications	SEdC

Source: Study Team.

The Roles of SEdC, Ministries and Provinces

Once the State's role has been defined, there still remains the question of how it is exercised at the center and as between the center and the provinces. One model that might be appropriate is to confirm the role of SEdC as that of the supreme policy-making and planning body for higher education and to split this from the detailed fund allocation and management functions. In its policy role, SEdC would advise the State Council on all matters relating to postsecondary education. It would be freed from the minutiae of day-to-day management of universities, but would be empowered to establish agencies or bodies to ensure that quality standards are maintained, that management information and statistics are provided, that resources are allocated equitably in line with its policy. Most of the more detailed macromanagement functions could be carried out by new grants committees or funding councils. These would act as buffer bodies between the universities and SEdC, in line with practice in many countries of the world (Figure 2.2). Their main advantage is that suitable representatives of society, industry or higher education would sit on their Boards and have an influence on the detailed management of universities so that it reflects their needs. One such committee or council could be established to oversee SEdC's 36 key universities (or its successor 100 universities planned for the early 21st century) and another to coordinate the funding for the 325 ministry-run universities. Similar committees already existed in the provinces visited by the mission and they might be redesignated, if they are thought competent to take on wider powers. Gradually, all provinces would have such funding councils. But, until this happens, either SEdC or a national grants committee would undertake the role. SEdC's overall role would include the allocation of funds to the various funding councils.

FIGURE 2.2: EXAMPLES OF BUFFER ORGANIZATIONS

In **India** a University Grants Commission (UGC) was established by the Government in 1956 with the main responsibility of regulating academic standards. Grants are given by the central government to universities through its agency to support and develop academic programs and the infrastructure of the universities. The Commission has 12 members and a secretariat of 760 staff, with five regional offices throughout the country to service and monitor its grants more effectively. In order to undertake its academic roles effectively it has created a large number of expert committees. These promote the development of new programs, assess proposals for change and monitor and evaluate ongoing academic activities. The Ministry for Human Resource Development retains responsibility for planning and policy but is advised on policy matters by a Central Advisory Board on Education, on which the Chairman of the UGC sits.

The **United Kingdom** changed its structure for the management of higher education in 1992 and each of the four countries now has a Funding Council whose main function is to advise the Minister of Education on the funding needs of higher education institutions and to distribute available funds. The Higher Education Funding Council for England is the largest one and distributes recurrent and capital funds for teaching and research to 144 institutions. The Council has 15 members including representatives of industry and the professions. Full responsibility for policy and planning higher education remains with the Ministry of Education.

Source: Based on information from Commonwealth Higher Education Management Services, Association of Commonwealth Universities, London, United Kingdom.

A central policy role for SEdC would include decisions on the designation of sponsors for universities. The Shanghai Higher Education Bureau has already been given responsibility for coordinating the activities of all the universities in the municipality regardless of their source of funding. There are clearly strong feelings on both sides relating to issues that in the long run provincial governments would have responsibility for all universities in their respective provinces, even those currently funded by SEdC. One of the issues which any transfer of responsibility would raise is whether the 36 SEdC institutions would retain a national entry system, taking students from all over China. In many countries Ministries of Education do set entry targets for students from particular regions or minority groupings. China could adapt the approach to ensure that provincial bureaus retain open entry in former SEdC-managed universities, if all institutions come under provincial jurisdictions in a timely manner. Perhaps the top 100 universities could have national entry policy.

Providing an Enabling Environment

One of the roles of a regulating government is to help universities manage themselves professionally. Several university presidents told the Bank mission that they wanted less control but more guidance. There are four ways in which the State can help:

(a)   SEdC or other sponsoring bodies should ask universities to prepare strategic plans and should encourage them to develop distinctive and, if necessary, diverse solutions to providing higher education. Strategic plans will incorporate existing institutional plans which have been SEdC requirements from the mid-1980s.

(b)   Universities must be given information to help them manage their institutions better.   Thus, not only will their internal information systems need to be strengthened considerably, but they will also expect to have a national reporting and information system providing comparative information on the performance of all universities.

(c)   Universities will need help in acquiring the necessary management skills and the development of extensive programs of training for the particular categories of staff involved in managing universities. This will require clarifying the expected role of university managers and administrators.

(d)   Universities will want to have access to advice and information on best management practice from universities in China and in other countries.

The four recommendations are described further.

Strategic Plans

Many governments have found that the best way to obtain results from their universities is to assist them in setting broad policy goals and to allow them to respond to the goals in their own way.   In the United Kingdom, for example, when it was decided to make a dramatic increase in the age participation rate, universities were not given higher enrollment targets, but were simply offered financial incentives and invited to submit their own ideas for expansion. One way for government to ensure that this relative freedom of action is soundly based is to mandate universities to think through their objectives and develop long-term strategic plans to achieve them. The results are often surprising to government as these plans unleash creative ideas and help universities embark on initiatives or innovative solutions that government on its own would never have imagined.

Before universities invest time and effort in such plans they will need to know why they are doing it and how their planning will fit in with national policy. It is therefore essential for the sponsoring body to prepare a framework document. This will cover areas such as: national objectives for higher education in the next five years, specific priorities in disciplines or subject areas for teaching and research, particular issues to be taken into account in planning (these might, for example, cover subjects such as minority students, gender balance, recruitment from poorer provinces) and guidelines on relationships with "minbans." In giving such guidance, it is important that constraints are clearly stated. For example, if the funding scenario is that allocations per student will fall by x percent, this should be stated in the document.

National Management Information

An important role of the government would be to develop information and reporting systems covering the performance of provincial university systems and individual institutions. Performance indicators, though based on the same data as management information, are evaluative measures relating to institutional or sector goals. They can be used at program/disciplinary level, institutional level, or system level. At present, annual statistics are reported and provide fairly comprehensive information for planning and management purposes. More complete and updated information on staff, students, courses, and finance should be publicly available to help both strategic planning by the government and managers of individual institutions. The coverage of any reporting system must embrace all activities of universities regardless of whether they are funded by government or not. A four-stage approach to developing the system is suggested:

(a)   research be commissioned based on the most suitable performance indicators that might help government, Funding Councils, and institutions (see Table 2.1) assess whether institutions have achieved the policy goals set for them;

(b)   a working group of university presidents and vice-presidents be asked to recommend comparative information that they would find valuable about other universities' outcomes and costs. They also be asked to comment on the feasibility of producing information resulting from the research in (a);

(c)   a survey of routine higher education management information that government ministries or provincial bodies need, including desired degree of aggregation be undertaken; and

(d)   on the basis of the three preceding studies, the government be required to define an annual reporting system for all universities and establish a suitable organization or agency to be responsible for information collection, processing and dissemination. There should be special emphasis on ratios, unit costs and other indicators of performance or achievement. Some examples of such measures or indicators collected in other countries are shown in Table 2.1. One prerequisite for such an exercise, which must not be overlooked and will need prompt attention, is the development of standard, national definitions of an undergraduate student, a staff member, a postgraduate, and of agreed categories of expenditure.

Training University Managers

Before management training can be planned and developed, SEdC needs to have a vision of how it expects universities to be managed. There are various models throughout the world:

(a)   Top management functions of the university are entrusted to respected senior academic staff who have given up their academic career permanently and have become full-time managers (the American model).

(b)   Top managers are academic staff who have been temporarily persuaded to become full-time or part-time managers, but who have no intention of doing it for longer than a short-term contract (the current Chinese model).

TABLE 2.1: PERFORMANCE INDICATORS AT THE NATIONAL AND INSTITUTIONAL LEVELS

Although indicators should always relate directly to the policy objectives that governments set for their higher education systems and institutions, many of these are sufficiently similar throughout the world for a generalizable set to be relevant in most countries. All data should be disaggregated by gender and by minority nationalities. It is important to distinguish between national and institutional indicators; the latter which relate to the internal management of an institution may be of little interest to government. A selection of possible national indicators, some of which reflect Chinese concerns, is shown below:

Students:
* numbers of full-time and part-time students in each institution
* students by family income
* numbers of postgraduates
* full-time equivalent student numbers
* percentage of applicants admitted by program of study
* percentage of students who are female and from minorities
* percentage of students funded through the State plan
* lowest entry score for which State students are accepted
* percentage of students in a year who drop out or fail
* percentage of entering cohorts who achieve good final degrees
* numbers of adults or others attending continuing education courses
* percentage of students who found jobs through assignment

Staff:
* number of full-time equivalent teacher
* percentage of teachers with higher degrees
* percentage of teachers aged 45 and under
* qualifications of teaching staff by age group
* average number of days formal staff development/training per teacher
* numbers of research publications, by category
* number of international conferences attended
* ratio of teacher numbers to nonteacher numbers

Resources:
* ratio of full-time equivalent students to open-access computer terminals
* expenditure per full-time equivalent student on books and journals
* square meters teaching space per full-time equivalent student
* ratio of full-time equivalent students to full-time equivalent teachers
* ratio of full-time equivalent students to total numbers of all staff
* number of book titles and periodicals in library

Finance:
* education expenditure per full-time equivalent student
* percentage of total recurrent expenditure on maintenance of premises and on administration
* percentage of expenditure on scholarships
* percentage of expenditure on health, education, housing.
* percentage of income from non-State sources
* university's unrestricted reserves as a percentage of annual expenditure
* percentage of expenditure on bank interest or loan repayments.

Source: Study Team.

(c)   Senior management functions are carried out by a mix of full-time permanent staff from either academic, nonacademic, or professional backgrounds and part-time senior academic staff with limited policy roles for a short period (the British model).

In all these models there must be a cadre of permanent, professional administrative and support staff working for the top managers. The more temporary the senior management, the more essential it is to have high-caliber administrators.

The situation in China is that of model (b) above without any formal acknowledgment of the need for permanent professional administrators. All the presidents and vice-presidents interviewed were keen to emphasize their prime loyalty to their academic careers. As regards administrative staff, there are the beginnings of professional disciplines emerging, but this was not universal and there are frequent examples of young teachers being allocated to fill administrative positions for a short period. It was not clear whether this allocation implies that they are inadequate academically. If China stays with model (b) (which seems to be culturally the most acceptable option), the status and role of administrative staff will need to be enhanced. Administration must not become a posting for failed teachers and it should be recognized as a family of professional disciplines that each deserves investment in training.

Management training for university staff at national level is currently provided by the National Academy of Education Administration (NAEA) in Beijing and by four affiliated colleges in other provinces. NAEA deals principally with training for education administrators below the postsecondary level; its training for university staff has been very limited, with only three core courses aimed at higher education. NAEA has offered only six- and three-month courses for presidents and vice-presidents and a few short courses for other categories of managers. Some provinces have been taking the initiative in developing courses of their own and in encouraging universities to provide some management training internally. In view of the size of national training requirements, SEdC will need to consider a more significant, structured approach. NAEA would seem to be the obvious focus for this, but it might require further investment in increasing the range of its specialist skills and capacity. The next steps could involve the following:

(a)   funding training—requires analyses of the various categories of university staff: presidents and vice-presidents, deans, heads of departments, senior administrative staff (by specialization), technical staff and middle managers in the administration;

(b)   development of a training strategy including resolution of issues such as the desirability of developing a qualifications framework for university management training, whether any training should be mandatory for any categories of staff, the options for delivery including distance learning, the scope for producing open learning materials for certain categories of trainee, the need for focus or centralization of training provision, whether by specialization or by geography, and a pricing/funding policy defining the scope of the state's financial support for continuing training provision;

(c)   deciding whether selected institutions, such as NAEA, should be preferred as key providers or developers of training material on university management; and

(d)   networking with international agencies and universities in order to draw on their experience and existing training materials[4] and to develop the opportunities for staff exchanges or secondments. It would be unfortunate if China is not able to tap the training material that is being developed for university management training elsewhere in the world.

---

[4]   For example, the International Center for Distance Learning at the British Open University operates a database of 26,000 courses worldwide. These include several on university management at diploma or certificate level, which could be adapted. Further details of such courses offered throughout the British Commonwealth are outlined in a publication by the Association of Commonwealth Universities.

Advice on University Management

University presidents frequently expressed the need for more advice on how to manage. How can this be provided? It is clearly not a task that either SEdC or provincial bureaus are competent to perform. However, in view of the scale of change facing universities, their limited access to management skills at present, the number of small universities, and the wide range of provincial management practices, there are good arguments for government to help develop some national initiatives. What is needed is no less than the development of a new profession in a very short space of time. One option would be for SEdC to subsidize an independent Higher Education Management Center (HEMC), which would provide help and advice to individual universities and provinces or municipalities. Possible roles for such a Center might be to:

(a)   undertake research into best management practice in Chinese universities—and relevant experience elsewhere—and disseminate the results to all;

(b)   work very closely with existing groups of university administrators to help them develop their professionalism and assist in the formation of other similar groupings for those managing physical property, the human resource/personnel functions, student admissions etc. Such work would include sponsorship of meetings, development of best practice, and publications relating to the specialist area of university management;

(c)   organize collective discussions and conferences on key management issues as they arise;

(d)   provide practical consultancy advice to specific university managers on troubleshooting, using a network of experienced practitioners;

(e)   publish guidelines and handbooks on good management and help develop comparative measures of managerial performance; and

(f)   advise the providers of management training about training needs of university staff and collaborate with them to develop and offer short courses.

SEdC could invite bids from universities to host such a center and then provide the selected university with "core funding" for a short period. During this time it would be expected to build up an income-generation capability from selling its courses, advice or software. If such a Center is established, it is important that its staff are not simply teachers with research interests, but are able managers with practical experience of university management.

These four steps by government will help individual institutions to build up their managerial capacity. Published national information will form the basis for critical self-examination as well as providing targets or comparative benchmarks. The staff development programs will allow individual presidents to develop their key staff as effective managers and the national HEMC can become a valuable sounding board for innovative, managerial ideas. Chapter 3, which follows, describes the management challenges that have to be faced.

3. CHANGES IN UNIVERSITY MANAGEMENT

Context

As was discussed in Chapter 2, one of SEdC's recent policy objectives has been to strengthen the management role of the university president. Although much formal documentation presented to the Bank mission showed the president as still being subject to the direction of the Party Secretary, there was no evidence that this was in opposition to the president's academic autonomy. What is less clear are the respective roles and powers of University Councils as regards the provincial bureau or SEdC. There is also a potential area of confusion in those cases where universities have established Boards of Trustees as well as a governing council.

Many universities have established Boards of Trustees in order to establish and develop links with society and local enterprises. However, the role of such boards is not always the same. Most institutions use it to provide contacts with a wide range of commercial enterprises and their funds, some stress the involvement of local provincial or municipal government officials, while Chongqing University actively involves its board in its internal management and expects it to review the University's development plans.

University organization structures have been changing. Many of those presented to the Bank mission appeared to be very flat with relatively large numbers of people shown as reporting directly to the president. After its recent merger (Chengdu Scientific and Technological University and Sichuan University), Sichuan United University has no less than six vice-presidents. In discussions with senior officials, a typical senior organization structure in universities emerged along the following lines:

> President
> > -Vice-President, Research
> > -Vice-President, Education or Dean of Studies
> > -Vice-President, Personnel
> > -Vice-President, Finance and Administration (and Enterprises)

In two universities, a post of secretary general was shown at the same seniority level as that of vice-president. The incumbents were senior, trusted academic staff who acted as the president's chief administrative officer. Other administrative job titles commonly found were: Director of Personnel, Director of Finance, Director of Academic Affairs, Director of Foreign Affairs (or International Relations), Director of General Affairs and Services, and Director of Science Research. In almost all cases these posts were filled by former teachers who had become administrators. In some institutions there were specialist offices for functions such as: Student Assignment, Campus Accommodation, the University Hospital, University Printing House, and management of university enterprises. The typical organigram was similar to that in the United States, with senior academic staff acting as vice-presidents and managing heads of administrative functions.

Management Issues

Respective Roles of President, Council and Board of Trustees

In a few of the universities visited, there was a University Council or Governing Body, but it had varying roles. In one case, it was described as advising the president, while in another it was clearly directing the president, as in the American or British model of governance. There was no consensus about the role or composition of a university council. This uncertainty will not be resolved until legislation is passed along the lines suggested in Chapter 2, which defines precisely what the respective roles of SEdC, the council and the president are. The role of Boards of Trustees will need to be confirmed in the light of formal powers given to councils. They might be expected to focus on fund raising and industrial liaison rather than on management.

One emerging problem is that of conflict between the president as manager/ fund raiser and as academic leader. On several occasions, senior academic staff told the Bank mission that they were not trained to take on management tasks and that they had difficulty reconciling the two disparate functions. Chinese university leaders are not alone in this dilemma, which is virtually a worldwide phenomenon in higher education. China does, however, lack an adequate infrastructure for either skills training or experienced technical support. If the recommendations in page 30 (Advice on University Management) are followed, the task of short-term academically inclined presidents would be made immeasurably easier.

The Management of University Enterprises

The management of enterprises is assuming growing importance as financial pressures increase and enterprises are seen as one of the principal sources of additional finance. Chapter 4 describes the income that has been generated to date from such sources and assumes that it will continue to increase. Responsibility for managing university enterprises appeared to be given usually to the vice-president in charge of finance, but there were indications in some institutions that this was becoming too difficult a job. All the universities visited had a number of enterprises employing their own workers; in one case 60 such companies were named, in another there were 400 employees in one enterprise alone; yet another had sales outlets in cities throughout China and several were run as joint ventures either with foreign investors or with former alumni in Hong Kong and Singapore. Fangzheng Corporation, owned by the University of Peking, was reported to have a turnover in excess of Y 1 billion and a profit of more than 200 million.

The increasing role that these enterprises play in Chinese universities (and reliance on them as providers of alternative income) raises two management issues:

(a)   whether they can continue to serve dual academic and financial objectives. There is a basic conflict between using a company as a research/consultancy test bed and teaching forum, and using it to generate profits. For example, the investment criteria for each objective are different; in one model, equipment purchases may be used to illustrate new technologies to students, while in the other equipment is purchased on purely payback or profit-making criteria. Although most university leaders have claimed that this has not yet a problem, financial pressures will make it increasingly difficult to serve purely academic objectives. Some university enterprises are already seeking to charge fees for the time they give to students.

The strategic question must be faced and universities should look closely at their portfolio of company enterprises and decide on which are purely commercial and should be managed as such, and on which have academic objectives. In the latter case, clear guidelines on investment criteria and the use of staff time need to be set. It may also be necessary to accept that such companies operate at a loss.

(b)   whether it is right that teachers who are appointed on essentially academic criteria should be expected to manage industrial holding companies in an increasingly competitive environment. One university has lost several million Yuan from one enterprise and now treats them warily. As China's market economy grows in sophistication, it is quite possible that those academic enterprises that have thrived until now will not prosper in the face of tougher, professional competition. The Bank mission gathered from one well-known key university that it did not wish to manage enterprises any more, but that it would prefer to be an investor receiving profits from organizations run by professional managers. This should be the route for all universities in future. It would be risky and expensive to allocate teachers to posts for managing enterprises unless they are particularly well qualified in the right technical skills.

Universities are clearly keen to get as close as they can to external enterprises, not only as sources of finance and work experience for students, but also as employers of their graduates. There was little evidence among universities visited of the close long-term relationships that exist in some universities which foster clubs or groups of their local enterprises and then jointly solve their technical problems by consultancy as well as providing training and short courses for all levels of staff. This scenario however is changing rapidly, particularly in areas of economic growth. In due course, China will need to develop the profession of Industrial Liaison Officer within universities in order both to professionalize the services offered by teachers and to ensure that universities get the maximum income possible from their inventions and intellectual property. As Chinese universities enter the world of commercial research, they can draw on international experience for managing the technology transfer process.[1]

The Management of Teaching Staff

Improving the quality of personnel and their performance has understandably been given top priority by presidents as their most important management issue. They now have the powers to make desired changes. Among the innovations being introduced were:

(a)   "Eliminating traditional ideas of giving promotion according to one's experience and age...and increasing the proportion of young and middle aged teachers in high positions." Some universities had radically changed their age profiles: at Southwest Normal University 67 percent of staff were under 45 and at Southwest Agricultural University 57 percent were under 35.

(b)   Attempting to recover suitably qualified academic staff from overseas or other provinces by offering specially attractive packages of accommodation and pay.

---

[1]   Council for Industry and Higher Education and Department of Trade and Industry (1989). Collaboration Between Universities and Industry. Six handbooks. HMSO. London.

There is active recruiting by some presidents of inland universities in an attempt to reverse the economic pull toward the prosperous coastal regions.

(c)   Restructuring administrative departments and sections and "merging overlapping functional sections so as to smooth their relations."

(d)   Placing strong emphasis on teaching quality through appraisal, examinations and the award of prizes to the best teachers.

(e)   No longer giving jobs to "those evidently unqualified for them"; opening up jobs to anyone who wanted to apply; and making appointments on the basis of merit and ability rather than age or seniority

(f)   Rewarding teachers according to their performance, as compared with the old method of giving everyone the same bonus. Several universities had developed systems that spread departmental surpluses (derived from a university-wide bonus and departmental earnings) among staff according to their teaching quality. The decision was entirely the dean's although the department's share of the university bonus was decided by the president.

(g)   Introducing special increases in the hourly rates paid for teaching in order to emphasize its importance.

Despite these changes many presidents felt constrained in their freedom to make major changes in the staff structure of their universities. They felt that, without the power to dismiss some staff entirely, they would always be compelled to retain some unproductive or ineffective teachers they would rather not employ. As long as society expected them to provide a total package of care for all their employees regardless of how much they contributed to the university, they could not become fully efficient. More recently the situation shows signs of change with the growing possibility of dismissal of inappropriate faculty.

Existing Inefficiencies

One main task of presidents is to improve the efficiency of their university. By international standards there is a long way to go. Overall student-teaching staff ratios, for example, in the most efficient institutions were 8.3:1 or 9:1, but in many others were still at levels of 5:1 or 6:1. This compares with European or Australian ratios in the range of 15:1 to 20:1. Presidents are now setting academic staff numbers using target student-staff ratios according to the type of department and the teaching it provides. Overall, they were planning to achieve tighter student-staff ratios, sometimes in response to ceilings set by the provincial authorities. For example, Southwest Normal University had 8.3:1 in 1994, but was targeting 9.5:1, Southwest Agricultural University had 9:1 and was aiming at 12:1, while Foshan University's current ratio was 11:1.

Another key ratio is that of total staff numbers to students. Because of the tradition of providing welfare and support services for the lifetime of staff, as well as complete municipal services, these figures are very high. Comparisons with European or North American universities (where ratios are around 1:7) are less relevant than with African institutions, where it is common to find one staff person for every two students. In China in 1993, the ratio was 1:2.5. In the near future the State will have to resolve the question of whether it expects public bodies to continue to offer life-long support to their staff; however, until some alternative sources of housing and social security support have been developed, it would be unrealistic to expect university presidents unilaterally to require their staff to retire from the university system (although a few isolated examples of this were found).

The use of space is another area where there is considerable potential for efficiency gains. SEdC norms say that each university must have 46 square meters of constructed floor space per student. In one New Zealand university the requirement per student has fallen from 15 to 9 square meters over the last five years. If SEdC acts to lower the space norms, this will have the effect of deferring the provision of further buildings and will force institutions to look hard at the way space is now used. Laboratory use in the mornings, lectures on Friday afternoons and early evenings will become the norm rather than a rarity. An item of expenditure that is often trimmed by poorly managed universities is that on the maintenance of buildings and equipment. In the long run this is a false economy and university councils should act to protect these elements in the budget.

Delegation of Management Decisions

University presidents have been quick to appreciate that they cannot exercise detailed control over the affairs of academic departments and most have moved rapidly to a system of delegating responsibility to deans or heads of schools/departments (Figure 3.1). One president agreed on individual performance targets with his deans and heads of departments and allowed them to build up financial reserves and to reward academic staff with different bonus levels as they thought fit. In another university the vice-president of finance was planning to delegate to heads the decision on whether to recruit staff on a full-time or part-time basis. Yet again, the move to such delegation is a worldwide phenomenon, but it is rare to find it adopted so rapidly after universities have gained their own as yet ill-defined autonomy. The lessons from international experience are that, if such delegation is to be effective, it has to be accompanied by sound information and reporting systems and good basic training in financial management for deans and heads of departments. Neither yet exists in many Chinese universities.

FIGURE 3.1: DELEGATING THE DIFFICULT DECISIONS

In Tianjin University the president has decided to delegate the personnel budget to deans and to combine the change with a formula approach that only pays people according to their teaching load. If a professor does only half the teaching load, the other half of the salary has to be earned from research or consultancies. This causes enormous difficulties for some deans. One now has over 100 teachers and only 150 students. The formula used by the university means that the department will only get enough money to pay for 15 people. The dean is not allowed to fire anyone and he knows that most of the staff in the department will be unable to earn the income needed to support themselves. When he allocates teaching duties, he will be giving out pay; those who get no teaching hours will have to find income from other sources.

Source: He Jin (1994), The Dean's Dilemma. Mission paper.

Faculty Development

Chapter 2 has described what the government can do nationally to help provide suitable management training for those academic staff with managerial responsibilities. However, presidents must bear the principal burden of ensuring that those to whom they delegate are qualified to do their job. This will involve the development of internal programs to supplement those at national and provincial levels.

Inadequate Information Support

While it was common to hear about the delegation of functions and budgets to deans and others, it was clear that the management information systems were unable to meet the demands which were made of them. There was a wide range of different evidence on the quality of university management information systems. In Guangdong province, most of the universities claimed to have most of their information systems operational, while in Anhui only a few made this claim. The usual approach to developing such systems appeared to be to commission the software development from teaching staff in the computing department. This has rarely been a permanent or satisfactory solution in other countries, since teachers are rarely familiar with the requirements of commercial operations. There were only a few instances of a university importing an administrative software package from another university, nor were there any reports of universities using any common software (as in the college sector) other than that required by SEdC to produce its standard financial returns.

There is a massive task of training ahead in all aspects of designing and implementing integrated MIS. The length and cost of this process is universally underestimated. SEdC has begun to take some initiatives in this area by arranging for meetings of those concerned with the development of MIS. However, presidents cannot avoid the responsibility of developing their own university administrative computing strategies and devising plans to achieve whatever kind of MIS they decide to adopt.

High Cost of Support Staff

One of the major management concerns of university presidents is the large number and high cost of their support staff. This was being tackled imaginatively by some but there were limitations on the flexibility and speed of actions that presidents could take because of social factors and the long-held traditions of care for workers. There were two main types of solution:

(a)   "commercializing" the support functions by making them better managed within the university system and encouraging them to undertake work for outside customers; and

(b)   "socializing" them by releasing them from full-time work for the university and permitting them to operate as free agents in the outside marketplace, as long as they perform some limited contracts for the university. At the end of the year, they would be expected to repay to the university the full cost of their salary.

Both these solutions are feasible in urban environments, but are not so easy in the more remote, rural areas or in poorer provinces. Neither solution removes the staff from the university that is still responsible for their total welfare. It was clear that many presidents would have liked to have made surplus support staff redundant, but were constrained because the necessary social protection was not yet in place.

Recommendations and Action Plan

A possible action plan for the government's consideration, with suggested tasks for both SEdC and individual presidents in the area of institutional management is shown in Figure 3.2.

FIGURE 3.2: ACTION PLAN ON MANAGEMENT

Goal: To improve the quality and effectiveness of university management

OBJECTIVE	MEANS	INDICATOR	ACTION
A. Government Level			
Ensure roles of government, university councils, and presidents are clearly understood	Pass a HE Act stating what respective powers and duties are vested with Government and University Councils	Act passed	SEdC
	Pass Regulations defining suggested contents of Statutes that university councils may submit for approval	Regulations issued	SEdC, State Council
Clarify universities' tax-exempt status on their earnings and confirm that donors can get tax benefits from gifts	Pass necessary legislation in a Finance/Taxation Act	Act passed Numbers of donations increase	SEdC, Ministry of Finance
Improve quality of management information	Sponsor or fund collaboration between universities in developing and implementing administrative software	Number of universities implementing MIS	SEdC
Ensure universities get maximum benefit from their enterprises and commercial activities	Issue guidance on types of enterprise and how they should be managed	Increase in income from enterprises and reduction in numbers becoming bankrupt	SEdC
B. University Level			
Provide strategic direction for universities	Develop a planning process from which a strategic plan emerges, to which all are committed	Completed plans linked to budgets	President
	Provision of training workshops on strategic planning for university staff	Numbers of participants	NAEA, etc.
Improve operational efficiency and reduce costs	Undertake regular reviews of potential efficiency savings	Reduced unit costs and improved efficiency ratios	University Council, President, Senior Staff
Maximize income from university enterprises	Review all enterprises, set financial targets for each one and professionalize its management where relevant	Profits from enterprises paid to university	Council
Ensure availability of high-quality management information	Prepare strategy for developing computer-based MIS, using bought software where possible	Reliable statistics, ratios, etc.	President

Source: Study Team.

What the Government Should Consider

The government can strengthen the internal management of institutions by:

(a)   Including **guidance** about the role and composition of the university Governing Body or Council **in its legal framework for universities**. Such a body could play a valuable role in linking the institution with society if its membership included not only students and senior academic staff, but also representatives of the local community, of the region, province or municipality, of a selection of enterprises and professional people such as lawyers, accountants and property specialists. The difference between a council and a fund-raising board of trustees should be clarified since many universities could get their functions confused.   The government could also issue a regulation suggesting the content of model Statutes that university councils should pass to control the detailed governance of the university. Annex 1 illustrates the possible coverage of university Statutes.

(b)   In consultation with the Ministry of Finance, **clarifying the position** of universities as regards their **tax-free status** and covering particularly their earnings from nonacademic activities and their consultancies. Tax incentives for donations to universities from enterprises and individuals should be considered.

(c)   **Modifying its encouragement for the expansion of university enterprises** so as to make clear that there are various options for managing the enterprises or for holding investments in them. The government might stress the distinction between retaining companies with wholly academic objectives and holding the others as investments within a commercially run portfolio. In general, direct management of enterprises by university staff ought to be discouraged.

(d)   In association with other sponsors of universities, encouraging them to **prepare their own strategic plans**; this would involve clarifying any policy parameters within which the universities should plan, defining the State's attitude to diversity in the way universities choose to meet national objectives and confirming the link between strategic plans and the annual funding processes. SEdC and others might derive performance measures from their policy objectives and ask universities to report on their success against such measures. A preliminary task for SEdC, ministries and provincial authorities would be to arrange the provision of training for university staff in the practical aspects of preparing strategic plans.

(e)   Continuing to encourage universities to collaborate in the costs of developing **computerized management information systems**. Even if existing software is imported from other countries, the cost of adapting such a system can easily exceed a million dollars for each institution. There is a strong financial and practical case for the government to follow examples of countries such as Australia and the United Kingdom where the government has funded universities to form consortia to share software development costs.

(f) **Providing funding** for ways of **promoting good management**, beyond those suggested in Chapter 2, and helping universities to learn from the experience of others in **improving their efficiency**.

What Universities Have To Do

The development of a **strategic plan** is the first major task for each university. Working within the framework provided by its sponsoring body, the university should assess its strategic options in the context of its history, academic strengths, and potential regional and local markets. The president should steer a planning process involving participation of the institutional body at various levels and members of the local community to produce a strategic plan to which senior members of the university are committed.

Plans for **improving management efficiency** will form an element of each university's strategic plan. Since the objectives and programs of each university will differ, there is no standard model of best practice. However, economy and efficiency exercises are being carried out in most universities throughout the world and Table 3.1 illustrates some of the questions and alternative approaches that are being considered. One of the roles of the university council (or equivalent governing body) will be to check that the president and his senior administrators are undertaking regular reviews of all these issues. No university can afford to stop questioning whether it can do things more efficiently. In many countries this process is taken for granted by funding agencies, which assume that universities are capable of making annual efficiency savings of between 2 and 4 percent per year.

University enterprises have enormous potential for losing university funds. Every council should therefore initiate a **review of all the existing enterprises** in order to make a clear distinction between those that are expected to generate profits and those that have primarily academic objectives. In the former case, the management of the activity must be as commercial as possible and external managers should therefore be closely involved. The council should consider whether it wishes to continue in the business of employing enterprise staff or whether it would be preferable to sell the operation to an independent private company. Where this is the case, the university will be freed of the burdens of management and will receive its income in the form of dividends.

In managing the university **reliable management information** is a prerequisite. The president will therefore need to have a strategy for computerizing the university's basic administrative systems so as to derive information from them. Such a program will take time to implement and could also be very costly unless advantage is taken of software developed elsewhere. It will therefore be in the interests of the university to collaborate with others either in sharing the costs of software or by purchasing ready-made programs. The government already has a plan for a nationwide information highway which should establish a framework for such collaboration. Any strategy that is agreed should be compatible with the network and communications policy of the university, so that administrative and academic users do not duplicate facilities.

TABLE 3.1: WAYS OF ACHIEVING ECONOMY AND EFFICIENCY

Teachers:
Set target student/staff ratios for each department

Set teacher workloads (class hours etc.) and allocate time between Teaching, Research and other activities such as Enterprises

Monitor and control teachers' time spent on activities

Use alternative teaching/learning method—CAL, Open learning, self study packs

Introduce Computer Assisted Testing for students to save teacher time

Share specialist staff with other universities (or employ them on a part time basis)

Use qualified people from industry/commerce as part time lecturers, where relevant

Support staff in departments:
Set target support staff ratios for particular departments

Ensure that Vice-Dean manages the time of departmental support staff

Use support staff as teaching assistants, for nonprofessional supervision, or management of open learning materials or terminals.

Delegate nonprofessional work of teachers to support staff wherever possible

Libraries and computer centers:
Set up local collaboration between libraries on journal purchasing, access via network to each other's catalogues,

Negotiate contracts between libraries for exchange of faxed articles or inter library loans.

Encourage access by teachers and students to *all* university libraries in the same city.

Use students as part time labor in stacking and shelving.

Get income from the sale of photocopies in the library.

Obtain income from sale of computers or accessories to teachers.

Use packaged administrative software or software developed by other universities

Administrative staff:
Simplify and redesign routine operational processes to remove delay and duplication

Integrate computerized operational systems to remove double/treble entry of same data.

Delegate some functions to teaching departments to eliminate delay and confusion.

Contract out routine administrative support functions to private enterprises, e.g.; printing, accounting, building design, legal advice, project construction management.

Restructure departments and divisions to reduce duplication and number of senior posts.

Equipment and teaching materials:
Form purchasing consortia of universities to get better terms/discounts from suppliers.

Establish central purchasing systems to identify the cheapest supplier for standard or bulk items

Encourage sharing of expensive equipment within the university and between universities in a city

Charge out the use of sophisticated equipment to commercial users

When technical staff are trained in the maintenance of such equipment, charge their services to other owners in the region.

Buildings and Space:
Ensure that timetables use all the working hours and that no hours are regarded as unusable

Make all classrooms centrally bookable and do not allow departments to claim any as their own

When modifying or rebuilding buildings, replace all old materials with maintenance-free materials

Before building a specialist facility, check that no one else in the region has one which could be shared

Design first and second year undergraduate laboratories as multipurpose for use by several disciplines

Design lecture and seminar rooms with movable walls to accommodate different class sizes

Use loose furniture that can be moved around to make flexible teaching layouts

Check to see how rooms are actually used compared with their timetabled and booked use by departments

Use statistics on room usage in planning the provision of new accommodation

Contract out building maintenance tasks on a competitive tender basis with fixed prices for standard tasks

Service staff:
Contract with staff on independent basis to provide services to the university

Obtain tenders for contracts with private enterprises to provide the services and compare their cost with the in-house staff

Place the internal services, wherever possible, on a customer service basis so that users are paying for service

General:
Ensure all division managers set performance targets for their staff each year

Encourage administrative managers to promote a culture of service and support to the rest of the university

Establish performance measures for administrative departments which assess their efficiency and the quality of their service

Reward excellent administrative performance as much as good teaching or research performance

Provide training and travel funds to let administrative managers visit other universities and conferences to learn good ideas

Source: Study Team.

4. FINANCING HIGHER EDUCATION: DIVERSIFICATION OF RESOURCES

Current Context of Higher Education Finance

Public Finance

Since China embarked on economic reform in 1978, the Gross Domestic Product (GDP) grew by an impressive 9.8 percent per year in real terms, from Y 1,006 billion to Y 4,501 billion in 1994 (in constant 1994 prices) (Table 4.1, Annexes 13A and 13B). However, the growth of government revenue fell far behind that of GDP, increasing at an annual average of only 2.6 percent over the period. This resulted from decentralization and from permitting production units to retain much of their earnings without simultaneously putting in place a national tax administration until 1994. The revenue-to-GDP ratio declined from 34 percent in 1978 to 13 percent in 1994 (Annexes 13A and 13B). Government expenditure, however, increased at 3.3 percent per year, higher than revenue, resulting in budget deficit in all but one year (Table 4.1). Between 1987 and 1993, the public sector deficit hovered around 11-12 percent of GDP and was a key factor underlying inflationary pressures in the economy. In 1994, however, the public sector deficit declined to 9.9 percent.[1]

Public expenditure on education increased from Y 21 to 98 billion (in constant 1994 prices), by an annual average of 10 percent between 1978 and 1994, far exceeding the respective growth rates of the total government revenue and expenditure (Table 4.1, Annexes 13A and 13B). As the overall public spending shrank over the years, public expenditure on education as a percentage of total government expenditure rose from 6.2 percent in 1978 to 17 percent in 1994. Public expenditure on education as a percentage of GDP rose from 2.1 percent in 1978 to the height of 3.1 percent in 1989, and then fell back to 2.2 percent in 1994 (Annex 13B). This level of public spending on education is low in comparison with least-developed countries' average of 2.8 percent, developing countries' average of 4.1 percent, and developed countries' average of 5.3 percent.[2]

Total public allocation to higher education grew from Y 4.2 to 18.6 billion (in constant 1994 prices), by an annual average of 9.7 percent between 1978 and 1994 (Table 4.1, Annexes 13A and 13B). Public spending on higher education increased from 20 percent of total public expenditure on education in 1978 to the peak of 29 percent in 1984, then declined to around 17 percent between 1989 and 1992, and climbed back to 19 percent in 1994 (Annex 13B). Since under 2 percent of the age cohort were enrolled in higher education in much of the 1980s, the high share of public spending devoted to them reflected the effort to rebuild the higher education system.

---

[1]   *The Chinese Economy: Fighting Inflation, Deepening Reform* (World Bank, 1996), p. 10.

[2]   UNESCO, *Statistical Yearbook 1995*, p. 2.28.

TABLE 4.1: AVERAGE ANNUAL GROWTH RATES IN REAL TERMS, 1978-94
(All Yuan are in constant 1994 prices)

	1978	1994	Average Annual Growth Rates
GDP (Billion Yuan)	1,006.3	4,500.6	9.8
Total Government Revenue (Billion Yuan)	345.8	521.8	2.6
Total Government Expenditure (Billion Yuan)	343.6	579.3	3.3
Total Government Education Expenditure (Billion Yuan)	21.4	97.9	9.9
Total Government Higher Education Expend. (Billion Yuan)	4.2	18.6	9.7
Total Institution-Generated Revenue (Billion Yuan)	0.2	4.2	22.3
Students in Regular Higher Education (Million)	0.9	2.8	7.7
Teachers in Regular Higher Education (Million)	0.2	0.4	4.2
Nonteaching Staff in Regular Higher Education (Million)	0.3	0.6	4.6
Total Staff in Regular Higher Education (Million)	0.5	1.0	4.5
Average Annual Wage in Higher Education (Yuan)	1,527	5,992	8.9

Note: The numbers on students, teachers, and staff in regular higher education institutions were rounded in this table. However, the calculation of the average annual growth rates was based on the original numbers (in hundreds of thousands).

Source: Summary of Annexes 1, 5, 6, 13A and B and *China Statistical Yearbook 1995*, pp. 115-117 for information on wages.

At the same time, given the very low enrollment ratio in China, public spending on higher education was high by international comparison. For example, Indonesia, Malaysia, Thailand, Taiwan (China), Republic of Korea, and Japan, which had a much higher enrollment ratio in higher education, spent only 11 to 17 percent of their respective total public education expenditure on higher education, and mobilized the rest of the resources from private spending; the rest of their public expenditure was spent on lower levels of education (Table 1.2). In 1980, China spent 27 percent of its public education expenditure on the primary level, 34 percent on the secondary level, 0.5 percent on preprimary education, and 18 percent on others.[3] By 1993, the share of primary education went up to 34 percent and that of secondary education to 38 percent, while preprimary and other types of education claimed 1.3 and 9 percent, respectively. Since the lower levels of education are where the poor have access to, whereas middle- and upper-class students tend to be overrepresented in universities, allocating more public resources to lower levels of education is more equitable. Table 4.3 provides a regional comparison of public spending per-student as a percentage of GDP per capita by level of education. In China, in 1990, public spending per-student in higher education was 193 percent of GDP per capita, that in secondary education was 15 percent, and that in primary education was 5 percent. In 1994, this was 175 percent.[4] While improvement has been made, this percentage is still considerably higher than the 1990 average of 98 percent in East Asian countries (Table 4.3). The relatively low per-student spending at the tertiary level in East Asia was made possible by the relatively large enrollment in higher education and efficient use of resources, resulting in reduced unit cost.

---

[3]   UNESCO, *Statistical Yearbook 1995*, p. 4-50.

[4]   This is calculated by dividing the public expenditure on higher education per student by the GDP per capita. In 1994, it was Y 6,645 divided by Y 3,800, which is equal to 175 percent.

Public allocation per student in real terms peaked in 1984, and then went on a decline with year-on-year fluctuation (Table 4.2, Column 6). The increasing share of university-generated income and student fees made up for the shortfall (Table 4.2, Column 7). In 1994, the total allocation per student amounted to Y 8,168 of which Y 6,645 were public allocation and Y 1,515 were allocated from university-generated resources (Table 4.2, Column 8). In other words, in spite of rapid enrollment expansion, the total public and institutional allocation per student maintained the average unit allocation at a relatively stable level for higher education.

Reforms in Higher Education Finance and Their Consequences

Before the reforms in the 1980s, higher education institutions received their funding almost exclusively from government appropriation according to the unitary State budgetary plan. Based on the previous year's allocation, the government would make some incremental adjustment according to the needs and development of the institution and the total budget for higher education. Unused funds had to be returned to the government at the end of the year. Thus, the tightly controlled budgetary system provided no incentive for efficiency gains, and hampered the initiatives of universities and lower-level governments. In recent years several significant reforms covering financial decentralization, new funding mechanisms and resource mobilization were implemented.

TABLE 4.2: FUNDING SOURCES FOR HIGHER EDUCATION AND SPENDING PER STUDENT, 1978-94
(In constant 1994 prices)

Year	Total Govt. Expenditure on Higher Education (Bil. Yuan)	Total University-Generated Income (Bil. Yuan)	Total Public & Own Spending (Bil. Yuan)	Student Enrollment (Million Persons)	Government Allocation Per Student (Yuan)	University-Generated Income Per Student (Yuan)	Total Spending Per Student (Yuan)
1978	4.2	0.2	4.4	0.9	4,892	196	5,087
1979	6.3	0.2	6.5	1.0	6,157	239	6,396
1980	7.4	0.2	7.5	1.1	6,448	161	6,609
1981	8.2	0.0	8.2	1.3	6,413	N.A.	6,413
1982	8.8	0.2	9.0	1.2	7,649	178	7,827
1983	10.8	0.3	11.1	1.2	8,963	208	9,172
1984	12.6	0.3	12.9	1.4	8,990	241	9,231
1985	13.5	1.2	14.7	1.7	7,913	716	8,629
1986	15.1	0.0	15.1	1.9	8,042	N.A.	8,042
1987	15.2	1.4	16.5	2.0	7,736	708	8,444
1988	14.7	1.7	16.3	2.1	7,131	803	7,934
1989	14.4	1.6	16.1	2.1	6,947	770	7,717
1990	13.2	1.9	15.1	2.1	6,414	904	7,318
1991	13.5	2.0	15.6	2.0	6,642	999	7,641
1992	14.9	2.7	17.6	2.2	6,820	1,252	8,072
1993	15.5	2.8	18.3	2.5	6,119	1,092	7,211
1994	18.6	4.2	22.8	2.8	6,645	1,515	8,160

Sources: The implicit price deflators from 1978 to 1993 were taken from *China: Macroeconomic Stability in a Decentralized Economy* (World Bank, August 1995), Statistical Annex Tables 1.1, 1.3 and 7.6; those figures for 1994 were taken from *China Statistical Yearbook 1995* (State Statistical Bureau, 1995), pp. 32 and 215. The price deflator was rebased, using 1994 prices as constant. Educational expenditure data were drawn from SEdC and State Statistical Bureau sources.

TABLE 4.3: CROSS-REGIONAL COMPARISON OF PUBLIC SUBSIDIES PER STUDENT AS A PERCENTAGE OF GNP PER CAPITA BY LEVEL OF EDUCATION, 1980-94

Region/Country (No. of countries)	Year	Preschool & Primary	Secondary	Tertiary
China	1980	4	13	362
	1990	5	15	193
	1994	-	-	175
Latin America (19)	1980	8	14	56
	1990	11	13	80
East Asia (8)	1980	5	14	182
	1990	8	19	98
South Asia (4)	1980	15	27	84
	1990	10	20	76
Middle East and North Africa (9)	1980	-	-	63
	1990	-	-	81
Sub-Saharan Africa (23)	1980	13	46	796
	1990	14	51	481

Source: UNESCO, *World Education Report 1995*, Table 12, pp. 104, 156-159.

Financial Decentralization

As part of the overall economic reform that allowed provinces and ministry-owned enterprises to retain a higher portion of their earnings for their own development, the central government has delegated financial responsibilities to provincial governments and line ministries in financing higher education.

Financial decentralization has encouraged experimentation and innovation. For example, Guangdong Province recently invested massively in education, raising teachers' salaries across the board to almost twice the national average, improving their housing, and matching central government's allocation to SEdC universities and colleges within the province. However, the financial capacity varies from province to province. Regional disparities in funding of higher education have serious implications for the ability of poorer provinces to attract and retain capable faculty members and to provide quality education. Table 4.4 shows the very wide range of allocations per student in a sample of provinces.

TABLE 4.4: GOVERNMENT ALLOCATION OF FUNDS PER STUDENT TO PROVINCIAL UNIVERSITIES AND COLLEGES IN SELECTED PROVINCES, 1992
(In Yuan)

Provinces	Total Govt. Allocation Per Student	Recurrent Allocation Per Student	Capital Allocation Per Student	Provincial GDP Per Capita	Percentage of GDP for Higher Education
Beijing	7,007	5,309	1,698	6,434	2.9
Guangdong	6,630	5,157	1,473	3,514	1.5
Shanghai	5,341	4,707	634	7,925	2.4
Anhui	4,154	3,613	541	1,243	1.8
Sichuan	3,471	3,019	452	1,357	1.6

Source: Constructed by the Bank mission according to information from the State Education Commission of China.

Even within a province, disparity is evident in the resources available for provincial universities and national universities. For example, of the Y 1,115 million revenue in higher education in one province, Y 787 million (including government allocation, own-generated income, and tuition fees) were spent on SEdC and line-ministry universities, and only 328 million on the provincial universities and colleges. Of that Y 328 million, 260 million came from the provincial government, and 68 million from student tuition fees and own-generated income generation. Consequently, the unit expenditure per student for provincial universities was Y 4,162, while that for national universities in the same province in the same year was Y 7,494 in 1992. Obviously, the provincial universities and colleges were heavily disadvantaged.

Changes in Funding Mechanisms

In conjunction with financial decentralization, the reform replaced the nonfungible line item budget with a block grant allocation from the state to the universities, and gave higher education institutions the autonomy to decide how to spend the money. The state has exercised only audit and supervisory functions holding universities accountable for the appropriate utilization of public resources. The state has also abolished the regulations for returning the unspent funds to the government at the end of each year.

The incremental approach to allocating recurrent funds was replaced by a formula-based approach. The major allocation parameter is the number of full-time equivalent students. Appropriation for special items and capital outlay is based partially on enrollment, and partially on ad hoc considerations. Although the enrollment-based approach has improved the transparency in resource allocation, it does not provide incentives to improve efficiency or quality. Moreover, some of the national norms for allocating public funds are extremely generous. For example, for each student enrolled, the institution is required to provide 66 square meters of land and 46 square meters of constructed floor space (including classrooms, dormitories, sports facilities, and laboratories) (Annex 10).

Resource Mobilization

In parallel with the reduction of public subsidies, government has encouraged higher education institutions: (a) to generate their own revenue; and (b) to charge tuition fees.

University-Generated Income. The reforms have given higher education institutions more autonomy to generate their own revenues. In 1992, central, provincial, and municipal government allocations accounted for 82 percent of the total revenue in public higher education institutions; income generated by higher education institutions themselves from various sources represented 14 percent and tuition fees accounted for 4.6 percent (Table 4.5).

TABLE 4.5: PERCENTAGE DISTRIBUTION OF FUNDING FROM DIFFERENT SOURCES

Source	1978	1990	1991	1992
(1) Total Budgeted Allocation From Government	**95.9**	**87.7**	**86.9**	**81.8**
1.1 Allocation for Recurrent Expenditure	74.8	64.9	65.3	61.4
1.2 Allocation for Capital Expenditure	21.1	22.9	21.6	20.4
(2) Total University Generated Revenue	**4.1**	**12.3**	**13.1**	**18.2**
Total of (2.1) and (2.2)	4.1	10.5	11.4	13.6
2.1 Net Income from University funded activities, among which:		10.3	10.7	12.8
income from university enterprises		2.8	3.1	3.7
income from commissioned training		2.1	1.9	2.3
income from educational services		0.9	0.9	1.1
income from research and constancy		1.0	1.2	1.3
income from logistic services (dining halls and guesthouse, etc.)		0.7	0.7	0.7
income from other funded activities		2.7	3.0	3.7
2.2 Donations and Others		0.2	0.7	0.8
2.3 Student Tuition and Fees		1.8	2.9	4.6
Total	**100.0**	**100.0**	**100.0**	**100.0**

Source: Estimated and constructed by the mission according to information from the State Education Commission, and from Chen Liangkun (1994).

The four principal sources of income are:

(a)   Income from university enterprises, which accounted for 3.7 percent of total higher education revenue. The most successful examples can be found in the major cities. In Shanghai, 50 higher education institutions operated about 700 enterprises in 1992, the total business volume of which in 1992 was about Y 1 billion. Fudan University's enterprises had a total output value of Y 20 million, among which Y 2 million were given back to the university. However, not all institutions have the relevant management expertise and not all investments produce positive returns. For example, a language institute in Sichuan Province lost about Y 3 million by investing in mining in a neighboring province. Success in generating income also depends a great deal on the location; universities in poor provinces are at a particular disadvantage.

(b)   Providing commissioned training for enterprises provides the second largest share of independent revenue (2.3 percent of total higher education revenue), while providing education services netted 1.1 percent. Departments that offer applied knowledge are in the best position to generate this type of revenue. For example, the Department of Law of Peking University generated much income by running short-term training courses on the large number of newly adopted laws to employees in state-owned and joint-venture enterprises. Commissioned training has great potential to generate further income because the demand for skill upgrading can only grow with economic development—although the potential for rural universities may be limited.

(c)   Income from research and consultancy accounted for 1.3 percent of total revenue in 1992. Research universities are in the best position to offer this kind of service. For example, the annual income from research in the 36 national key universities was Y 1.12 billion, compared with their state allocation for recurrent expenditure of Y 1.17 billion in 1993. Universities are also able to charge an overhead ranging from 5 to 15 percent, depending on the nature of the research and the source of funding. For many provincial colleges or teachers' colleges, where the research budget is very small, their ability to provide research and consultancy is limited. Logistic services (such as running dining halls and hostels) were not very lucrative, netting only 0.7 percent.

(d)   Donations now contribute 0.8 percent of income compared with zero in 1978. However, most of these donations are for the construction of buildings, which bear the name of the donor or are in the form of merit scholarships for students in China or for faculty members to study overseas. The beneficiaries tend to be prestigious universities with large networks of influential alumni. Small provincial universities in the interior are rarely the recipients of donations. This again heightens the disparity between national universities and the others.

Tuition Fees. Before 1978, university admissions were tightly controlled by the state, students paid no fees and were assigned jobs upon graduation. The 1985 reform allowed higher education institutions to admit students outside the state plan, as long as they are either sponsored by enterprises or self-financed. In 1992, students in the state plan were charged an annual tuition fee of Y 300-600 and room and board of Y 100-300. Enterprise-financed and self-financed students were charged an annual fee ranging from Y 2,000 to Y 6,000 inclusive of room and board. Regional figures display even higher proportions of self-financed students than the national figure. For example, in 1993, 50 percent of the new student intake in Shanghai was self-financed or commissioned by employers. In Anhui, these categories of new students amounted to 63 percent, the highest in the country. In fact, enrollment grew by 22 percent in 1994, far above the growth target of 6 percent in the state plan, and a large part of the growth was attributable to the increase in self- or enterprise-financed students. This reflects the strength of social and private demand for higher education.

Since 1989, universities and colleges have charged a low level of fees to state-financed students. The fee level varies by region and subject specialty. Students in agriculture, forestry, normal education, minority education, physical education, and maritime education are exempted from tuition fees. In 1992, they enjoyed subsidies of about Y 80-150 per month to compensate for the future low salaries in these public services or to support special subjects. Revenues from tuition fees at the national level in 1992 accounted for less than 5 percent of total revenue on higher education (Table 4.5).

The policy changed in September 1994 and the distinction in fee levels between students financed by the state, enterprises, and themselves was eliminated. For most universities, the tuition fee level was set around Y 1,300 per student in the state plan in 1995, although for a few subject specialties in some universities, the fee level can be higher, but cannot exceed Y 2,700. Students in teacher training programs are exempt from fees. The goal is to recover 20 percent of the cost of higher education by 1997.

This policy has implications for enrollment, job placement, and student financial aid. Previously, the rationale for setting enrollment quotas was to ensure that needed personnel were trained and the state had the financial capability to finance their training. Once a uniform rate is charged to all categories of students, the justification for setting enrollment quotas disappears.

Instead, enrollment would be driven by the private demand for education, which, in turn, is responsive to labor market signals of employment prospects and wages. In this sense, raising tuition fees closer to the level that reflects the cost has put in place a self-regulating market mechanism.

There are, however, two negative impacts, and that is where the state can play a role in regulating the system. First, institutions have incentives to increase their revenue by expanding enrollment, irrespective of their capacity to deliver and of quality. Since students have no information on the quality of education provided by individual institutions, they can be misled into paying an enormous amount. Therefore, the state has both a role in the accreditation of universities and colleges, particularly newly formed private institutions, and the obligation to publish institutional performance indicators to enable students to make informed decisions about which institution to attend. The details will be discussed in Chapter 5.

Second, charging tuition fees can have a negative impact on equity if qualified students who cannot pay are forced to give up their places. Therefore, in conjunction with charging tuition fees, the former merit scholarships and grants system introduced in 1983, which distributed funds equally to all students, was changed into a new system of merit scholarships, grants, and loans for needy students in 1987. The coverage varies from one institution to another. Some universities charge a higher tuition fee while providing more scholarships. In 1992, financial aid covered between 50 to 80 percent of students. However, the sums awarded were very small, ranging from Y 60 to 300 per year, which provided inadequate support (Table 4.6).

TABLE 4.6: FINANCIAL AID TO STUDENTS, 1992

	Annual Amount (Yuan)	% of Students Covered
Scholarship	over 100-1,000	less than 10
Grant-in-aid	200-600	40-50
Student loan	300-600	less than 10
Work Study	hourly pay	less than 10

Source: Universities' reports.

When the total amount of tuition fees received in 1993 was compared with the amount of financial aid universities have to provide to its students, it was found that the financial aid varied from a 39 percent equivalent to more than twice of tuition revenue (Annex 18). Henceforth, the expectation that charging tuition fees can recover the target share of the cost should be tempered by the realization that cost recovery must be accompanied by student financial aid if equity is to be protected.

Conclusions. Financial decentralization has made possible the mobilization of previously untapped resources and encouraged innovation on one hand, but has heightened the disparity based on natural endowment and comparative advantage on the other hand. Since most provincial universities are much more disadvantaged than national universities (and yet enroll over 50 percent of students), their financial plight has serious implications for the higher education system as a whole. Moreover, while the new funding mechanism has raised universities' cost-consciousness, the norms for resource allocation have not provided any incentives to improve operational efficiency.

Changing Pattern of Higher Education Finance: Institutional Perspective and Implications

Annex 14 provides a summary of the revenue and expenditure of 14 universities in 1993. Data on revenue and expenditure for these same universities from 1980 to 1993 are presented in Annex 15. It should be noted that these universities were not drawn from a representative sample, and, therefore, the data have no nationwide generalizability. Nonetheless, they provide a glimpse of the financing issues confronting individual institutions.

On the revenue side, the institutional data confirmed that state allocations constituted the bulk of revenue for them, except where the university can obtain a large share of its resources from "other source or donation," as in the case of a university in Guangdong province. It is also clear that revenue fluctuated widely across institutions and within institutions from year to year. This makes long-term planning difficult, and there is a case for state funding of nonpersonnel cost on a triennial basis, channeled through a university and college council, which would allocate funds on the basis of strategic plans and evidence of improvement of efficiency and productivity.

On the expenditure side, the major components of recurrent higher education expenditure are: personnel cost (salaries and benefits), student financial aid (which each institution provides to its students in need), administration, instruction, equipment, maintenance and repair, and logistical services (such as running canteens and dormitories); capital expenditure is mainly for construction of buildings for instructional and administrative purposes, student dormitories and residence for faculty members and other staff. Research is not funded on a regular basis, but research expenditure is considered as part of total spending. Several observations can be made from these institutional data.

First, no uniform pattern of spending has emerged from these institutions' data. Each institution's history, the size and age profile of its staff, assets, programs offered, and other related factors play an important role in affecting spending. For example, universities with an aging staff find themselves having to spend more and more on personnel cost, due to the need to pay for medical care and pension of these staff, and to continue to recruit new staff to replace them.

Second, salaries and benefits have been on the rise in all institutions in real terms, although their percentage share rose or fell as the total revenue and spending changed (Annex 15). The increase in salaries and benefits averaged 10.7 percent per year between 1980 and 1993, faster than the 8.9 increase in average annual salaries. This reflected in part the increasing pension and welfare responsibilities of universities. For example, Hefei University of Technology, with an enrollment of 7,200 regular students and 2,000 adult students, will have 2,000 retirees by 2000. Unless alternative provincial, regional, or national health insurance and retirement pension systems are developed, the welfare burden of universities is likely to grow.

On the other hand, however, personnel cost did not exceed 50 percent of total spending in these institutions; some even spent as little as 11 percent on salaries and benefits. This is unusual in comparison with other countries, where personnel cost in higher education can be well over 50 percent. This is attributable to wage compression in the public pay scale. In 1994, the average annual wage in higher education institutions was Y 5,992 ($704), which was 23 percent above that in secondary education, 33 percent above that in primary education, and 32 percent above the national average in all sectors (Table 4.7). These relatively higher wages reflected the policy to increase wages of "intellectuals" in order to attract and retain capable persons in higher education. On the other hand, these wage differentials were small relative to the substantial differentials in skill requirements between faculty members and secondary and primary school teachers. In view of the fact that holders of doctorate and master's degrees have highly portable skills, unless the terms of service and research environment are sufficiently attractive, higher education institutions would be hard pressed to attract and retain capable individuals in the future. To the extent that wages reflect quality of the service provider, the quality of education in private universities and colleges in China is highly questionable. The state can avoid aggravating the situation by removing any ceiling on tuition fees to enable public and private universities to charge fees at a level that students are willing to pay in order to attract capable persons into teaching, but to ensure that financial aid is available to help the needy students.

TABLE 4.7: AVERAGE ANNUAL WAGE OF STAFF AND WORKERS BY LEVEL OF EDUCATION, 1994
(In Yuan)

Level	Average	State-owned Unit	Urban Collective Unit	Other Unit
Higher Education	5,992	5,993	4,569	3,944
Secondary Education	4,943	4,949	3,686	12,177
Primary Education	4,514	4,537	3,055	11,383
National (All Sectors)	4,538	4,797	3,245	6,303
GNP Per Capita	3,679			

Source: *China Statistical Yearbook 1995*, Tables 2-10, p. 32 for GNP per capita; Table 4-26, p. 116-117 for annual wages.

Third, administrative costs are not very high, fluctuating between 2 to 6 percent in these institutions. Spending on logistical services varied between 5 to 12 percent across institutions, but mostly stayed on the low side. Instructional expenditure fluctuated from 4 to 14 percent across institutions, with most around 6 percent. Spending on equipment fluctuated even more widely across institutions from 2.4 to 18 percent of expenditure. These data indicated that the leadership in these universities has done a good job in containing administrative costs, spending as much as possible on instruction and equipment. That, however, does not mean that universities have sufficient funding for improvement of instruction. Devaluation of the Chinese currency[5] and the rising prices of international journals and books have an adverse impact on the ability of higher education institutions to access the most updated knowledge and to purchase new equipment. Institutions are under pressure to reduce their purchase of library books and subscriptions to academic journals. For example, Fudan University, one of the national leading universities, reduced its journal subscriptions from 1,600 in 1988 to about 800 in 1993. The

---

[5] According to *China Statistical Yearbook 1995* (p. 799), the exchange rates of the Chinese currency fell from Y 3.2 to $1 in 1985 to Y 8.6 to $1 in 1994. This report adopted the exchange rate of Y 8.5 to US$ in 1994, which was used in another World Bank report (1995), *China: Macroeconomic Stability in a Decentralized Economy*, in order to attain consistency within Bank documents.

University of Malaya in Kuala Lumpur, to use an Asian comparator, holds well over 1,300 titles. Harvard University holds about 100,000 periodicals and 13.5 million books.

Fourth, research spending ranged considerably across institutions, going from zero to 39 percent. This revealed extreme variability in the ability of universities to attract funding, with implications for the quality of research and instruction associated with it.

Fifth, capital expenditure varied from 7 to over 52 percent over the period within and across institutions (Annex 14). This fluctuation indicated the lack of predictability in resource availability and could easily crowd out other expenditures. National data show that capital expenditure accounted for 20-22 percent of total public allocation between 1978 and 1992; however, this share declined to 7 percent in 1993 and 16 percent in 1994. This extreme fluctuation of capital expenditure at the national level corroborated with the trend shown in institutional data, reflecting that in the face of resource constraints, capital expenditure was cut to give priority to recurrent spending.

The reason that institutions spent a considerable portion of their total expenditure on capital construction is because of the need to finance the construction of student hostels and housing for university staff. Of the total floor space in regular higher education institutions, only 33 percent were used for instructional purposes and 6 percent for administrative purposes, but 62 percent for residential purposes (see Annex 10 for sources). Of the residential buildings, 31 percent of the floor space was for housing for faculty members and staff, while 15 percent for students' dormitories. Of those buildings under construction in 1994, staff residence accounted for as much as 40 percent of the total floor space. The total floor space per student in 1994 was 44 square meters, of which 14 square meters were for instructional use, and 7 for student hostels and the rest for other purposes such as sports and recreation. The total and instructional floor space in China was much higher than the Republic of Korea's total square meters of 8 in 1985 and 10 in 1991. This wasteful result is probably due to the common problems of most Chinese state-owned units, namely, overstaffing, poor use of existing capital assets, emphasis on creating new ones and higher priority to the interest of staff than those of clients.

A major impediment to improving the efficiency of use of capital expenditure is the obligation to provide housing for staff. Under the socialist system, all government units, state-owned enterprises, and universities are obligated to care for the welfare of their staff. A private housing market was nonexistent. Retired staff and descendants of deceased staff continue to stay in their university housing. Even today, the absence of affordable housing in the private sector does not provide any alternative arrangement for universities. Any enrollment expansion and staff increases necessitate a proportional investment in capital construction. And the lack of resources for capital construction have been cited frequently as a major constraint to enrollment expansion.[6] One option (already adopted in some universities) is to sell the right to live in university accommodation either at or slightly below construction cost. However, there are a number of unresolved issues. First, the legal right of the university to dispose of its property has not been spelled out by law. Second, selling the quarters at the cost of construction will not reflect the value of the land, which has skyrocketed in recent years; also the proceeds from sales

---

[6]   An article in *People's Daily (October 6, 1995)* pointed out that because the capital investment cost for every new enrollee to be Y 60,000 in 1993, the government cannot finance such construction to enable an annual growth rate of enrollment at 8 percent.

of housing units at or below construction cost cannot provide substantial capital for university development. Third, after the sale, certain portions of the university's property will not be available for redevelopment, thereby limiting the management and financing flexibility of the institution. Therefore, a major policy issue relates to ensuring that the university does not give away its valuable assets and that university housing is not inheritable by descendants of university staff. The complexity of this issue requires housing reform on the national level, and is beyond the scope of this study. However, the issue does require immediate attention because 25 percent of all the faculty members in the country are currently in their 50s, and due to retire in the first decade of the 21st century. Unless housing reform is in place, universities would have to house minimally 25 percent of the staff recruited to replace the retirees. This financial burden would undoubtedly crush any hope for expansion and qualitative improvement.

Nonetheless, institutional data show that most of the 14 universities do have surpluses which indicates that the policy of requiring universities to be responsible for their own finances has some success in fostering fiscal discipline (Annex 15). Because institutions' financial situations differed, expenditure per student also varied enormously from under Y 6,000 to over Y 14,000 in 1993 (Annex 17).

Conclusion

This analysis of the reforms for diversifying sources of funding and changing the pattern of spending has found that part of the financial difficulties experienced by institutions stems from disparities in their natural endowment and location, part is due to the funding mechanism which does not provide incentives for efficiency improvement, and part stems from the welfare burden that the socialist system requires institutions to bear. Changing the funding mechanism will improve efficiency and reduce some disparity in natural endowment, but systemic change is required to reduce the welfare burden.

Policy Options for Funding Higher Education, 1995-2020

The demand for highly educated personnel will depend to a large extent on how fast the economy grows. According to the Ninth Five-Year Plan (1995-2000), the Government's target for GDP in 2000 is to quadruple that in 1980, and that for GDP in 2010 is to double that in 2000. This entails an average annual growth rate of 8 percent between 1995 and 2000, and over 7 percent between 2000 and 2010. Given the momentum of China's historical growth rate, it is realistic to expect the GDP to continue to grow at an annual average of 7 to 9 percent in real terms over the next 25 years. Annex 22 provides estimated GDP per capita based on three scenarios of average annual GDP growth rate: (a) slow growth at 7 percent; (b) medium growth at 8 percent; and (c) fast growth at 9 percent and projected population based on a set of assumptions outlined in Annex 21. According to these projections, China's GDP per capita would be $600-$700 by 2000; $1,100-$1,600 by 2010; and $2,100-$3,500 by 2020. In other words, in five years' time, China would be on its way to becoming a lower-middle-income country, and in 25 years' time, it would be poised to join the league of upper-middle-income countries[7] (Table 4.8 and Annex 22). To sustain these growth rates, the demand for well-educated personnel is likely to be high.

TABLE 4.8: PROJECTED GDP PER CAPITA, PERCENTAGE OF RELEVANT AGE GROUP ENROLLED IN HIGHER EDUCATION, AND TUITION FEES AND SPENDING PER STUDENT, 1995-2020
(In Constant 1994 Yuan)

	1994	2000	2010	2020
GDP Per Capita in Yuan				
Slow Growth (r=7%)	3,800	5,400	9,900	18,300
Medium Growth (r=8%)	3,800	5,700	11,500	23,300
Fast Growth (r=9%)	3,800	6,000	13,300	29,600
In Dollars (8.5 Yuan = $1)				
Slow Growth (r=7%)	447	630	1,200	2,200
Medium Growth (r=8%)	447	670	1,300	2,700
Fast Growth (r=9%)	447	710	1,600	3,500
Country Income Level	Low	Becoming Lower-Middle	Lower-Middle	Becoming Upper-Middle
Enrollment Ratio (%)				
r=7.6%	2.4	4.9	7.7	18.8
r=9.8%	2.4	5.5	10.7	25.4
Enrollment (Million Students)				
r=7.6%	2.8	4.4	9.0	18.7
r=9.8%	2.8	4.9	12.5	25.4

Note: The numbers are rounded.

Sources: Summary of Annexes.

To enable higher education institutions to educate as many students as possible under conditions of public resource constraints, it is imperative to pursue three policies simultaneously: (a) improving the operating efficiency of the system; (b) enhancing institutional capacity for resource generation; (c) implementing cost-recovery policies while providing financial assistance (see Figure 4.3).

Efficiency Improvement

Contain staff growth. Enrollment expansion must be accompanied by efficiency improvement in order to attain savings. The underutilization of staff is a prime case. Between 1976 and 1994, total staff increased at an annual rate of 4.5 percent, with teachers increasing at a slightly lower rate than nonteaching staff (Table 4.1). At this rate, if enrollment expands at 7.6 percent per year over the next 25 years, the student-to-staff ratio would be 3.7:1 by 2005, and 5.8:1 by 2020, still lower than the current European and North American average of 7:1 (Annex

---

[7] The World Bank's definition of country income level is as follows: low-income countries are those with a GNP per capita of $695 or less; lower-middle-income countries are those with a GNP per capita between $696 and $2,784, and upper-middle-income countries are those with a GNP per capita between $2,784 and $8,626 (World Development Report 1995).

24). However, if staff growth is slowed to 1 percent per year, and if enrollment expands at the historical rate of 9.8 percent over the next 25 years, the student-to-staff ratio would be 6.7 by 2005 (closer to the current European and North America average), and 19:1 by 2020 [closer to the current Korean and Taiwanese (China) ratio] (Annex 24 and Table 1.6).

Given that the average wage increased by 8.9 percent in real terms between 1978 and 1994[8] (Table 4.1) and the scarcity of skills that is likely to occur in a rapidly growing economy, higher education cannot compress wages without losing its ability to attract and retain capable teaching staff. Therefore, the key is to contain the growth of nonteaching staff, not to suppress wages. Projection shows that if staff growth continues at the historical rate of 4.5 percent, and if wages also grow at the historical rate of 8.9 percent at the GDP growth rate of 7 percent, the wage bill would grow from 41 percent of the public expenditure on higher education in 1994 to over 100 percent after 2005, and over 500 percent by 2020 if other things remain unchanged and public expenditure continues to grow at the historical rate (Annex 25). This is clearly unsustainable. Even if staff growth rate is reduced to 1 percent per year, if wages grow at 8.9 percent per year and GDP at 7 percent, they will take up 89 percent of total public spending on higher education by 2020, and universities would have to generate sufficient revenue to cover spending on administration, instruction, and capital construction, which may consume half of the total higher education expenditure.

Encourage the growth of existing public institutions in size through expansion or merger, and the expansion of private universities. As Table 1.1 has shown, the average size of a university was 2,390 students in 1993. This compares poorly with many other countries; in New Zealand no university has less than 7,000 students, in the United Kingdom a small percentage of the 130 institutions have less than 4,500 students, and Australia has recently merged all its universities into large comprehensive institutions. Mergers help pool resources (such as libraries, laboratories, specialties of faculty members) together and better serve the diverse needs of students. At the same time, it is important to allow for the expansion of private universities in order to meet increasing demand and to create competitive pressure for public universities to improve their performance. The government, however, has a role to provide the infrastructure and information to the public about the quality of all public and private institutions through various mechanisms to be discussed in Chapter 5.

Devise funding mechanisms that encourage efficiency and reward cost-effective provision. The current resource allocation formula of x Yuan per student takes no account of marginal cost. In the United Kingdom, a new bidding system was introduced in which universities were asked to tender for teaching more students at less than the average cost. To the surprise of the funding body, all the universities submitted bids for far lower unit costs than they were being funded for. Other incentives to foster efficiency could also be built into the system; for example, funding bodies could ask universities to report on the number of courses for which fewer than, say, 10 students were enrolled. Rewards could be offered to those universities that rationalized their program offerings. A multiparameter funding formula could be devised to take into account policy issues such as the number of poorly subscribed programs, the relative wealth of the province, or the size of the university.

---

[8] In current prices, these were Y 545 in 1978 and Y 5,992 in 1994 (*China Statistical Yearbook 1995*, p. 115 and 117).

Review the norms and space formulae for allocating capital funding as it is clear that they are extremely generous by international standards, and do not encourage institutions to make effective use of their space by such methods as double shifts, or seven-day timetables. Many Chinese universities are extremely well endowed in terms of the size of the land and the spaciousness of the buildings and classrooms. While student hostels and staff quarters are often overcrowded, facilities for teaching and research are not. Thus, these available facilities can accommodate the expansion of enrollment.

Allow flexible duration of study as long as course requirements are fulfilled. In order to maximize the use of available buildings and staff, it is worthwhile considering shortening the duration of a bachelor's program from the current four to three years, but run regular courses in the summer to ensure that the total amount of instruction time is not shortened and the content of study would not be compromised. From the university's point of view, the merit of this system is to enable maximum use of classroom, student hostels, staff time, and staff quarters. This would enable universities to enroll 33 percent more students every four years. From the student's point of view, they can finish their study a year faster and can begin to reap the economic benefits of their own education earlier.

Universities in Hong Kong have adopted a uniform three-year system in 1993 in order to promote rapidity in student enrollment. They follow the British system in having seven years of secondary education so as to compensate for a shorter duration of study at the university level. If China shortens the duration of its bachelor's programs, it does not have to make systemic change in the secondary education. It can consider adopting the American model of the credit unit[9] system, which enables students to take courses in the summer and graduate within three years or less, as soon as they fulfill all the course requirements. Many foreign students in American universities speed up their studies by taking an above average course load in regular semesters and in the summer, in order to save the additional year of room and board, and to enter the labor market ahead of time. Running regular courses in the summer can also apply to short-cycle programs.

Consideration of appropriate compensation is a prerequisite to ensure that academic staff have the incentive to teach during summer months. In fact, many already engage in part-time employment anyway. Therefore, mandating them to take up additional teaching during the summer would only legitimize activities that have been ongoing, and would work to the advantage of all parties.

Better use of educational technology to reduce cost and assure minimum quality. China is not alone in facing the challenge of having to expand enrollment under conditions of resource constraints. Table 1.2 shows that many countries have increased enrollment in higher education massively between 1980 and 1993. One way to meet the challenge is to take advantage of modern instructional modalities by using radio, television, and computer to supplement classroom teaching, or to provide open learning and distance education opportunities. The use of educational technology can reach a large number of students quickly and at relatively low cost. There is no necessity to wait for new buildings, student hostels, and

---

[9]   Currently, a few universities are experimenting with a fledgling credit unit system. The full range of flexibility, however, calls for a quality assurance and accreditation system upon which recognition of equivalencies should be based.

staff residence to be built, and hundreds of thousands of faculty members to be upgraded to expand higher education. The success in training a large number of students in China's television universities (1.3 million graduates with college diplomas in the 1979-91 period and over 3 million students who had passed TVU courses not for credit) illustrates the potential of using educational technology to extend access (see Annex 29 on the history of television higher education).

Since high quality products require high production costs, an option is to purchase existing telecourses and distance education packages, particularly those on natural science, technology, international commerce, foreign languages, for adaptation and use them in China. Providers of these courses can be found in Britain, Canada, the United States, and Japan. The University of Singapore has purchased the franchise from the British Open University to conduct their academic programs. The Open Learning Institute in Hong Kong has also purchased a range of British Open University courses. The "University of the Air" in Japan produces high-quality programs, which could serve specific needs of Chinese students. The benefits of purchasing existing materials from reputed universities and distance learning institutions are that they are usually well-tested and are of reasonable audiovisual quality, and that through the use of these materials, Chinese students can obtain a window to the world and learn what students in other countries are learning. There are, of course, the added benefits of cost savings and extending access to more students within a relatively short time span. The cost of adaptation and translation, however, is likely to be substantial, and this calls for central government, provincial authorities, and/or a consortium of universities to act together in the purchase and use of the materials.

Enhancement of Institutional Capacity for Resource Generation

The projection on growth of personnel cost shows that wages can easily consume the entire public expenditure on higher education (Annex 25). This requires the generation of additional resources through the universities' own means, an imperative in order to finance administration, instruction, equipment, maintenance and repair, and capital construction. The trend between 1990 and 1992 shows that different components within own-generated revenue grew at differentiated rates. Revenue from enterprises increased at an annual average rate of 15 percent, revenue from commissioned training at 4.5 percent, revenue from educational services at 10.5 percent, revenue from research and consultancy at 14 percent, revenue from logistical services did not grow at all, revenue from other sources by 17 percent, and revenue from donation by a significant 200 percent.

Most of these historical growth rates are used as baseline data for projecting future self-generated income, except from enterprises, other sources, and donation mainly because revenue generated from these three channels has increased so rapidly that it is unrealistic to expect it to grow at the same speed in the future. A more realistic expectation is for enterprises to generate incremental increased income at 9 percent on par with economic growth, for other income to grow at half its historical level, and for donations to grow no more than by 1 percent annually. If this growth rate continues, university-generated income will be around 10 percent of total income by 2000, and 13 percent by 2020 (Annex 26). The potential for universities to increase their own income can be enhanced by the following strategies:

Implementing Cost-Recovery Policies and Provide Financial Assistance

Charging Tuition Fees. As China's economy grows, it would be realistic to expect tuition fee income to represent a growing percentage of total university income. Current government policy is to target 20 percent of the cost to be recovered from charging tuition fees by 1997, although institutions are given considerable flexibility in implementing this policy. Within each province, the percentage would obviously differ. Given current economic and higher education policy trends, the income from this category could be close to the target by the turn of the century (see Table 4.9 for the current status). Annexes 28A and 29B project the total public and private resources at different enrollment and GDP growth rates. According to these projections, if the assumptions hold, student tuition fees could contribute between 24 to 38 percent of the total resources for higher education by 2020. (See Annex 20 for explanation of the assumptions of the projection.). Nonetheless, growth estimates are not precise because they depend as much on unknown variables such as political changes. In the United Kingdom, a 15 percent share of income in 1988-98 shot up to 34 percent in 1992-93 and then fell back again because of a political decision in 1993-94. Income from student tuition fees in public universities constitute over 25 percent and 40 percent of recurrent expenditures in Chile and the Republic of Korea, respectively. These two countries have also had extraordinary growth rates in higher education in the past decade. (See Figure 4.1 for a cross-country comparison of the percentage of cost recovery in public institutions.)

TABLE 4.9: PER STUDENT COST IN ADULT POSTSECONDARY EDUCATION

	Total		% of Total Revenue	
	1993	1994	1993	1994
State Allocation (Million Yuan)	1,151	1,750	75	71
Recurrent	1,013	1,369	66	55
Capital	139	381	9	16
Institution-generated Revenue (Million Yuan)	74	88	5	4
Tuition Revenue (Million Yuan)	312	597	20	25
Total Revenue (Million Yuan)	**1,537**	**2,435**	**100**	**100**
Enrollment (Million Persons)	2.0	2.3		
Spending Per Student (Yuan)	769	928		
Tuition Fee Per Student (Yuan)	168	254		

Note: Percentages are rounded.

Source: SEdC and *China Statistical Yearbook 1995.*

Institutions should be allowed to set their own fee levels for all categories of students, irrespective of whether they are from the state plan, self-financed, or enterprise-financed. The level might vary for different categories of students, and for students in different academic disciplines, depending on the private and social demand for each subject specialty. In this way, institutions can align their income with the teaching and research demands imposed on them. Institutional control over tuition levels has helped North American universities to withstand cuts in public funding. Responsiveness to the general market from competitor institutions will provide the pressure to keep fees within limits, if there is an abundance of providers. Competition will provide the motivation to maintain quality of instructional programs.

FIGURE 4.1: TUITION FEES AS A PROPORTION OF RECURRENT EXPENDITURES IN PUBLIC HIGHER EDUCATION INSTITUTIONS
(percent)

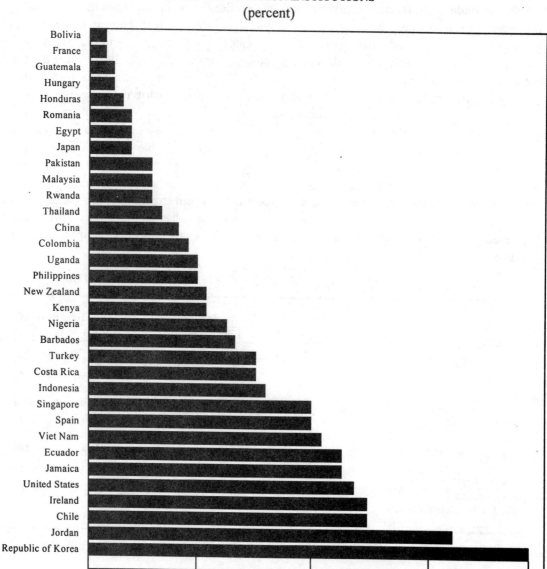

Source: World Bank estimates.

An alternative cost-sharing approach might be considered in which for particular fields of study at certain institutions, students might be asked to pay for the first one or two years only; if they perform satisfactorily, the government and employer will support them for the last year of study. This will provide an incentive for efficiency gains, because if students drop out or repeat, they will have to be responsible for costs.

Certain methods of payment and measures can assist families to pay tuition fees. First, payment by installment permits the financial burden to be spread over the year. Second, banks should encourage to set up education savings accounts with the explicit aims of promoting family savings for education long before the child has reached the college-going age. Savings accumulated over the years would cushion the sudden need to set aside family income to support students through college. Third, it is important to promote a flexible schedule for completion of study so that students can reduce their direct and opportunity cost.

To what extent fees should be raised is an empirical question that requires further data collection and analysis. It is important to differentiate between three groups of students: (a) those who attend without much financial difficulty; (b) those who are marginally able to finance their education; and (c) those who will be denied access because of absolute inability to pay. For Group (a), their demand for education is not likely to change very much even when tuition fees are raised. Group (b) might join the rank of Group (c) if fee increases exceed their financial capacity. On the other hand, the demand for education is likely to increase as household income increases. Given that most urban households have only one child and that household income will rise as the economy grows, Group (b) might join the rank of Group (a). Household demand for education is expected to grow stronger, even when tuition fees are high. Cost recovery, therefore, should remove subsidies for Group (a) in order to free up public resources, but should target assistance in the form of loans for Group (b), and a mixture of grants, loans, work study, and national service for Group (c).

Policymakers are advised to monitor the price elasticity of demand to see how the demand for education by various groups changes as tuition fees increase. In group (a), the demand for higher education does not change very much in response to tuition fee increases because the majority of students is from families of means. Not only can they afford to forgo their earnings by attending school, but they also would have had access to high quality primary and secondary education, thereby being well prepared to pass the many levels of examination to move up the education pyramid.

However, tuition fees tend to have differential adverse impact on the poor, minority groups, rural students, and women. The first three categories of students tend to suffer from lack of access to good quality schooling. Furthermore, poor rural households tend to have more than one child, and thus face more difficulty in supporting all children to pursue education. When faced with choices, parents often hold daughters back to enable sons to pursue education. Female enrollment, as a consequence, tends to be lower across all levels of education. Elasticity of demand, therefore, should be disaggregated by student family income level, gender, rural background, minority status, and geographic location. If an academically-qualified student is forced to turn down the admission or to drop out because of financial difficulties, and the place be given to a less qualified student who is able to pay the fee, not only would the system be unjust and social mobility be sacrificed, but there will also be an efficiency loss to society because talented but disadvantaged people have been excluded.

Financial Assistance to Students. The key policy question is: if substantial cost recovery is implemented, what is the economic burden on the poor, particularly rural households whose per capita income is half that of urban income, and what kind of financial assistance can be provided to the qualified but disadvantaged? Data on student background from selected Chinese institutions found that throughout the 1980s and in the early 1990s, children of peasants accounted for about 30 percent of the student population in comprehensive universities, over 40 percent in medical and normal (education) universities, and some 75 percent in agricultural and forestry universities. Given that over 70 percent of China's population reside in rural areas, higher education is one of the very few channels for mobility for young people from rural backgrounds; it also provides the technical skills for rural development. In 1994, rural income per capita was Y 1,798 and urban income per capita was Y 3,502. Figure 4.2 illustrates the unequal economic impact of university tuition fees on rural and urban households. This calculation uses the figures of 1994 as the basis, and assumes that the level of unit cost of higher education, and rural and urban per capita income remain stable over the years.

FIGURE 4.2: DIFFERENTIAL ECONOMIC BURDEN ON RURAL AND URBAN HOUSEHOLDS

	Rural	Urban
Income Per Capita (Yuan)	1,789	3,502
Family Income with 2 wage earners (Yuan)	3,578	7,004
Unit Cost	8,160	8,160
Tuition Fees Per Child Per Year		
@ 24% cost recovery (Yuan)	1,958	1,958
@ 31% cost recovery (Yuan)	2,530	2,530
@ 38% cost recovery (Yuan)	3,101	3,101
Tuition Fees Per Child as % of Family Income with 1 wage earner		
@ 24% cost recovery (Yuan)	109%	56%
@ 31% cost recovery (Yuan)	141%	72%
@ 38% cost recovery (Yuan)	173%	89%
Tuition Fees Per Child as % of Family Income with 2 wage earners		
@ 24% cost recovery (Yuan)	55%	28%
@ 31% cost recovery (Yuan)	71%	36%
@ 38% cost recovery (Yuan)	87%	44%

Source: Study Team calculations.

If the same level of tuition fees is charged to rural and urban households, the economic burden will fall disproportionally on the former. Tuition fees would account for 109 to 173 percent of the average rural family income with one wage earner, or 55 to 87 percent with two wage earners. However, they constitute 28 to 89 percent of the average urban family incomes, depending on the number of wage earners in the household. Given that rural households tend to have more than one child, in spite of the single-child policy, rural students (particularly girls) are even less likely to be supported by their families to pursue higher education, whereas it is well within the means of the average urban households to do so. Minority families, who tend to live in poorer areas, and who tend to have more children because they are exempt from complying with the one-child policy, also tend to face more difficulties financing their children's education. Furthermore, because rural students account for a disproportional share of the total enrollment in agriculture, forestry, medical and normal universities, who will enter the low-wage profession in the public sector, they are even more adversely affected by tuition fees. To the extent that their future life-time earnings will be low, and that they provide important social services, they can be considered to have paid their tuition fees through national services. The Chinese government's policy of exempting students of normal universities from tuition charges is, therefore, justifiable and commendable.

Agricultural, forestry, medical, education, and minority students together account for nearly 40 percent of total students in higher education. These groups, together with poor students in comprehensive and other universities, account for over 50 percent of the total student body who need adequate financial assistance in order to pursue higher education. For the poor, the foregone earnings often are more substantial than the direct cost of higher education. Of the direct costs of education, housing and food are as substantial as tuition fees, transportation, and books. That is why any form of financial support for Group (c) should cover not just tuition fees, but also living expenses, transportation, and books.

Loans would enable students to finance their education by borrowing against their future earnings. Loan schemes can either be open to all students, regardless of their parents' wealth, or only to those who have satisfied means-tested requirements. For very poor students, however, even the availability of credit is associated with high risks because at the time of entering university, successful completion of study programs and finding employment after graduation are unknown factors. This will discourage many from taking loans and they may opt out of further studies. Therefore, the form of financial assistance for the very poor should encompass a package of **grants** and loans, as well as **work study** programs or **national service**. Eligibility for grants should be means-tested.

If it is assumed that about half of the students do not contribute significantly to fees either through tuition fee exemption or through grants, what is the net contribution of tuition fees to the total revenue of higher education? The implicit assumption is that the other half of the student body will in some form or other enjoy less public subsidies proportional to those who benefit from them. These include students in subject fields which have high private economic returns (such as law, business, and engineering), and those who live in higher income cities and provinces, particularly along the coast. Differential fee payment is justifiable because these students also benefit most from high-paying occupations and working in a labor market which is freer than those in the interior.

Given the diverse jurisdictions and modes of financial support institutions of higher education function within, it is very difficult for individual institutions to come up with resources to provide financial assistance to students. For comprehensive universities, it is possible to use the differential fee scheme to cross-subsidize students. However, for universities that have a single mission—such as education and forestry—they do not have the diversified programs and students to do so. Therefore, the role of the central government is crucial in providing student financial assistance. The central government can target general tax revenue to fund agriculture, education, and medical universities where graduates are likely to work in low-wage occupations but perform important social services so that these institutions either do not have to charge fees or charge very low fees. This method of channeling funds to institutions directly can cut down the administrative cost, but is likely to weaken institutions' responsiveness to labor market demand. Furthermore, this method is likely to be caught up in the politics of the budget process.

An alternative is to set up a national fund that provides needs-based grants and student loans. Applications for financial assistance from individual students will be reviewed and approved at provincial offices of the national fund. Given the enormous number of students and potential applications, the administrative cost to operate this system is likely to be high. Nonetheless, if the funds can be made available at the national level, this will have an equalizing effect for the country as a whole. Financial institutions usually require physical capital or financial resources to guarantee the loan, but students can only offer their human capital as collateral. Without the State's provision of funds initially, it is difficult to start a loan scheme, although commercial banks or new independent financial organizations can be contracted to administer the lending and collection processes.

Student loan schemes have been implemented in over 50 countries. The vast majority of these countries offer a traditional loan, which enables repayment over a specified period.[10] Sweden and Ghana offer income contingent loans, and Australia has a form of a graduate tax to recover cost. Loan programs in developing countries generally provide assistance with living expenses, and cover only a small percentage of the student population.

A student loan program should be self-financing, otherwise it is a grant in disguise. Therefore, it is important to set positive real interest rates in order to reduce hidden subsidies, and to use a variety of approaches to minimize default. Collecting repayments has often been a problem because of lack of collateral. There are several strategies to limit default: (a) income contingent loans, which ensure that repayment is in proportion to the income earned by the graduate, provide a mechanism for achieving a balance between cost recovery, minimum risk to the borrower, and effective targeting of lower wage earners for subsidies; (b) rationing loans to those students whose family income fall below a threshold level; this will limit the government's financial burden; (c) rationing loans on the basis of good academic performance that will also reduce the risk of providing loans to students who are likely to repeat or drop out, thereby containing the cost of loan programs; (d) using social security or national insurance payroll deductions to help minimize evasion; and (e) authorizing employers to deduct repayment amount

---

[10] In the United States, the federal government has been sponsoring a student loan program since 1966. By 1995, it lent out 6.8 million loans, totaling $27,126 million, at an average amount of $3,948 per loan. Besides the federal government, there are three other major organizations that provide student loans—Citicorp, New England Education Loan Market (nonprofit), and Sallie Mae. Repayment begins six months after graduation. These four organizations offer four basic repayment options : (a) a level-repayment plan in which an equal amount of principal plus interest is paid over a 10-year period; (b) a graduated plan, where the repayment is low in the beginning and rises gradually over a 10-year period; (c) an income-contingent plan, where the payment is a percentage of the income of the graduate over a 15-year period; and (d) a loan-consolidation program, which allows graduates to refinance all the federal student loans and stretch the payments out more (totally 15 to 30 years). As an example, for a loan of $15,000 made at an 8 percent annual interest rate, the monthly payment and the total cost will be different under each of these plans:

	Monthly Payment	Total Cost (principal +interest)	Terms
Standard	$182 (Years 1-10)	$21,198	Equal monthly payment for 10 years
Graduated	$126 (Years 1-2) $177 (Years 3-5) $230 (Years 6-15)	$22,906	Low initial payment but gradually rising. Paid off over 10 years.
Income-contingent (assumes initial payment of 4% of initial salary of $30,000)	$100 (Year 1) rising to $143 (Year 3) rising to $236 (Years 12-15)	$29,740	Monthly payment based on % of borrower's after-college income. Paid off in 15 years.
Consolidated	$144 (initial payment).	$25,802	Allows several loans to be folded into one package and repayment to be stretched out to 15-30 years.

(Kristof, 1996)

from the salaries if debtors are in arrears. All of the above methods have been implemented in other countries and Annexes 30A and 30C provide information on existing student loan programs.

The government is well advised to organize an international conference on higher education finance and student loans by inviting experts and administrators from countries which have been successful in combining the setting up student loans in conjunction with charging tuition fees. Countries which have been in the forefront of these experiments include Australia, Chile and Sweden. Such a conference would provide a forum to examine policy options for China. In order to identify the most efficient and equitable loan scheme for China, the Government will need to mount in-depth studies of the existing financial institutions, and of the administrative capacity of the central, provincial and local governments, and conduct simulations of various schemes. Annexes 30A, 30B and 30C provide a checklist of policy options for student loans; a methodological note for calculating subsidies on mortgage loan programs as an example of the type of consideration required before a decision can be made. Other options such as income contingent loans or graduate tax should be explored and simulations carried out for them as well.

Conclusion. The cost-recovery measures described are, in effect, long-term financing strategies for higher education. Current trends of financial resource generation efforts indicate the potential for enhancement of these measures in certain categories. Along with China's rapid economic development, the social and private demands for higher education will continue to grow. The implementation of the measures will enable the higher education system to provide more student places, which are now being limited proportionally by the high level of student subsidies and low level of cost-recovery, as well as to provide quality inputs. Cost recovery must of course be accompanied by student financial support to enable disadvantaged but talented students to pursue higher education.

FIGURE 4.3: ACTION PLAN FOR FINANCING HIGHER EDUCATION: DIVERSIFICATION OF RESOURCES

OBJECTIVE	MEANS	INDICATOR	ACTION
Improve the efficiency of the higher education system	Encourage enrollment expansion and institutional mergers where they are cost-effective	Average size of universities and student-to-teacher ratio increased	SEdC, ministries, provinces
	Amend funding formulas so that they encourage expansion at marginal cost and allow for special provincial factors. Reward teachers who have greater workload and are also productive researchers		SEdC, ministries
	Review space norms and formulas used for decisions on capital allocations	Reduced norms per student and higher utilization	SEdC
Enhance institutional capacity for resource generation	Encourage *all* universities to market short courses to enterprises	Increased income generated	SEdC, ministries, provinces
	Develop research capacity in smaller universities by encouraging collaboration between large and small institutions for research grants	Increase research income in smaller universities	State Council, research funding bodies
	Provide incentives so that more enterprises and private citizens give donations to universities	Increase in volume of donations	Ministry of Finance, SEdC
Implement a cost-sharing policy to spread burden of higher education cost	Continue policy of increasing tuition fee levels and allow institutional autonomy, subject to policy parameters on scholarships and loans	Percentage of total university income from tuition fees	SEdC, ministries, provinces
	Provide initial capital for provincial and national schemes for student loans and encourage their operation by independent financial organizations	Increase in percentage of enrollments from poor, minority or female students	SEdC, provinces

Source: Study Team.

5. QUALITY IMPROVEMENT IN INSTRUCTIONAL PROGRAMS

Global attention to quality issues in higher education has reached an unprecedented level in recent years as countries recognize the correlation between educational quality and economic growth; the need for greater accountability in times of declining resources; and the demand for systems to deliver value for money. A strategy to improve the internal efficiency and therefore the performance and quality of Chinese higher education institutions includes, at its core, efforts (a) to develop a curriculum that is both internally coherent as well as externally responsive to labor market changes; (b) to enhance teaching and research activities, while setting up processes to attract and retain qualified and experienced staff and monitoring equity issues in relation to women and minority faculty members; (c) to institutionalize quality assurance practices in order to meet agreed quality criteria, by reinforcing and extending fledgling accreditation practices, linking monetary and nonmonetary incentives to good performance; and (d) to institute and sustain structures and procedures that will enable institutions to maintain levels of educational inputs (books, equipment and other instructional materials) and facilities relative to national norms.

Context: Changes of the Reform Decade

Curriculum

Striking changes have taken place over the 1980s in China's higher education curriculum, with (a) adjustments in enrollment emphasis that reflect both the personnel needs of a rapidly changing economy and rising social demand in certain popular areas; (b) a partial relaxation of central control over curricular content with institutions having more control over specialties and syllabi, while working within the guidelines of teaching hours and basic requirements provided by the government; (c) significant efforts in moving from narrow, highly specialized programs at undergraduate level to more broad-based structures of knowledge; and (d) experimentation with course organization and delivery methods. These are not evenly spread across the regions, however, as many institutions, particularly those in the poorer provinces, lack the technical and professional expertise that would allow them to take advantage of the policy changes.

Between 1980 and 1993, basic disciplines such as natural sciences and agriculture have seen a drop in enrollment as have the social sciences and humanities. The largest gains have been made in engineering (37 percent of all enrollments in 1993) and applied disciplines such as law, finance and economics—enrollment in economics rose from 3 percent in 1980 to 13 percent in 1993. In all areas efforts to move toward implementing broader-based curricula are evident but the absence of suitably trained and experienced faculty poses severe problems in many provinces. Each of the smaller number of programs in the applied sciences has a broader definition and wider professional employment scope; basic sciences have introduced links to new applications and providing hands-on experiences; and in the humanities the emphasis has been on enhancing potential areas of application, such as archives, tourism and urban studies in the case of history. In course organization, significant efforts are being made to provide more choices to students, demonstrated in partial credit systems that make some provision for elective courses. Double major programs have been established in some cases for high-achieving students able to qualify in two different areas.

Research

University-based research is recognized to be the necessary foundation for good graduate study, curriculum development in new fields, and teacher preparation in all subject areas. The sources of funds are varied and include national five-year plan key projects, the National Natural Science Foundation of China, the State Science and Technology Commission and SEdC key project funds. A greater portion of the funds are distributed on the basis of a rigorous peer review process, but the largest share is on the basis of national allocation to priority projects. With science and technology advances seen as the cornerstones of economic development, applied projects garner the bulk of resources. Funding remains very limited for the social sciences, and in the basic natural sciences it is likely only to be available for scholars associated with science departments in prestigious comprehensive universities.

Faculty

The curricular changes that have taken place over the reform decade make considerable demands on the faculty contingent in Chinese universities. These demands vary by field, by region, and by level of institution, all of which require competent and highly motivated staff, working within a strongly supportive professional environment. The quality of instruction delivered by faculty is determined largely by the numbers available, their qualifications, how they are deployed, and their levels of remuneration. Important differences exist between faculty based on their geographical location, in the center of economic growth or at the periphery, and at national, provincial or local level of institution. Data comparing inland institutions with those in economically thriving coastal universities will be used in this section to highlight the differing problems and challenges.

There have been solid achievements in faculty development since 1980 but higher education institutions face a crisis situation in attracting and retaining high quality staff. Over the past decade, the Chinese government has made a number of policy changes[1] in order to raise the status and quality of university teachers, through improving remuneration, specifying detailed principles regarding teacher quality, training and responsibilities, and by instituting preferential policies in housing and social welfare. Faculty structure at the end of the Cultural Revolution decade was heavily skewed toward a middle-aged group that had entered faculty positions in the late 1950s and middle 1960s. With the lacuna in recruitment during the Cultural Revolution decade, by the end of the first decade of the next century, retirement of this age group will precipitate an issue of crisis proportions. Net decreases in teaching faculty numbers were 3,760 in 1991 and 502 in 1993, and the trend is expected to continue in the next few years.[2] Coupled with this eventuality, as discussed in Chapter 1, the small proportion of highly qualified

---

[1] CPC Central Committee and State Council document "Program for Reform and Development of Chinese Education," February 1993; and "On Implementation of the Program for China's Educational Reform and Development."

[2] Department of Planning and Construction, State Education Commission, China, *Educational Statistics Yearbook of China for 1991-1992*, People's Publishing House, Beijing, December 1992, p. 34.

personnel (only about 2 percent had PhDs in 1994) jeopardizes leadership in teaching, research and publications activities. The 18 institutions visited in the field showed almost 40 percent under 36 years of age, representing an accelerating rate of faculty renewal that is fairly representative of national trends. The distribution of faculty rank structure has also changed greatly over the same time period, moving from a small number of lecturers and teaching assistants to more balanced distributions as Table 5.1 shows.

TABLE 5.1: TRENDS OF CHANGING FACULTY STRUCTURE BY RANK
(In percent)

	Professor	Associate Professor	Lecturer	Teaching Assistant
1980	1.52	6.20	53.32	38.96
1985	2.49	13.12	45.38	39.01
1989	6.00	23.99	42.84	27.17
1993	8.91	32.79	41.39	16.91

Source: Study Team calculations.

Teachers' salaries have been constantly adjusted since 1990, with additional bonuses added to basic salaries for teaching hours, teaching years, responsibilities as class director, academic title, performance and other contributions. An important incentive to retain qualified staff was the establishment of a national salary scale for all faculty ranks where between-rank differences are substantial, and salary levels are higher than that of equivalent personnel in government positions. Before reform in 1990, the base salary for a lecturer was Y 97, 128 for an associate professor, and Y 200 for a full professor (Johnston, 1991). By 1992 the salary levels for these three ranks were Y 200, 300, and 500 respectively. It is unlikely that this trend will continue. Provincially-administered institutions in poor areas are particularly hard-pressed to pay these higher salaries while, by contrast, wealthier provinces such as Guangdong have been able to provide additional subsidies to the base salaries, thus increasing inequalities between regions and jurisdictions. As elsewhere in the world, however, institutional salary levels cannot match those offered in industry. In spite of these attempts, the average salary of teachers was listed as the ninth in a list of 12 occupations.[3] A recent investigation at a national key university, Nanjing University, showed that 43 percent of the faculty thought that financial remuneration was the key consideration relative to continuing or giving up their teaching careers.[4]

Measures to increase remuneration have not been able to render teaching as a sufficiently attractive and appropriately rewarding occupation. Consequently, the problems of recruitment and retention or "brain drain" of staff are not unexpected. The three dominant features of the "brain drain" in China are the movement of teaching faculty from teaching positions to other occupations; from hinterland to coastal areas; and from mainland China to other countries—the nonreturn rate of Chinese scholars studying abroad between 1978 and 1992

---

[3] Guo Fei, "On Salaries of University Teachers," China's Education Daily, July 7, 1993, p.3.

[4] He Xiaoxin, Mu Ronghua, Zhou Yian, Mao Rong; "Investigation and Analysis into the Changing Psychology of Teachers in University, Nanjing Academic Journal, No. 1, 1995, p.175-181.

reached 50 percent[5]. It happens most noticeably among young and middle-aged faculty in most needed, newly-established and market-oriented specialties such as economics, finance, trade, foreign language, etc., and the trend looks set to continue for the next few years. The results of an investigation into 121 universities and colleges in 22 provinces in 1993 showed a decline of 16.4 percent in the total number of faculty, with 62.4 percent of them being young and middle-aged.[6] Findings of a study of 12 institutions in the Beijing area indicated that the number of younger faculty who had left during the period of 1987 to 1992 accounted for 78.8 percent of the total number of those who were recruited during the same period.[7] With the increasing gap between salaries and living conditions between interior and coastal regions, it was shown that in 1993 about 18.2 percent of the emigration was to the coastal areas while only 6.1 percent was in the opposite direction. This trend is expected to continue in the next few years.

Incentives other than salary, especially those tied to rewarding improving quality of teaching, research and publication opportunities have become increasingly important both in recruiting and retaining able faculty. Emphasis has been placed on promoting excellent young faculty, eschewing traditional promotion procedures and quotas: the vigorous activity which was evident in some institutions visited was attributed to this reform. The development of graduate programs, begun in the 1980s, leading to masters and doctoral degrees, continues to be the most important source of career development, particularly in light of the policy to raise formal qualifications of faculty under 40 years of age. Table 5.2 gives the qualification profile of the total faculty contingent in the 18 institutions visited, and shows the strides that have been made in raising qualifications since 1980. However there are tremendous differences in the qualifications of faculty in different geographical regions, fields of study and levels of institution, with provincially-administered, interior universities faring most poorly.

TABLE 5.2: TRENDS OF FACULTY QUALIFICATION STRUCTURE
(In percent)

	Bachelor	Master & Doctorate
1980	92.34	7.66
1985	77.95	22.05
1989	64.68	35.32
1993	59.41	40.59

Source: Study Team calculations.

Support strategies for professional development that have worked include: (a) encouraging staff to qualify for further degrees through inservice programs; (b) developing training plans for enhancing teaching and research skills; (c) giving young faculty priority for attending international conferences; and (d) organizing special collections of publications

---

[5]   Hu Zhongtao, "Ideas and Policies for Strengthening the Building of a Contingent of Young Faculty," Beijing Normal University Academic Journal, March, 1994 p.84-87.

[6]   Bai Zhou, "A Survey Concerning the Contemporary Situation of the Faculty Contingent in Higher Education Institutions," China's Higher Education, No. 12, 1993, p.12.

[7]   Hu, 1994.

including theses and research articles. Institutions in poor provinces which do not receive central government support continue to be markedly disadvantaged. Sichuan is a case in point. While faculty qualifications in most national level institutions in the province had reached 70 percent or 80 percent, Sichuan Industrial University which is funded by the province was a low 20 percent.

Quality Assurance

In China as a step toward quality assurance, the accreditation system ("ping-gu") began in 1985. Common to all quality assurance practices are the following elements: (a) the development of standards; (b) the application of those standards to a program or institution by third parties for the purposes of assessment and enhancement; and (c) the subsequent improvement of the educational entity. In some countries, as is the case in China, this basic process is enhanced by provisions for a self-evaluation process (by institutions and programs) and site visits by a team of expert peers. Third-party evaluators add force to the process, although it is ultimately the program or institution's ultimate responsibility to maintain and improve quality. To be accredited means that the characteristics of a total institution or educational program within an institution have been considered and that institutional or programmatic strengths and weaknesses have been weighed. The various levels of accreditation (Bachelor's, Master's, Doctoral) undertaken may involve multiple agencies—national, provincial, municipal, professional bodies—depending on the level and scope of the exercise. Accrediting activities are still very modest, with some parts of the country, notably the municipality of Shanghai, providing good models for emulation.

Issues

Curriculum

Balancing Considerations. In the curricular change process over the decade, universities and their faculty have had increasing freedom to shape their own programs, upgrading the knowledge content through links to ongoing research, and making them more directly relevant to professional employment needs. With increasingly rapid economic change, and greater latitude for student job choice on graduation, the latter concern has become predominant. As institutions take on greater managerial, professional and academic responsibilities, they will be making, and are already having to do so, decisions that they have little training and experience to fall back on. An appropriate balance needs to be found among various considerations in improving the higher education curriculum. These include:

(a) considerations of maintaining academic standards and the constant upgrading of the knowledge content;

(b) concerns about macroregulation of emphasis on various fields in relation to national needs for personnel; and

(c) concerns about providing a foundation of knowledge and nurturing a professional attitude, which fosters abilities for an ongoing self-development process that goes beyond immediate market demands.

Curriculum Monitoring and Renewal. Education systems and institutions everywhere lag behind changes in society. With the speed of socioeconomic and cultural/ lifestyle changes in China, parts of curricula of educational institutions become obsolete from time-to-time. A system of quality is also a system of relevance: experimentation and piloting of innovative approaches to the planning and implementation of curricula need to be built into the system, and as the monitoring and participating in the generation and dissemination of new knowledge through research activities. This would include the responsibility of monitoring labor market outcomes for graduates, following up on characteristics of job placements and levels of remuneration. Such monitoring would include national and local shifts in supply and demand of skills, feeding this information into the curriculum evaluation and renewal process. Within the framework of decentralization, insufficient resources and attention have been given to equipping faculties in departments at institutions and Provincial Education Commissions (PEdCs) with the tools of training and experience to lead in curriculum development and implementation at local level. Strong central leadership is urgently required from SEdC to establish a national curriculum monitoring, review and renewal mechanism that responds to: (a) national and local needs; and (b) international development in knowledge generation.

Research

Funding and Opportunities. Increasing higher education and national research and development investments have become important components of economic growth strategies of industrialized and developing countries. Recent studies by economists indicate that the social rate of return from investments in new industrial technology in developed countries seems to be high (20 to 30 percent) and that technological change in many industries and increased economic output of society have been based on recent academic research (Mansfield, 1994). Despite the fact that absolute levels of research have increased in China, their distribution among institutions, between discipline areas, and the relationship between research and increased economic output need close attention. A more appropriate balance is required between basic and applied research, and for such research findings to feed into curriculum, faculty development, and industry. Differences in research and funding opportunities for scholars in the various fields are a concern for all faculty, particularly as research results have become an important criterion for promotion decisions. Of equal concern is the need to expand enrollment at the graduate level, providing attractive and competitive conditions. Besides promotion opportunities, developing a research culture needs to be cultivated for its contribution to improved teaching. Higher education institutions are also important sources of personnel for public and private research and development units and their graduates should be available to support varied developmental activities nationally as well as locally. Incentive mechanisms, improved training for faculty, and increased mobility of researchers are required for universities to transform research and development into increased productivity.

Faculty

Pedagogical Approaches. The key people who make curricular change happen are the teachers. While changes have taken place in the character and definition of instructional programs, making them more flexible, broad-based and overtly market-oriented in terms of content/knowledge, there has been less change in teaching methods and fundamental pedagogical approaches, which opens up questions of effective change. Reasons identified include a continuing paucity of appropriate training of faculty in content and new teaching methodologies; significant research not as widespread as it should be; lack of good reference material and library resources as well as better techniques of accessing and utilizing such resources; lack of adequate equipment for experimental work, particularly in poorer institutions; and a general content-oriented ethos that puts pressure on coverage of prescribed amounts of curricular material in a short time. In interviews conducted with students at Nankai and Tianjin universities (He Jin,

March 1994), teachers were perceived as overconservative and reluctant to consider new teaching approaches. Other studies conducted in the Central South and Northwestern regions have indicated that many teachers who have returned from abroad are eager to introduce more open and effective teaching methods, but have found strong student resistance to change. Part of this was attributed to student apathy, part to concern for getting high marks, and gaining desired levels of expertise quickly (Hayhoe, 1992 and 1993).

Downgrading Teaching Responsibilities. A problem area noted is the tendency for younger faculty to seek second jobs, as a supplement for income levels that are regarded as very low. That promotion opportunities are linked to research results, that remuneration levels are low as compared with the growing industrial and service sectors, and that effective mechanisms are lacking to ensure material reward for high performance, provide additional reasons for downgrading the importance of teaching responsibilities.[8]

Female Representation. The issue of female representation constitutes both equity as well as quality considerations. Surveys in the field revealed that fewer young women were supported for master's and doctoral degree studies than young men. Nationwide in 1992, women made up only 27.3 percent of all master's students and 11.2 percent of all doctoral students although, for the same year, 37.3 percent of all faculty under 30 were women (SEdC, 1993). Generally, women are encouraged to complete the four graduate-course credits necessary for promotion to lectureships. However, graduate enrollment figures by gender indicate that a disproportionately low number are gaining the graduate degrees necessary for promotion and career development beyond lecturer status. In 1993, women made up only 23 percent of all faculty with masters degrees and 8.6 percent of all with doctoral degrees. Tables 5.3 and 5.4 which give a breakdown of faculty by gender and qualifications, as well as gender and rank, in the 18 institutions included in this study show striking gaps in qualification levels between male and female faculty and the concomitant gap in rank. Fewer women than men have the degrees that will be essential for promotion in their academic careers.

TABLE 5.3: FACULTY BY GENDER AND QUALIFICATION

	Doctorate	Masters	Bachelors
Male	284	2,034	2,772
Female	22	768	1,777

Source: Study Team calculations.

TABLE 5.4: FACULTY BY GENDER AND RANK

	Professor	Associate Professor	Lecturer	Teaching Assistant
Male	950	2,975	3,169	1,138
Female	134	1,014	1,865	919

Source: Study Team calculations.

---

[8]   Bai, 1993, pp. 21-22.

Among reasons given for this situation were: (a) women's family responsibilities that, it was claimed, militated against them in undertaking graduate work; (b) policies on age restrictions could be the same for men and women—35 being the maximum entry age for a formal master's program and 40 for an inservice program—but they tend to present more serious barriers for women; and (c) a general social culture in which middle-aged women in formal study programs are regarded as anomalous. Women also tend to be overrepresented in basic science and basic humanities courses, areas where teaching responsibilities for the whole university are heavy. Given the growing trend of associating high status with specializations, teachers in basic fields may be seen as an emerging underclass, many of whom are women. Unless special efforts are made to provide full graduate training and research and publication programs for women faculty, the quality of the overall faculty contingent will suffer.

Minority Representation. Relatively little information is available on faculty from minority backgrounds. In 1992 they represented 4.9 percent of total faculty, about half the level of their representation within the total population. They are less likely to have graduate degrees and so will tend to move slowly through the ranks. Policies to ensure equal participation of women and minorities are particularly important in economically disadvantaged hinterland provinces, where the brain drain of young male faculty is acute (contrasting with coastal provinces where it is relatively easy to attract qualified scholars in all fields), yet creates new opportunities for women and minority scholars.

Academic Inbreeding. Previous World Bank project-related conclusions on the unhealthy practice of academic inbreeding were reinforced by this report's findings. A tradition exists where universities recruit their own best graduates and these young faculty are mentored by older scholars and past teachers. Efforts to break this pattern have been difficult. Prestigious universities, in the event they are unable to recruit from the small number of overseas-trained returnees, recruit from among their own graduate schools. Universities in the interior fare particularly badly as their best students are attracted to the coastal provinces. This problem is so serious that many universities in the poorer and more inaccessible regions fear encouraging their young faculty to go elsewhere, even within the country, for graduate study.

In well-resourced and top-level key institutions, academic inbreeding is clearly not an issue in relation to quality outputs. In poorly resourced universities located in disadvantaged areas and with significant contingents of staff with limited academic qualifications and research experience, the university may be unable to fulfill the important goals of providing: (a) developmentally relevant research results to the locality and the province; (b) adequate assistance to the community in order to keep pace with technological change; and (c) appropriate technical and managerial services to the productive systems in the province, bringing them into the emerging competitive ethos of the national economy. The implications are serious for developing and supporting a curriculum relevant to societal needs; and for institutionalizing and sustaining high-quality graduate training and research programs critical for local capacity building.

Outlook for the Future

Given the issues discussed above, the current scenario has a number of features that would yield dividends for the future of the higher education sector. Young intellectuals do pay considerable attention to supportive work environments and to enhancement of their social status even if material benefits are relatively low.[9] There is evidence that the academic quality of young faculty is increasing and so is their participation in leading teaching and research positions. In 1991 43.63 percent of new recruits had doctoral and master degrees; in 1993 the corresponding figure was 32.45 percent[10]. Supervisors of postgraduate programs under 45 years old increased by 42 percent in 1992 and 73 percent in 1993 compared with the 1991 level[11] and more than 25 percent of young faculty had important publications of either teaching materials or research achievements. The same numbers were responsible for opening some, most-needed, newly established interdisciplinary courses.[12] Although the rate of "brain drain" was down to less than 5 percent in 1993 and trends seem uncertain, it has a potential to continue, if unfavorable working conditions persist. Appropriative incentive mechanisms need to be put in place in order to make best use of resources and to ensure the long-term benefits of advanced training abroad for institutional development. Also, personnel mobility could be seen as a positive force in reducing academic inbreeding while developing diversity within the country. Smaller but qualitatively strong personnel could lead to welcome increases in efficiencies. Therefore, the anticipated peak in faculty retirement by 2010 provides a compelling rationale for the implementation of effective staffing policies, particularly in poor provinces. As discussed earlier, institutions in coastal regions such as Guangdong do not face such a crisis since they are able to attract and keep staff from all over China. Priority policies would include the creation and implementation of favorable working conditions; insisting on high academic qualifications; investment in inservice graduate study; and implementation of national policies on better living conditions.

Quality Assurance

Criteria and Quality Indicators. Accreditation as applied to specialties and courses is rigorous, highly quantitative, and prolonged. Institutional leadership has suggested that although this relatively new and objective process (often graded on a Pass/ Fail or an A, B, C, D scale) has distinct advantages over the former potentially subjective opinion of a few "experts," it nevertheless could benefit from streamlining to make it more responsive to rapid educational reforms. The evaluative standards themselves are often carried out at two levels: general criteria and the more specific quality indicators. The general criteria are usually qualitative in nature, but the quality indicators are more apt to be quantitative and often are not directly related to educational quality. Examples of quality indicators for a specialty described in Anhui Province call for not only the total number but also the square footage of books in the library dedicated to the specialty with little attention paid to whether the books are current or are used exhaustively.

This problem is being studied by the Higher Education Division of SEdC. In the meanwhile, the quality indicator system has become complex enough to require a software package for institutional use such as the one developed by Southeast University in Nanjing. The issue of quality indicators, their utilization and effects requires close scrutiny. Some descriptive

---

[9]   Beijing Normal University, "On the Situation of Scholars Studying Abroad and Their Intention of Returning to China," Educational Research, May 1994, p. 71-76

[10] See *Educational Statistics Yearbook of China* for 1991-92, and 1993, Peoples Education Publishing House, Beijing, 1992, p. 34 and 1994, p.28.

[11] Ibid. 1992, p.34.

[12] Hu, 1994.

materials reviewed paid more attention to how to compute the coefficient for the grading than how to improve educational quality.

National Implementation. The various stages and technical procedures call for a core of trained personnel who are able to implement the national plan at the provincial and institutional levels. Currently, numbers of trained staff and available funds fall far short of making a nationwide impact. Without institutional accreditation in the repertoire of quality-assurance practices in China, insufficient attention is being paid to the institutional infrastructure required to improve overall quality. As greater responsibilities are devolved to institutions while funding decisions still remain highly centralized, the range of information derived from accreditation exercises should enable centralized funding decisions to be made differentially across the system, as well as assist responsible policy-making agencies in their monitoring tasks.

Rewards and Sanctions. The current debate needs to identify and clarify issues related to follow-up action to accreditation exercises. This will include the reward system for those who achieve qualitative standards of excellence beyond minimal criteria; the sanctions should an institution fail to meet established standards; and strategies for encouraging underperformers to better levels of performance. Care must be taken that the rules and structures do not harden into rigidity resulting in a process that inhibits institutional innovation rather than releases the potential for higher levels of quality attainment.

Recommendations and Action Plan

A set of actions directed to the issues identified is presented below. The institution's strategic plan would include activities such as those in the detailed plans of action in Figures 5.1, 5.2 and 5.3 at the various levels of participation (governmental, institutional, individual). These provide major pointers for consideration, debate and possible implementation. Priorities among the actions would depend on each institution's unique needs. The plan for the curriculum section needs to be seen as complementary to that for faculty development, both of which are closely linked to the action plan for accreditation assurance activities. They have been arranged in three packages in order to maintain the importance of the curriculum and faculty components as sets of activities which are to be pursued in their own right, with the third providing periodic checks on institutional abilities and capacities to meet nationally approved quality criteria.

The action plans were developed with the following principles in mind:

(a)   Support for change must come from the top of the management and administrative chain in order to ensure its place in overall planning, budgeting and scheduling procedures.

(b)   Changes should be the outcome of appropriate consultative processes with all major stakeholders as informed participants. National, provincial and institutional plans need therefore to ensure that relevant training, targeted research, and consultations with appropriate bodies such as employers, professional associations and civic organizations have been put in place prior to decision-making discussions as the curriculum is not an inert instrument but an evolving process that ought to reflect societal changes.

(c)   Incentives and sanctions, both monetary as in funding for research, and nonmonetary such as an annual "Best Teacher Award," need to be institutionalized at the appropriate levels to propel the shift toward desired outcomes; to sustain the momentum for change; and to provide much-required motivation for action.

(d)   Training and professional support for change has to be an ongoing process rather than a one-shot activity: recurrent funds need to be tied to these budget items.

Priorities for Government Action

Once the institutions have worked out the strategic plans for the institution as a whole as recommended in Part 2 of this report, studied the three sets of Action Plans in this Part (Curriculum, Faculty, Accreditation—Figures 5.1-5.3), analyzed and prioritized their needs, government guidance and funding support will be required across the board to assist them in moving forward. Government advice and support will be required for setting up appropriate structures at central, provincial and institutional levels such as those suggested in the following recommendations, as well as setting up the appropriate consultative and executive processes. The incentive structure at the institutional level will benefit from the experience of government as would information exchange mechanisms, and overseas research and training. Government inputs will be crucial in setting policies and providing the seed funding for institutions to boost research in the basic sciences and humanities and/or offer specifically targeted scholarship schemes to ensure enrollment numbers, faculty training, recruitment and promotion of women and minority faculty; and the continuing vitality of instructional programs.

Improving Quality

The recommendations made in this section focus on four key aspects in the improvement strategy: curriculum, teaching and research, quality assurance, and educational inputs and facilities. The various components of the strategy are as follows.

The strategy recommends that a nationwide system of accreditation be supported in order to maintain systemic and institutional quality in government and nongovernment institutions.

(a)   The strategy builds on the achievements made in the accreditation process by the Academic Degrees Committee of the State Council and SEdC, and the initiatives triggered by the World Bank University Development Project II in 1986. Accreditation activities have been slow thus far: with the growth of new programs, experimentation with course structure, the problems of staffing, the search for greater internal and external efficiency, and the concern with meeting national and international criteria of excellence, accreditation can contribute to regulate monitoring and self-evaluation and assessment processes that are crucial to the vitality of institutions.

(b)   The primary purpose of this five-year program is to integrate quality improvement efforts relative to institutions, programs and teaching. The objective is to establish a workable system of accreditation as a first step toward systemwide quality assurance. The goals would include the following at national, regional and institutional levels:

(i)   Broadening the practice of institutional accreditation while minimizing the bureaucracy required to achieve it; includes institutional processes with periodic external/audit reviews;

(ii)   Strengthening and expanding the development and accreditation of professional licensure where it is needed professionally;

(iii)   Encouraging the management of the accrediting process and the development of a council/committee that will perform the "recognition" function—developing standards and identifying the entities (such as an interuniversity council, State and Provincial Education Commission subcommittees.), which will carry out the minutiae of the evaluative process;

(iv)   Providing information relative to criteria and quality indicator development and application to institutions;

(v)   Collecting and analyzing data at a central level and, if data are sufficiently robust, then publishing and using them to inform decision making;

(vi)   Strengthening undergraduate course and specialty accreditation;

(vii)   Improving pedagogical techniques in concert with other aspects of faculty development; and

(viii) Providing opportunities for educators to study international practice in accreditation and teaching appraisal and improvement.

(c)   Structural Components

(i)   **National Steering Committee and Secretariat.** The program could be coordinated by a national Steering Committee, which would operate in the provinces through a number of "quality centers" located in provincial higher education institutions. The Steering Committee, working with the body responsible for accreditation procedures, will be composed of key people in central and provincial/municipal governments and institutions who can provide leadership over a continuous time period. A small secretariat needs to be identified, located either at the center or at one of the provincial higher education institutions, and this could be expedited with the assistance of local/international consultants.

(ii)   **Accreditation Bodies.** The composition of bodies responsible for accreditation functions is crucial to the effectiveness of the process. Ideally agencies should be entirely self-regulatory with institutions paying for their services. In reality, since the public higher education system is dependent on public funds, governments tend to pay for self-regulatory functions.   China has separated the accreditation responsibilities for graduate and undergraduate degrees: in many countries it has been found advantageous for one body to bear overall responsibility. Central bodies responsible for accreditation activities will train appropriate personnel from the provincial education commissions and from institutions in institutional evaluation techniques, assisting them to carry out performance reviews that are central to accreditation activities. The selection of peer scholars who carry out reviews is a critical part of the overall process. In every review committee, regardless of the level, there should be at least one member who is from a jurisdiction other than the one in which the university is located.

(iii) **Quality Assurance Centers.** A small number of pilot centers could be located in selected provincial institutions. Their brief would be to offer seminars and training sessions related to accreditation procedures; coordinate efforts at institutional and program levels; promote the integration of evaluation practice in the improvement of instructional practices; and encourage international exchange, joint research and publications in accreditation and associated areas such as assessment, promotion, and production of evaluation materials. The Steering Committee would determine resources necessary to conduct accreditation activities through centralized and decentralized efforts.

(iv) **Centers of Excellence.** Linked with the issues of accreditation and achieving national standards are those associated on an ongoing basis with improvement in curriculum and faculty development. Connections between the two areas of quality improvement have to be made evident through mechanisms that are planned and budgeted for. A major thrust for faculty development internationally is the development of staff development centers that deal with local and national educational challenges. It is recommended that, sharing existing institutional, provincial and national funds, capacity and capabilities for research and training in specified cognate areas, "centers of excellence" be established to serve provinces or regions. Among their prime functions would be provision and coordination of inservice training, both higher-degree programs and nondegree courses for ongoing professional development and updating purposes; and stimulating, conducting, and coordinating research and publication activities. Joint interuniversity councils would manage the centers.

A center, whether serving a province or a region, could be an important forum for appropriate professional bodies that represent the collectivity of universities. In the long term, as the decentralization process continues, provinces and institutions may well find their contributions to local, provincial and regional scholarly activities becoming increasingly significant in targeted improvements to quality through the development of appropriate research policies, research agendas, fostering training, research and consultancy skills locally. Enhancement of local research, training and consultancy facilities will help to increase the attraction of local institutions in the poor provinces, helping to secure the services of qualified faculty.

Essential complementary inputs are required in order to bring about coherent quality improvements in instructional and research programs. The development of libraries and training of library staff are essential elements to which managers and administrators need to give attention. Training should include programs for laboratory staff—managers and technicians—in equipment maintenance and use. Also as part of its service to higher education institutions strategic areas such as the more complex aspects of computer training should be included as part of a center's brief. Managers need to take care that resources are not expended on activities that are better organized in individual institutions. Underscoring the supportive framework is the need to institute and develop modern communications systems which can provide access, irrespective of geographic location, to new knowledge and information.

A center of excellence would be funded by: (a) core funding from government; and (b) participating institutions on a: (i) cost-sharing basis for joint activities such as research; and (ii) fee-for-service basis to institutions for specific, customized programs such as curriculum materials. Centers would be in close touch with "quality centers" whose activities in monitoring and evaluation/assessment would provide a constant flow of information on needs. Both categories would come under the planning responsibilities of the central and provincial education commissions, with inputs from all participating institutions. Increased support for cooperative interinstitutional research and teaching activities would be an attractive incentive for institutions to support such a venture, while allowing individual institutions to cope with the rising costs of research.

FIGURE 5.1: ACTION PLAN FOR NATIONAL SYSTEM OF ACCREDITATION

Goal: To strengthen and enhance a national system of accreditation

OBJECTIVES	MEANS	INDICATORS	ACTION
A. Government Level			
Move toward the macromanagement of accreditation	Centralize the national authority for standards into a single coordinating committee such as the Academic Degrees Committee of the State Council (ADCSC); and enhance management capability	Clarification of a single authority	State Council
Provide a centralized process of educational standards development and entrust the accreditation review process to decentralized entities	Strengthen the provincial/municipal academic degrees committees and related bureaus of higher education	Evidence that educational entities have sufficient personnel and administrative support	ADCSC, SEdC
	Concentrate on development of national standards for institutions and degree programs (rather than specialty and course levels) to make the broadest impact at the outset.	Development of broadly stated standards of institutional quality can be applied to a wide spectrum of institutions	
To develop national standards for the professions which will lead to the creation of professional associations, domestic licensure and international recognition	Hold national discussion on "professionalizing the professions" and invite all affected constituencies.	Provision of a national forum; the development of professional associations; and the creation of professional licensure	Line ministries & faculties with support of the State Council, ADCSC & SEdC

FIGURE 5.1: (cont'd)

OBJECTIVES	MEANS	INDICATORS	ACTION
A. Government Level (continued) Create a National Educational Data Base	Develop data of information derived from common standards	Evidence that institutions and programs are provided with data which enables them to compare themselves with norms and learn from peers	ADCSC
Provincial programs to improve the quality of learning and pedagogical techniques	Establish **quality centers** which can serve to integrate quality improvement efforts relative to institutions, programs and teaching. The centers can be equipped over time to offer seminars and training sessions and promote the integration of evaluation practice in the quality improvement of teaching and learning.	Establishment of quality centers	SEdC, PEdCs, Line Ministries
To increase faculty with higher degrees; to coordinate research and publication activities	Establish **centers of excellence** linked with the issues of accreditation and achieving national standards that build on and enhance existing capacity and capabilities for research and training in specified cognate areas for faculty of participating institutions	Establishment of centers of excellence to serve provinces or regions	SEdC, PEdCs, Line Ministries, participating institutions
B. University Level			
To participate in the process of institution and/or programmatic accreditation, understanding the dual purposes of accreditation/ assessment and improvement of quality	Develop an institutional response to the process of accreditation at two levels (1) assessment and (2) improvement	Assessment: appointment of a person or persons with responsibility to monitor and/ or coordinate all accreditation activity at the institution. Improvement: preparation of an administrative/management plan for short- and long-term improvement.	Institutions and Faculties

Source: Study Team.

FIGURE 5.2: ACTION PLAN FOR CURRICULUM DEVELOPMENT

Goal: *To improve the curriculum toward a general education to better serve economic development and educational needs by means of management, enhancement and quality control.*

OBJECTIVE	MEANS	INDICATOR	ACTION
A. Government Level			
Curriculum reform with a vision of both quantity and quality goals for higher education in the annual and five-year plans	Strengthen the Academic Degrees Committee of the State Council (ADC) in its control of the quality of higher education by giving it the power to oversee curriculum development and the spending of government funding for curriculum-related activities (If this is beyond the capacity of ADC, set up an independent council)	Clear regulations that the ADC has the proper input in regard to quality in the policy-making process of SEdC; and more important, it should also be given some veto power.	State Council
	The duties of ADC are the following: 1. Repeatedly emphasizing and illustrating the importance of curriculum revitalization and its relationship with quality improvement. Use seminars to provide information regarding the need for ongoing curriculum reform	Input of ADC in the policies Regular seminars for various levels of leaders and staff	ADC
	2. Ensure that the Curriculum Division (CD) in SEdC has the authority and the means to carry out its duties.	Special liaison setup between ADC and CD	ADC
	3. Work closely with the CD to bring about a set of qualitative indicators or criteria for each type of postsecondary institution in higher education. Four aspects should be included: • teachers' qualification and training plans, • textbook production and development • quality of and demand for graduates, and • course content and arrangement.	Qualitative indicators for future plans	ADC and CD
Strengthen the Curriculum Division in policy-making and implementation, research and supervision	Endow the Division with adequate annual financial support for curriculum development activities at SEdC and university levels	Increased financial support for curriculum-related activities	ADC and SEdC

Figure 5.2: (cont'd)

OBJECTIVE	MEANS	INDICATOR	ACTION
A. Government Level (continued) Highlight quality improvement in higher education and the role that curriculum plays	Cooperate with ADC to come up with viable rules for curriculum development and quality requirements: • priority for higher education development should be quality improvement, • curriculum is core to quality improvement, • specify the roles for provincial education commissions and universities, and • given the autonomy endowed in universities CD and ADC retain the rights to check and discipline when quality deteriorates.	Clearly define duties for provincial education commissions and postsecondary institution More autonomy for universities in areas that affect curriculum, e.g., admission and graduation policies, faculty employment regulations	Curriculum Division
	Work closely with the National Institute of Educational Research (NIER), research institutes and universities to conduct systematic research on curriculum and related activities: • designate a central research institute to act as the center for all curriculum research activities, and provide it with an annual budget, • list all projects for competitive bidding, but fund them in relation to their popularity (i.e., the most popular ones will get 50% and 80% funding, while the less popular ones will get more); • designate essential project (e.g., how to protect basic disciplines, programs and courses from being sacrificed by market impact) to research institutes with full government funding; • assist the research institutions to build connections with enterprises for fund-provided services; and • publish a regular (quarterly or semiannual) newsletter to provide information on research (the projects and their results and findings).	Annual list of research projects A selected research institute with funding secured Specific rules on the bidding A list of services universities can do for enterprises and vice versa The newsletter or journal	The CD and NIER

Figure 5.2: (cont'd)

OBJECTIVE	MEANS	INDICATOR	ACTION
A. Government Level (continued)			
	Coordinate with ADC to conduct regular supervision of curriculum development in universities randomly selected: • Curriculum should be linked to future plan and policies, and financing and research; • Feedback promptly given to everyone involved, universities should be warned that quality problems will gradually cause them to lose their market share of good students, and therefore, the reputation of the school, the obvious consequences for financing decisions.	An annual report on the supervisions and steps to be taken for problems to be solved Public and distribution of findings	CD and ADC
B. Institutional Level			
Enhance the sense of responsibility and ownership for each university in their curriculum development and related activities	Establish a Special Office (SO) (or use part of the Office of Academic Affairs) to be in charge of regular curriculum development. It oversees and coordinates curriculum reform and planning, teacher training, textbook development and equipment provision.	University statement and an annual budget for the office Publication of course offerings with information relating to teacher training, textbook and equipment	SO
Develop institutional plans based on long-term strategy as well as annual plans for curriculum development. The long-term strategy should be in tune with the institutional goals; the annual plan includes priorities for each year.	Examine the goals and present conditions of the institution to decide what the school wants to be in the next 5, 10 or 20 years. Set one specific goal for each year as the priority.	Drafting and completion of strategies and plans that should be made known to everyone	
Bring curricular processes closer to world of work	Set up high-level joint university employers (or corporations) curriculum council to monitor labor market outcomes of graduates including job placements and remuneration and yearly shifts in supply and demand in skill areas.	Annual report with recommendations for curriculum change or shifts in emphasis	SO jointly with the President's Office

Figure 5.2: (cont'd)

OBJECTIVE	MEANS	INDICATOR	ACTION
B. Institutional Level (continued) Experiment with course organization to test viability of new courses and/or their income-generation capability with aim of incorporating in regular program if successful	• Pilot short programs in new areas, responding to rapidly changing needs; • Establish continuing (adult) education programs in these areas of self-financing basis; and • Recruit part-time teachers in specific areas from industry as required.	Evaluation of programs over a three-year cycle in terms of demand, financing and knowledge/skills base	SO and department
Assign the process of curriculum development and standardize in accordance with the national quality assurance system when the latter has been established	Set clear rules on changes in curriculum, such as procedures for initiation and approval of changes and above all, the financial and administrative support for such changes	Announcement of the rules	
	Set specific rules on curriculum-related activities, such as teacher training, textbook development and equipment provisions.	Complete set of rules in light of the strengths, weaknesses and constraints	SO
	Carry out annual assessment improvement and set up an annual award for teachers and staff judged as best contributors/performers. The purpose of the award is mainly for acknowledgment and recognition	An annual report on curriculum improvement with an emphasis on priority areas; the selection of the award-winning teachers	SO
Further the scope of training	Improve the present credit system by giving students more choices with specific guidance: for instance: • instead of giving the students a timetable, tell them what each course is about, what type of knowledge it will provide and how it may affect their future, and let the student decide what to learn; • instead of dividing the courses into required and elective, group them by subject themes and levels and give students some freedom to choose in each group; and	An improved course list with proper information on each course: its content and connections with other courses	SO and departments

Figure 5.2: (cont'd)

OBJECTIVE	MEANS	INDICATOR	ACTION
B. Institutional Level (continued)			
	• for core course, both general and specialty, more be offered by different levels for students or different interest and capacities.		
	Enlighten students to see the necessity of a solid foundation in general education for their future career by holding seminars, running exhibitions and inviting past graduates as guest speakers. The purpose is to show the students the link between their learning and their work in the near future	An orientation at beginning of each semester to provide the opportunity for previous students to help newcomers in course selection.	SO and departments
Ensuring the quality of teaching by securing books, journals and equipment for teachers	Secure annual budget for books and equipment and oversee its spending at the institutional level.	Input of SOE representative at the budget and expenditure review meetings should affect the department budget for future years	SO
	State budget for routine items for each department to reduce waste while retaining bidding items purchases at the institutional level for better management.	Adoption of the system with proper training planned and carried out	
	Find new ways to better utilize existing equipment and books; for example: • extend hours of labs and libraries, • enlist student help to reduce overhead costs at labs and libraries, and • arrange joint-institution (or cross-departments) utilization of books and equipment.	Negotiate with universities to change rules Motivate libraries, labs and department to agree on better utilization of existing facilities	SO and departments
	Look for ways to obtain external funding for books and equipment: • internally, foundations and research funds; and • domestic enterprises that need the university's services (graduates, research).	Set up information center for external funding possibilities	SO

Figure 5.2: (cont'd)

OBJECTIVE	MEANS	INDICATOR	ACTION
C. By Related Activities			
Improve the training system for administrators and teachers	Run regular training programs for administrators of all levels (from SEdC to universities). If possible, training should be based on real cases and new research findings.	Regular training programs held at different levels; evaluation of impact on training on quality of programs.	SEdC, provincial education commissions and universities.
	Training should expose everyone to the entire process of curriculum making, from planning, implementation to management so that coordination is possible	Appoint a professional to be in charge. Training using case method	SO
	While teachers have opportunities to advance their specialties, they also need to improve their pedagogy. SEdC should make general guidelines on this, but it is the universities' duty to set up teaching improvement centers, or run innovative teaching seminars to help teachers improve.	Seminars on teaching methodologies; core courses and discipline-specific	SO and department; resource persons from center and other higher education institutions
	Set up a teaching award for best teachers, who will be asked to give demonstration classes.	Regular demonstration classes held	Department and SO
	For those who are willing to innovate, support them not only with moral encouragement, but also actual assistance, such as reducing their workload or assign a small team to cooperate, and providing pockets of discretionary funds.	Fund for innovative teaching set aside	University and SO
Improve the textbook production process	This needs government support in proper changes in royalty regulations, printing and publishing rules. Once these rules are in place, the present textbook production should follow the market economy, running on a competitive base. Staff should be encourage to participate in writing, individually or in teams.	Once government support is obtained, make explicit rules for competitive undertaker of textbook projects.	SO and SEdC and the central government

Source: Study Team.

FIGURE 5.3: ACTION PLAN FOR FACULTY DEVELOPMENT

OBJECTIVES	MEANS	INDICATORS	ACTION
I. Upgrade the overall quality of the faculty contingent			
1. Continue improving the qualifications of faculty	(1) Targets of faculty qualification upgrading are set up in the framework of national research capacity development blueprint. (2)Resources are committed for graduate programs enrolling current faculty members.	Share of graduate degree-holders continue to increase	SEdC, PEdCs and institutions
2. Improve the pool of potential faculty for basic disciplines and service fields	(1) National academic societies, such as the National Physics Society, are entrusted to set up scholarship committees; (2) the scholarship committees identify and support promising undergraduate and graduate students; and (3) scholarship recipients are required to enter teaching positions upon graduation and remain for a minimum number of years.	Enhanced quality of graduates entering faculty positions in the esoteric disciplines	SEdC and national academic societies
II. Reduce brain drain in institutions in hinterland areas			
1. Improve academic and research environment	(1) Establish a committee to address comprehensively the human resources needs of hinterland areas in terms of teaching and research; (2) substantially increase funding to upgrade libraries and research facilities in national institutions; (2) encourage national and provincial foundations as well as government-dedicated research funds to assign additional weight to applications for research funding from university faculty; (3) SEdC provide assistance for international academic exchange.	Libraries and equipment comparable to national institutions in other regions; more international exchange opportunities for all institutions in outlying areas; reduced brain drain	The ad hoc committee, State Science and Technology Commission, SEdC, line ministries, provincial education authorities, foundations
2. Improve living conditions	Provide wage premium as an incentive to work in these areas.	Faculty basic salaries higher than in other areas, housing comparable.	SEdC, Ministry of Finance, provincial governments

Figure 5.3: (cont'd)

OBJECTIVES	MEANS	INDICATORS	ACTION
3. Retain faculty through locally provided training	(1) Appoint committees to evaluate graduate training programs in institutions in each region; (2) identify and designate a selected number of programs as regional training center(s) for specific academic disciplines; and (3) formulate policies to encourage faculty to attend such programs.	Cooperative training programs established and operating	SEdC, line ministries, provincial education authorities, ad hoc committees
III. Improve qualifications of women faculty			
1. Increase awareness of the problem	Campaign to make administrators and policymakers at various levels aware of the statistics concerning feminization of faculty, inadequate research opportunities and low qualification.	Statistics on women faculty compiled and published	SEdC and PEdCs
2. Improve the chances of promotion for women faculty	(1) Establish an affirmative action program to encourage enrollment of women students in formal graduate programs; (2) provide inservice graduate training programs (or cooperative training programs) to facilitate attendance by women faculty; and (3) relax age restrictions on enrolling women in graduate programs.	Increased enrollment of women students in formal and inservice graduate training programs	SEdC, PEdCs, universities and colleges
IV. Improve the teaching conditions of basic sciences and service fields	(1) Appoint ad hoc committees to study and propose broadening the definition of "basic sciences" and identify curricular changes; (2) eliminate basic studies section or department where applicable and incorporate the "basic courses" into departments of more broadly defined academic fields; and (3) increase research opportunities of faculty teaching "basic courses."	Basic studies section or departments eliminated; increased research participation of faculty teaching basic courses	SEdC, PEdCs, universities and colleges

Figure 5.3: (cont'd)

OBJECTIVES	MEANS	INDICATORS	ACTION
V. Reduce and eliminate "inbreeding" in faculty development			
1. Continue efforts to attract doctorate holders from overseas universities			
a. Increase awareness of degree candidates	Utilize various publications, mass media, etc., to keep potential returnees informed of personnel needs in domestic institutions, improved academic and living conditions, and research opportunities	Personnel needs of institutions and improvements in all areas publicized	SEdC, PEdCs, universities and colleges
b. Improve academic environment and research conditions	Increase funding to upgrade libraries and equipment	Libraries and equipment improved	All concerned
c. Improve living conditions	Coordinate and manage research and teaching outside of institution in order to raise more funds.	Increased share of revenue from outside teaching and research	Universities and colleges
VI. Reduce "inbreeding" in institution in hinterland areas			
1. Improve the research and academic environment	(1) Substantially increase funding to upgrade libraries and research facilities in national institutions; (2) encourage national foundations to assign additional weight to applications for research funding from university faculty; (3) SEdC provide assistance for international exchange.	Increased share of funding for library and equipment; increased international exchanges	SEdC, line ministries, provincial education authorities and national foundations
2. Improve living conditions	Provide wage premium for working in these areas.	Faculty basic salaries higher than in other areas, housing comparable	SEdC, Ministry of Finance, provincial governments

Source: Study Team.

6. ACHIEVING REFORM GOALS: STRATEGIC PRIORITIES

The mission of any higher education system includes: (a) the advancement of understanding and the generation of new knowledge; (b) contribution to the economic well-being of the community it serves; (c) enabling the development of effective social institutions; and (d) the enrichment of the cultural environment. The government has taken a pragmatic, gradualist approach to implementing changes, proposing a gradual devolution of the state's overall management function from the center to provincial and municipal authorities. This report has reviewed policies and implementation to date and provides advice in four key areas of China's reform agenda in higher education: (i) the changing role of government in relation to higher education institutions; (ii) the implications for institutional management; (iii) the diversification of the structure and sources of financial support and its utilization; and (iv) quality improvement in higher education with particular emphasis on staffing and curricular issues.

At the institutional level, the motivation to change appears to be driven by the government's plan to support the development of 100 key universities and some key areas of study in order to reach international standards, with every college and university aiming to become a member of this exclusive collective. "To meet the challenge of the world's new technological revolution, the resources of central and local authorities and of other sectors must be pooled to properly manage about 100 key universities and a number of key areas of study and specialized studies. China should strive to raise to the world's higher levels in the early 21st century with regard to educational quality and scientific study and management of a number of institutes of higher learning, fields of study, and specialized studies."[1] To the extent that the plan has stimulated institutions to strive for greater efficiency (mergers of small institutions, improving staff-student ratios, etc.) and for enhanced quality (rationalizing curricula, upgrading staff qualifications and facilities), China has met with success. Despite the progress made thus far, institutions that are handicapped at the start of the race with minimal financial resources and even less managerial, technical and professional know-how, are likely to face the probability of even greater divides and disparities by the end of the next decade. There are clear implications for political and economic destabilization as a consequence. The analytical outcomes of this report, based on experience and cumulative information from higher education projects undertaken by the World Bank since 1982, that the variations and disparities within the system—of geographical region, of physical terrain, of economic and social development, of technical expertise, of human and financial resources—preclude courses of action that hold true uniformly for the 1,065 institutions (1995 figure is 1,054 institutions as a result of mergers).

This section of the report identifies courses of action and recommends that implementers of reforms see as priorities. The three clusters of strategies outlined here were selected based on the following criteria and subsume the action plans suggested earlier:

---

[1]   "State Issues Educational, Development Program," Beijing Xinhua Domestic Service, February 25, 1993, translated in Foreign Broadcast Information Services, March 3, 1993, FBIS-CHI-93-040, pp. 16-17.

(a)   provision of critical assistance to provincial institutions in poor provinces that are resource-starved and have little access to professional and technological support for quality improvement activities;

(b)   goal of widespread impact visibly increasing access, equity, efficiency and quality in the provincial higher education system;

(c)   incremental development building on previous World Bank investment in higher education in China and inputs from national and local education authorities; and

(d)   achievement of sustainability in financial and human resource terms over the long term with built-in monitoring, evaluation and revitalizing capabilities.

Operational Strategy

The strategies would be operationalized within the reform framework of devolution from government to provincial, municipality and institutional authorities. Central to government functions is SEdC and its provincial counterparts, the PEdCs. The 1985 "Decision on Education Reform" reconstituted the Ministry of Education (MOE) into SEdC, making it a supraministerial body reporting directly to the State Council. SEdC's new functions incorporated a broader national perspective and the interests of the overall education sector, not only those it directly finances. Its mandate is to formulate and guide implementation of policies on education and not to control the system directly. Its responsibility is seen as: (a) maintaining macrolevel control through overall policy and planning; and (b) providing the key elements of an enabling environment that oversees and assists in planning, guiding, reflecting, evaluating, training, and research, leaving direct implementational activities to institutions. It links directly at the provincial level with provincial education commissions and their higher education bureaus. Based on the broadened framework of SEdC, the report strongly endorses the government's gradualist approach to change, recommending careful planning and monitoring, building on good practices. Three major thrusts are recommended in the next three sections—Enabling Environment, Financing Higher Education, and Improving Instructional Quality—which identify strategic priorities for urgent action.

Enabling Environment. The pace of changes in the various jurisdictions has been varied: implementation is characterized by dynamism punctuated by uncertainty. Organizational structures and academic practices are evolving to keep pace with demands.

(a)   A priority is the completion and ratification of the Higher Education Law, which should provide guidelines putting forth definitions of the respective roles, responsibilities and powers of the national, provincial and municipal authorities and the universities themselves. Suggestions based on international higher education laws and statutes are provided in Annex 2.

(b)   Crucial to achieving success in the reforms is the principle of autonomy as evidenced in the devolution of new managerial, administrative and academic responsibilities and powers to institutions. Institutional autonomy should be maintained in all these areas and not be eroded. One way of strengthening this is by encouraging each institution to develop a strategic plan for its future, taking the needs of its region and community into account. Expert technical assistance should be provided to poorly-endowed and inexperienced institutions in this undertaking.

(c)   New tasks and responsibilities demand new skills: academicians have become institutional managers and require training and exposure, both national and internationally, to best management practices. At another level, policymakers are encouraged to consider providing a cadre of permanent, professional and support staff who will maintain stability and continuity when top managers change. To facilitate this, a national Higher Education Management Center could be established to provide help and advice to individual universities and provinces or municipalities. The roles and functions of such a Center are indicated in Chapter 2.

(d)   Integral to sound management practice is the quality of its information base. The report recommends that a designated agency be responsible for collection, processing and publishing data and information that emphasize indicators of performance or achievement of the kind suggested in Chapter 2.

(e)   The initial stages of establishing nongovernmental (private) educational institutions should be encouraged and guidelines be set up to expedite the approval process. A clear link exists between the caution with which the government and its institutions regard this phenomenon and the strategy recommended for instituting widespread accreditation procedures and facilities in Chapter 5. All institutions would be subject to standards that have been set nationally and from which monitoring and evaluation practices would flow.

Financing Higher Education. If the state is to achieve its target of increasing the participation rate in higher education, it has to actively pursue policies for improving efficiency at both system and institutional levels and for seeking sources of alternative funding. The report suggests the following key measures:

(a)   Curbing the creation of new public universities so as to increase the average size of the present ones; and encouraging the expansion of private sector universities in order to provide competition;

(b)   Reviewing the funding methodologies for both recurrent and capital funding so as to reward efficiency and encourage expansion at below average cost. In the case of capital allocations, the existing space norms should be modified and brought closer to international standards. Mechanisms might be explored that encourage universities to accept students on a commuter, rather than residential, basis;

(c)   Stressing the importance of internal efficiency in universities by devising reward schemes for well-managed institutions;

(d)   Developing policies and programs that encourage universities to generate further income from the provision of short-term training, professionally managed enterprises and donations or endowments from all sources; and

(e)   Continuing the policies of cost sharing through universal tuition fees as well as of adequate measures for providing loan schemes in order to protect poor, minority or female students. It is suggested that any student loan schemes would have to receive initial financial capital from government sources.

Improving Instructional Quality

In order to build a culture of quality in the system, several factors need to be considered. Among them are the setting of educational standards as reference points for all stakeholders; professional incentives to provide and sustain motivation, impelling actors to attain and maintain standards; a system that is visibly equitable; and access to instructional materials, equipment and facilities. The strategy recommended in Chapter 5—the establishment of "quality assurance centers" and "centers of excellence"—is based on institutionalizing best practices that have emerged locally and internationally, and include initiatives jointly developed by the state, provinces and institutions. The report recommends that:

(a)   Accreditation procedures be extended to poor provinces, particularly those that are economically disadvantaged. In order to do this, two bands of training are required that intermesh: training in academic and professional knowledge and methodologies; and training in organizing and conducting accreditation procedures with rigor. The experience of local and international expertise may be required to set this in motion.

(b)   Managerial initiatives and greater autonomy on the part of institutions, supported by the State, could put together incentives and disincentives to move institutional practices toward qualitative goals. The rewards and sanctions should be clearly spelled out to all involved.

(c)   Funding policies for research and training (discussed in Chapter 5) in relation to rectifying the balance between institutions, between discipline areas while keeping gender and minority priorities in mind, need to be taken into consideration.

(d)   Programs and activities established by centers of excellence must commence with strategic plans of their own, taking plans of participating institutions into account, and beginning with pilot programs, identify areas best managed through core government funding, those through institutional funding, and those that require combinations of resources. Without clarity about funding from the outset, the sustainability of the initiative would be in danger.

(e)   Quality assurance centers, centers of excellence, and governmental training and research units need to define their different missions so as to clarify territories of action in order to avoid wastage of resources through duplication.

Chinese Universities in the 21st Century

Given China's own clear policy that education will provide the strategic initiative in international competition in the 21st century, and using international benchmarks of effective higher education systems, the vision of higher education institutions that emerges for the next century might be characterized in the following way:

(a)   The government will have moved from a state-control model of higher education governance to a scenario where it plays the crucial role of macroplanner, coordinator and supervisor, involved nationwide in quality assurance in terms of standard setting, monitoring and evaluation. Clear policies are already in place regarding the utilization of evaluation results.

(b)   A ratified Higher Education Law will provide the framework for independent growth as well as accountability.

(c)   The higher education system is strongly market-driven, competitive, output rather than input-oriented, with strong planning and monitoring capabilities. Universities keep a clear-eyed view of educational goals, assiduously nurturing disciplines and activities (such as in the humanities) that are not immediately popular as market-oriented programs.

(d)   Government funding will steadily decrease as institutions become increasingly autonomous and self-financing, with growing participation by privately funded institutions, joint efforts with social organizations, overseas compatriots, interested foreign institutions, and local and international corporations.

(e)   Sensitive multiparameter funding mechanisms and reward systems will have brought about leaner, more efficient systems with indicators such as faculty/student ratios, research and publication outputs, and facility utilization rates moving toward or on par with international standards. Institutions have more autonomy and powers in terms of resource allocation, mobilization and utilization.

(f)   Cost-sharing especially through considered student fee regimes will be accompanied by well-tested and targeted loan and award schemes, encouraging universal access to higher education.

(g)   Better alignment of wages with skills and levels of productivity will increase financial returns to higher education. Differentiated salary levels will better reflect levels of education.

(h)   The Government will give institutions the highest degree of freedom in terms of enrollment and curricular decisions so that human and material resources (libraries, etc.) will have broad social influence.

(i)   The system will have the characteristics of a mass rather than an elitist higher education system, characterized by greater student choice of disciplines.

(j)   Institutions will have the flexibility and the know-how to develop curricula in tune with changing socioeconomic environments while maintaining a balance by supporting core knowledge-generating and life-enhancing programs of study.

(k)   With better and more accessible technology, personal, individualized instruction will be the norm rather than teacher-centered, rote learning, paving the way for greater creativity and for expanded enrollment at the degree level.

(l)   Research, teaching and publication activities will flourish through the synergy contributed by institutional links with government, business and community bodies, and through ongoing interchange with international universities and organizations. A major focus will be an increasingly proactive role in science and technology research and development and greater interaction in this area between industry and the higher education sector.

(m)   Increased enrollment in graduate-level programs in response to student and labor market demands will be characterized by growing numbers of women.

(n)   Well-organized and ongoing staff development programs will provide continuous upgrading and updating facilities for all, while providing opportunities for women and minorities to move up the professional career ladders of their choice.

(o)   The outcome of such deep qualitative changes will be a self-renewing and internally energized capability to change skill mixes of faculty and students as necessary.

(p)   There will be increased numbers of nationally accredited institutions, which will include nongovernmental institutions, with provincial and multinational support for qualitative and quantitative standards. The large number of accredited private institutions allow the higher education sector to better meet labor market demands of the economy.

(q)   Leading Chinese universities, in collaboration with other leading universities in East Asia (e.g., Japan, the Republic of Korea), will be setting important agendas in research and development in the region, bringing about a better balance of scholarship, research and publication activities between Western and East Asian universities.

Constraints for achieving this vision in the short run include serious shortfalls in financial resources, a dearth of managerial, technological and other high-level skills. An absence of growing markets in disadvantaged areas underscores the disparities existing in the system. The contrast between institutions in the thriving coastal regions and poorer provincial and local institutions is a case in point. Inherent tensions exist that may continue to keep universities and colleges in bondage unless vigorous efforts are made to upgrade the weaker institutions and unleash their potential for growth.

ANNEX 1: CHINESE HIGHER EDUCATION: HISTORICAL BACKGROUND

China's present higher education system was established in the early 1950s with the deliberate intention of training higher level personnel as effectively as possible for service in all sectors of the new socialist state. The model was derived directly from the Soviet Union, with the assistance of Soviet experts in both its design and implementation, and it was intended to counteract some of the well-known weaknesses of higher institutions during the previous Nationalist period: a tendency toward overly high enrollments in areas such as law, political science and humanities, which were strongly favored due to persisting values from the traditional civil service system, considerable geographical imbalances between coastal and central/hinterland regions and a degree of diversity that did not ensure common academic standards.

The new system was created initially between 1950 and 1955, with a complete reorganization of old institutions and the creation of new ones around a national plan, which emphasized curricular patterns that would ensure close coordination between higher education programs and personnel needs of the state as well as a rational geographical distribution of higher education. The country was divided into six major geographical regions, and, from 1950 to 1954, each of them had an educational bureau that coordinated planning for the region. At the core of the system were three or four main types of institution that were directly administered by a new national ministry of higher education: polytechnic universities with a wide range of applied scientific and engineering programs, comprehensive universities, with programs mainly in the basic arts and sciences, and normal universities with arts and sciences programs combined with education, which were responsible for setting national standards for teacher training at tertiary and secondary level. Each region had at least one of each of these three types of institution, some had two or three, and their role was both a national and regional one. In addition to these core institutions, there were a large number of sectoral institutions, in areas such as agriculture, medicine, steel, finance, law, railways etc. They were managed by appropriate ministries and were distributed across the country, taking into account differences of regional emphasis by sector. Each institution was narrowly specialized in its programs, and its role was to train personnel for its specific sector.

Between 1950 and 1954, each region had the responsibility of enrolling students through entrance examinations, but in 1955 a national unified entrance examination was established. The recruitment base was still a selective and highly academic upper secondary education system, and competition was not as intense as it later became. A unified national job assignment system was put in place in 1956 and was managed jointly by the State Planning Commission, the sectoral ministries, and the Ministry of Higher Education, to ensure that each graduate was assigned a position as a state cadre in a setting where their knowledge could be put to good use. It was the norm for graduates to be sent far from their homes, often to serve in the development of new institutions or industries in hinterland areas.

The main function of this new higher education system was teaching, with a separate system for research established under the Chinese Academy of Sciences and various national ministries. A large number of research institutes developed, with research topics and funding assigned by plan from the state, and with very little connection to the higher education system, except for the fact that research staff were drawn from its graduates. A few institutes under the Academy undertook programs of graduate training in the late 1950s and early 1960s.

In 1957-58, with the Great Leap Forward, a second important stage in the evolution of the socialist higher education system took place, with the vigorous development of new institutions at the provincial level and the decentralization of authority over some national institutions. The Ministry of Higher Education was merged with the Ministry of Education. Many provinces created their own comprehensive and normal universities as well as various specialized institutions during this period in order to serve provincial personnel needs. This was a time when a large number of graduates from the best universities in coastal areas were sent to remote regions as core faculty for newly established local institutions. Also some coastal institutions were moved to the hinterland.

In a situation where the priorities were to build heavy industry as the basis for a modern economy and establish a strong socialist governmental and education system, these patterns set in place in the 1950s worked well at first as there was a fairly high degree of predictability in personnel planning for these areas. However, with a new emphasis on agriculture and light industry in the late 1950s and the rapid growth of secondary education, which increased the pool of graduates competing for entry to higher education, many concerns about equality of access and the suitability of the system to China's indigenous economic and cultural development came to the fore. The Cultural Revolution was a period in which some of these concerns were aired and strong criticism was expressed of the Soviet-derived pattern. For three years, from 1966 to 1969, all regular recruitment to higher education was halted. Between 1971 and 1976 much smaller numbers of students were enrolled. Unfortunately, efforts to run open-door institutions and link academic knowledge with social transformation failed. This caused inestimable damage to the economy and society, especially affecting intellectuals and government cadres.

In the late 1970s, the concern for modernization through economic revitalization became paramount. The leadership of Deng Xiaoping opened up a new era of reform, which brought about fundamental changes in higher education. In an important national conference for science and education held in 1978, clear goals of service to economic modernization in the four areas of agriculture, industry, national defense and science and technology were set forth. This national policy emphasis on the economy has resulted in dramatic changes over the 1980s.

In 1985, the Chinese government's new policy entitled "The Reform of the Education System" emphasized the implementation of a three-level school management system at the central, provincial, and major municipal levels. The same reform plan gave universities new powers, particularly with regard to the content and methods of teaching, as well as freedom to develop new programs and even new local institutions at the short-cycle level and in adult education.

ANNEX 2: SUGGESTED TOPICS FOR THE HIGHER EDUCATION LAW AND UNIVERSITY STATUTES

Higher Education Law

The Higher Education Law should be at a very high level, assuming that there are secondary levels of regulation at national level (via State Council, SEdC and other edicts) and university level (via the university's own statutes and regulations). The Law should thus focus on providing the framework for detailed monitoring and regulation at both levels. If it concentrates on general principles and guidelines, it will not need to be revised at intervals. Its clauses should include:

General Principles

- A general statement of principles concerning the autonomy and rights of the universities.

- The right of SEdC to increase, or amend, at any time by regulations the powers, rights and duties of universities.

- A summary statement of universities' overall mandate, their duties as regards society and its purposes.

- Universities to have nonprofit status and to be independent legal entities capable of entering into contracts. The Chair of the Supreme Board or the President should be the legal representative.

- Statement of the general principle that ministries or provincial and local governments shall have macrocontrol over universities, but shall not intervene in their management.

- The right of any locality or group of enterprises and individuals from China or overseas to open an institution of higher learning, subject to the approval of SEdC or provincial government.

- Confirmation of the exemption of universities from all taxation, as long as the profits from any noneducational activity are dedicated to educational activities.

Controls and Powers

- The right of SEdC to alter at any time by regulations the ways in which macrocontrol shall be exercised by itself, ministries, provinces or local governments.

- The rights of the Chinese Academy of Sciences and any other body named by the State Council to set quality standards, undertake evaluations or tests, or otherwise review the educational performance of the university.

- The powers and rights of provincial governments to control and monitor the quality of teaching and research in the university.

- The right of SEdC and provincial governments to set regulations concerning universities' disposal of any assets, their reinvestment of the proceeds, and the construction of any building.

University Council

- Definition of the roles, broad powers, and duties of a university's Supreme Board or Council.

- The number of members of Council, where they come from and how they are to be appointed.

- Procedures for the appointment or removal from office of the Chair of Council.

- The appointment of an Academic Council with responsibility for upholding the quality of teaching and research and guidelines as to its membership and appointment of the Chair.

- The broad duties of the Academic Council as regards the approval of new course, the award of degrees, diplomas, etc.

- The duty of the University Council to draft (or amend) internal statutes (for approval by SEdC, the Ministry or province) to describe how the University shall be managed.

- A similar duty of the Council to issue regulations to control the day-to-day academic, financial and other management processes of the University and the right to delegate the power to issue or amend such regulations to committees or university officials.

- The duty of the University Council to publish an Annual Report with such contents including financial accounts, as shall be prescribed in regulations.

- Duties of the Council to uphold the highest standards of financial management within the University and to ensure the absence of fraud or misuse of funds.

University Management

- The powers and responsibilities of the President.

- How he or she shall be appointed or removed from the office.

- The rights of the University to own land and other assets, borrow money, enter into contracts, undertake trading activities, and to operate outside China as long as the activities are undertaken for the purposes of clause 3.

- Definitions of the role and duties of any Statutory Officers of the University, e.g., Secretary to the Council.

University Statutes

The University Statutes should again be written with a long timescale in mind, so that they do not need to be amended regularly. Their first draft and later amendment should require approval at provincial or State level. Internal university regulations, on the other hand, will be changed often and some (such as those relating to fee levels) may alter each year. Their amendment will be an internal university matter that requires different levels of approval depending on the topic. Some will be decided by the President, some by the University Council, and some by senior leaders.

The Statutes should include:

- detailed powers of the University Council and Academic Council;

- power of either body to create such subcommittees as are required;

- specification of any subcommittees either body must have (e.g., relating to Finance or Academic Quality);

- the term of membership and how new members are selected or put up for approval;

- detailed powers and duties of the President and the extent to which they may be delegated;

- powers and duties of Vice presidents and Dean's Directors; how they are appointed or removed from office;

- the need for internal procedures for development and submission of proposals for higher degrees;

- the need for internal procedures for approval of courses leading to undergraduate degrees or a lesser qualification;

- the need for internal processes for review and maintenance of quality in teaching and research;

- role of the University Council in authorizing major capital expenditures projects and in approving detailed financial regulations;

- duties of the University Council as regards the University's Annual Report and financial accounts and their independent inspection or audit;

- role of the University Council in approval tuition fee levels and the power to delegate such decisions;

- duties of the University Council and Academic Council concerning equal opportunities and enrollment or recruitment of minorities among staff and students;

- need for procedures for handling appeals by staff or students on decisions of appointment, promotion or discipline;

- the role of the University Council if any, in approving international joint ventures, or in accepting funds from overseas Chinese donors or international agencies.

ANNEX 3: RETURNS TO HIGHER EDUCATION: TOOLS FOR ASSESSMENT AND INTERNATIONAL COMPARISON

Tools for Assessment

Policymakers in every country are confronted with two fundamental questions in considering whether to expand a particular level of education and the desirability and nature of public intervention. One important input in this consideration is whether expansion is economically attractive, given the labor market conditions and the marginal cost of expansion. The other is the consideration of market failure and how government policy can address it. The purpose of this annex is to address the first question, while the issue concerning market failure and the need for student financial assistance is discussed in Chapter 4.

There are two basic tools to assess the economic attractiveness of further investment (public and private) in higher education: (a) the rate-of-return analysis (or cost-benefit analysis) to estimate the economic returns to education for the individual and the society; and (b) the analysis of labor market outcomes of graduates to evaluate whether the supply has met the demand for skill requirements. These approaches and experience of countries are discussed below.

(a) The Rate-of-Return Analysis (Cost-Benefit Analysis)

The underlying assumption of this analysis is that education enhances productivity of individuals. As a private investment, education incurs immediate direct cost in the forms of tuition fees, books, and transportation, and indirect costs (opportunity cost) in the form of forgone earnings to the family or the individual, and it yields benefits in the form of increased future earnings. Over the lifetime of individuals, the benefits of education generally outweigh costs, thereby providing positive rates of return to the investment.

This analysis estimates the internal rate of return to investment in education by equating the present value of costs to the present value of expected monetized benefits. To estimate the private rates of return to education, individuals' post-tax earnings are taken to calculate the private benefits (which are measured by the difference in the average earnings of graduates of one educational level and those of a lower level) and direct private cost and foregone earnings while in school are used to calculate the cost of schooling. To estimate the social rates of return, pretax earnings are used to calculate the social benefits, while public expenditure on education is added to private costs to calculate the total resource cost to society for investment in education (Psacharopoulos, various years).

Empirical studies in over 60 countries found that, worldwide, all levels of education are profitable for both the individual and the society. In countries that have not achieved universal primary education, the first level yields the highest social returns and the tertiary level yields the lowest, because both costs and the degree of pubic subsidy tends to increase markedly with the level of education. However, as a country's per capita income rises and the educational attainment of workers increases, social returns to lower levels of education decline. On the other hand, the private returns to tertiary education are higher than those to primary and secondary education in countries of all income levels, because of the relative scarcity of high-level skills and often substantial public subsidies that reduce private costs. These findings provide the economic justification for public subsidization of basic education and for charging tuition fees at the higher levels of education, because graduates who will enjoy higher life-time earnings are the beneficiary of their own education. However, if the social returns to higher education exceed those to other levels of education, then there is considerable relative underinvestment and under supply at this level, which could be due to inappropriate government policies that artificially restrict expansion (as in Hong Kong in the 1970s and 1980s), low public subsidies for higher education relative to other levels (as in the Republic of Korea), or market failure (as in Taiwan for women and rural people). In the case of government policies that restrict higher education expansion, the remedy is to remove these constraints. In the case of a high degree of cost recovery and market failure, it is important to provide student financial assistance. Therefore, on grounds of both efficiency and equity, charging tuition fees should be accompanied by student loans and scholarships to ensure that talented students from low-income families, women, and ethnic minorities are not denied educational opportunity by obvious imperfections in the private credit market for education.

The rate-of-return analysis, however, does not measure nonpecuniary private benefits and the positive externalities (spill-over effects) of education. In the case of higher education, the external benefits of the development of high-level technical and managerial capacity that underpin economic growth, advancement of the civil society, the public good nature of basic research, and the contribution of higher education to the nation-building process have never been estimated (Birdsall, 1995). Furthermore, it does not take into account the positive social effects of extending opportunity from the elite to the masses and of reducing the wage inequality that the expansion of higher education can bring. Thus, these benefits of higher education call for the government to play a key role in promoting higher education to ensure equal opportunity for access and quality, in subsidizing to the degree that it generates public goods, and to provide student financial assistance to correct for capital market failure.

(b) Analysis of Labor Market Outcomes

To inform policy direction, more dynamic indicators on the labor market outcomes of education (such as the probability of employment and unemployment of graduates, and the effects on higher education expansion on the earnings of graduates) are needed to complement the results of cost-benefit analysis. Given China's rapid economic growth and the low stock of highly-educated workers, what needs to be monitored to guide higher education policy are: (i) how do the wage differentials between secondary school and university graduates change over time?, and (ii) what is the source of the change in the wage gap?

This type of analysis can only be conducted in a labor market where wages are driven by the forces of supply and demand. The assumption is that wages are equal to or less than marginal productivity. Because the demand for labor is derived from the demand for goods and services, it is affected by the shift in the composition and level of output and inputs, and by technological change. The very existence of the wage differentials between secondary and tertiary educated workers indicates that the former could not substitute for the latter. The college wage premium (and the wage gap) will rise if supply has not caught up with demand.

To answer these two questions entails obtaining basic data on wages (preferably distinguishable between main and secondary jobs, and from bonus and benefits), hours worked per month or week, age, gender, years of education, level of educational attainment, years of work experience, work history (such as duration and frequency of unemployment), and occupations (such as professional and technical, managerial and administrative, clerical, sales, production, and agricultural). It would be highly desirable if information is obtained on such variables as place of education (rural and urban), parental education and income, ethnicity, public or private sector employment, and firm size. Data in a single point in time will suffice if the purpose is to examine the wage differential of a given year. However, to examine change of wage differentials over time (for example, between 1986 and 1996), at least two cross-sectional datasets are needed for these two years. The wages of young workers between the ages of 25 and 24 are of particular relevance to educational policy because their wages are more sensitive to the shifts in the supply of and demand for educated workers and because the educational composition of the labor force changes most rapidly in this age group.

The analysis entails working in two steps. First, it requires conducting a multiple regression analysis on each of the datasets separately to estimate wages as a function of a worker's characteristics. Other variables can be included to control for their effects—for example, test scores of reasoning ability and of academic achievement (to control for innate ability and cognitive skills), socioeconomic variables such as paternal and maternal education and income, gender, ethnicity, or rural and urban origins (to test for discrimination or labor market segmentation).

As a second step, a shift-share analysis can be used to decompose the sources of change in the wage differentials between secondary school and university graduates. There are a number of ways of doing this, and the data requirements vary with different approaches (Katz and Murphy, 1992; Knight and Sabot, 1990; Kim, 1994; Wu, 1995). The most basic approach requires two cross-sectional datasets to identify occupationally-related sources of change in the wage differentials between high school and college educated workers. This requires fitting four regressions for secondary school and university educated workers, separately, for each of the two years. The coefficients generated from these regressions can be used to estimate the effects of redistribution of workers between occupations, and the effects of changes in relative wages within occupations. If the wage difference between occupations is larger than the wage difference within occupations, then a larger portion of the difference in the wage gap is attributable to the occupational redistribution of secondary school and university graduates. This would suggest that difference in the college premium is attributable to shifts in the supply of college educated workers. Conversely, if the wage difference within occupations is larger, then difference in the college premium might be due to changes in the demand for college educated workers.

The Changing Worth of a University Education: International Trend

In the 1980s and 1990s, high-income economies such as the United States, Canada, Britain, and Australia have witnessed a sharp rise in the college premium, resulting in growing income disparity between the better educated workers and their less educated counterparts. Countries with more rigid wage structure, such as those in continental Europe, do not have the same extent of increased disparity in wages, but suffer from rising unemployment (World Bank, 1995a, 1995f). Both growing wage inequality and rising unemployment have been attributed to the declining demand for the less well-trained in a world of increasing technological change and global economic integration. The widespread use of computer technology has raised skill requirements, while competitive pressures generated by global economic integration have forced both manufacturing and service firms in high-income countries to restructure and increase productivity rapidly. These processes, in turn, have led to increased demand for highly educated labor relative to that for labor with less skills. College graduates have been able to move into high-skilled, higher-paying occupations, while high school graduates have been trapped in low-skilled, low-paying jobs with uncertain prospects (Levy and Murnane, 1992; Spenner, 1985, 1988; Blackburn, 1990; Blackburn, Bloom, and Freeman, 1990, 1991; Bound and Freeman, 1992; OECD, 1993; Davis, 1992; World Bank, 1995a, 1995b, 1995f).

Some middle-income Latin American countries—such as Argentina, Chile, and Mexico— which have liberalized their trade regimes in recent years, have also seen increased wage inequalities. In Chile, for example, the wages of university graduates rose by 56 percent relative to those of high school graduates between 1980 and 1990 (World Bank, 1995f). Analysts are still disentangling the various effects at play in these Latin American countries—complementarities between inflows of new capital and skills, demand for well educated workers (relative to their supply) immediately following liberalization, labor saving technological change, and competitive pressures from lower-wage unskilled workers in poorer countries. These factors also seem to affect the demand for highly educated labor in Hong Kong, Malaysia, and Indonesia. The following are three short case studies on the effects of higher education expansion on the wages of graduates in the Republic of Korea, Taiwan (China), and Hong Kong.

Republic of Korea

The case of the Republic of Korea, China's eastern neighbor of 42 million population, is highly illustrative of the relationship between education and economic development. The Republic of Korea now has a GNP per capita of over $7,000, and is the second Asian country after Japan that is in the process of joining the Organization of Economic Cooperation and Development (OECD), which consists of high-income countries in Europe, North America, and Oceania. It is also the fifth biggest investor in China. The rebirth of the Republic of Korea after the Korean War (1950-53) has been deemed an economic miracle (World Bank, 1993). The Republic of Korea has made sustained investment in education, concentrating about 90 percent of public resources on basic education, and encouraging private provision and financing of tertiary education. Primary education was universalized by the late 1950s; by 1970, 64 percent of primary school graduates entered junior secondary schools, 71 percent of junior secondary school graduates entered senior secondary schools, and 35 percent of senior secondary school graduates entered higher education. By 1994, the gross enrollment ratio in higher education is 51 percent.

How have the social rates of return changed over time? The following table shows that for males, the social returns to college and university education exceeded those to high school education since 1977 and continued to climb in the 1980s. This indicates that the demand for highly educated people was stronger than the supply throughout much of the 1980s due to strong growth of the economy. By contrast, at the margin, the country has an over supply of lower level graduates relative to demand. Between 1985 and 1994, however, the social returns to higher education declined by half due to rapid expansion of higher education. This decline was relatively modest considering the remarkable increase of 218 percent in the gross enrollment rates from 16 percent to 51 percent between 1980 and 1994[1] (see Table 1.2).

A recent analysis of the 1980 and 1990 data from the Korean Occupational Wage Surveys[2] confirmed that the average wage gap between male, full-time, high school and college educated workers between the ages of 25 and 34 declined substantially over this period--whereas college-educated workers on average earned 67 percent more than high school educated workers in 1980, they earned only 26 percent more in 1990 (Kim, 1994). In other words, college graduates continued to command a wage premium over their high school counterparts, although at a lower rate in 1990 than in 1980. The overall result of the tremendous expansion of higher education is a substantial reduction of wage inequality.

SOCIAL RATES OF RETURN BY LEVEL OF SCHOOLING (MALES ONLY)
(In percent)

Researcher	Year	High School	College and University
Kim, G.S.	1967	9.0	5.0
Florida State Univ.	1969	11.0	9.5
Jeong, C.Y.	1971	14.6	9.3
Bae, J.G.	1977	9.9	13.8
Park, S.I.	1980	8.1	11.7
KEDI	1982	12.3	13.0
KEDI	1985	7.6	14.5
KEDI	1994	7.3	7.2

Source: Paik, Sung-Joon, *Educational Finance in Korea*, Korean Educational Development Institute, Seoul, 1995, p. 29.

A shift-share analysis which decomposed the occupation-specific change in the wage gap between high school and college graduates at the level of labor market entry between 1980 and 1990, however, revealed interesting variation within each occupation group: while there was a substantial reduction in the wage gap in production and service occupations, a modest growth in the wage gap between high school and college graduates still existed in the professional and technical occupations (for example, physical scientists and engineers, medical and life scientists, statisticians and economists) (Kim, 1994:91). In short, in spite of the tremendous expansion of higher education, given the industrial upgrading and rapid economic growth of the country, the wage premium of university graduates in professional and technical occupations still grew, reflecting a continued demand for highly specialized skills. Returns to higher education in the future will depend on the growth of industries and sectors predominantly requiring university graduates, rather than high school graduates.

Taiwan (China)

Taiwan, the Chinese province of 22 million population, now has a per capita GNP over $10,000 and is considered another "East Asia Miracle" (World Bank, 1993). In the early 1950s,

---

[1] The Republic of Korea's enrollment increase more than doubled China's increase in gross enrollment ratio from 1 to 2 percent over the same period.

[2] The sample contains some 21,800 workers in 1980 and 29,700 workers in 1990.

about 42 percent of the working population was illiterate. The priority then was to ensure that the next generation will not suffer from the same incapacity. Primary education was universalized in 1960. As the demand for secondary education grew, nine years of basic education were made free and compulsory in 1968. The next stage was expansion of senior secondary education, including senior vocational education, as well as junior colleges in the 1970s. The 1980s marked a period of expansion of universities and colleges. By 1992, 88 percent of junior secondary graduates enrolled in senior secondary schools and about 60 percent of senior secondary school graduates enrolled in tertiary education. The gross enrollment ratio in Taiwan grew from 18 to 39 percent between 1980 and 1994 (see Table 1.2).

A recent study using the rate-of-return analysis on Taiwan's Household Income and Expenditure Survey[3] found that during the 1976-90 period, the most profitable level of schooling shifted from secondary to four-year college education, in spite of the rapid expansion of higher education (Fwu, 1993). For males, the private returns to college education increased from 9 percent in 1976 to 11 percent in 1990; while those to high school education declined from 10 to 8 percent. For females, the private returns for college education rose from 13 to 14 percent, and those for high school education fell from 9 to 7 percent (see Table below). These findings suggest that given the increasing private returns to higher education, the incentives for private investment in education (by implication, the willingness to pay tuition fees) would continue to be strong.[4]

PRIVATE AND SOCIAL RATES OF RETURN TO SECONDARY AND TERTIARY EDUCATION, 1976 AND 1990

	1976				1990			
	Secondary		Tertiary		Secondary		Tertiary	
	Private	Social	Private	Social	Private	Social	Private	Social
Complete Data Set	10.50	8.24	10.75	7.98	9.11	6.13	12.65	7.78
Male Subset	9.88	7.72	9.28	7.70	7.27	4.78	10.90	7.56
Female Subset	10.13	8.62	12.93	5.97	9.27	5.90	13.88	7.22
Urban Subset	8.15	6.72	10.05	7.48	8.57	5.62	12.43	7.68
Rural Subset	11.25	8.32	9.63	5.49	9.33	6.91	12.90	6.99

Source: Fwu, 1993, p. 511.

The study also found that the social returns to education differentiated by gender and region. The social returns to higher education remained largely stable at nearly 8 percent for males between 1976 and 1986, but rose from under 6 to over 7 percent for females. By contrast, the social returns to high school education for males declined from 8 percent in 1976 to 5 percent in 1990, and for females, from 9 to 6 percent. For urbanites, the social returns to college education increased marginally, but for rural people, the social returns increased from 5.5 to 7 percent over the period (see Table below). These findings suggest that further public investment in higher

---

[3] The survey contained some 9,400 households in 1976 and 16,000 households in 1990. The unit of analysis of the study is the individual worker.

[4] The finding that in Taiwan, private returns are much higher than social returns, is consistent with the trend in most market economies in the world. It is probably opposite in China, where wage structure is administratively compressed and wages of highly educated professionals do not reflect the social value of those professional capabilities.

education would enable females and rural people, the traditionally disadvantaged groups, to attend universities and this would have continued economic benefits for society.

Hong Kong

Of particular relevance to China is Hong Kong, a territory of 6 million population with a GDP per capita of $18,000, which is due to return to Chinese sovereignty on July 1, 1997. Hong Kong is the opposite case of the Republic of Korea and Taiwan because of the historical restriction of higher education. Although primary education was universalized in 1970 and junior secondary education in 1978, these came almost a decade later than the Republic of Korea and Taiwan. The Hong Kong Government historically restricted university enrollment to about 2 percent of the relevant age group, although enrollment in nondegree programs in polytechnics doubled (Cheng, 1987). The Government controlled the supply of higher education graduates through restricting them to publicly funded institutions, and nonrecognition of local private colleges and nonrecognition of degrees conferred by universities in non-Commonwealth countries. Expatriates were recruited to fill decision-making and other key positions in the civil service. Because of limited higher education opportunities at home, families of means sent their children abroad for further studies, resulting in 64 percent of tertiary educated workers in the labor force holding overseas credentials in 1986, according to the census. In the late 1970s and early 1980s, Hong Kong was similar to China in the low stock of university educated workers. Thus, Hong Kong provides a natural experiment to illustrate the potential consequences of restricting or neglecting higher education. The expansion of nondegree programs began to pick up the pace in the first half of the 1980s, and degree programs were rapidly expanded in the late 1980s and 1990s. By 1993, the gross enrollment ratio in higher education was about 20 percent.

The social rates of return to higher education in Hong Kong also exceeded those to secondary education by 1986. The table below presents the findings.

SOCIAL RATES OF RETURN TO EDUCATION IN HONG KONG

Researcher	Year	Secondary Education	University Preparatory	Higher Education
Hung	1976	15	-	12
Wong	1976	14-15	23	5
	1981	10	18	10
	1986	10	11	12

Source: Chung and Wong (Eds.), 1992, p. 32.

A study using census data[5] found that between 1976 and 1986, during which Hong Kong was transformed from a low-cost manufacturing base to an international center of commerce and finance, the college wage premium increased, despite an increase of 55 percent in the proportion of male, full-time workers between the ages of 25 and 34 with university degrees (Wu, 1995). Whereas university educated workers earned 190 percent more than the secondary school graduates in 1976, they earned 227 percent more in 1986. The payoffs to higher education were found to lie

---

[5] The sample contains some 19,500 workers in 1976 and 43,800 workers in 1986.

principally in its interaction with job experience. The returns to experience increased more rapidly for university educated workers in 1986, particularly for those in professional occupations. The rapid wage growth experienced by university educated workers over their secondary school educated counterparts demonstrated the value of a university education in enhanced capacity to learn and adapt on the job. These general skills, provided by university education, were in short supply in Hong Kong. The shift-share decomposition analysis found a rising demand for experienced, highly educated workers in a fast expanding and increasingly complex economy. This suggests that expansion of higher education to meet the social and private demand would have continued economic benefits.

ANNEX 4: SCIENTIFIC RESEARCH AND TECHNOLOGICAL DEVELOPMENT

The Current Status

In a country of 1.2 billion people, who make up 23 percent of the world's population, on only 7 percent of the earth's cultivable land, Chinese science and technology has the dual missions of "solving a number of major strategic problem including adequate levels of food, shelter, transportation, education, and health care," and in improving the country's "scientific and technological infrastructure" (*Science*, Nov. 1995, p. 1154). Both missions intersect with those of higher education, although China's scientific establishment is far more encompassing than higher education. It comprises 23,613 institutions, of which 7,805 are research institutions, 12,499 industrial enterprises, and 3,309 research institutes within higher education. About 2.6 million persons are employed in these institutions, of whom 1.5 million are scientists and engineers. Research and development (R&D) spending accounted for about 0.5 percent of the GNP in 1994 (*China Statistical Yearbook 1995*, Table 18.40, p. 619). About 7 percent of R&D was spent on basic research, 30 on applied research, and the rest on development (*Science*, Nov. 1995, p. 1135).

The leading research institution is the Chinese Academy of Science (CAS), which was established in 1949 and has 123 research institutes under its jurisdiction. Since 1978, the CAS has also undergone reform to make its research institutes more open to university professors, increased mobility into and from the institutes, strengthened international collaboration, introduced a system of peer review, and provided more opportunities to a younger generation of scientists. It has established 100 open laboratories and has set aside funds to improve collaboration with universities. It has also established relations with more than 3,000 enterprises to facilitate technology transfer through contract research. About 30 percent of its activities are devoted to basic research, another 30 percent to population, resources, and the environment, and the remaining 40 percent to technology development. About half of its budget is obtained through competition from government and industrial projects. The CAS's achievement is recorded in Annex 8.

In the effort to advance science and technology, the Government created state key laboratories in 1984 to break into the forefront of global science and established the National Natural Science Foundation of China (NSFC) the following year to coordinate, review, and evaluation research efforts. These key laboratories received an initial grant of $1 million or more to modernize their facilities and are eligible for additional funding. Although it was not a large amount by international comparison, it was large relative to China's average research grant of $10,000 over a three-year period. Ten years into the program, the key laboratories proliferated into 155 labs, of which only 11 are world-class and received top rating by the NSFC. The inability to weed out weak labs even though they have been identified has resulted in spreading the research funds more and more thinly, a consequence similar to that of the proliferation of higher education institutions (*Science*, Nov. 1995, pp. 1137-1139).

Two recent developments are noteworthy because of its long-term potential consequences. The first is the policy to provide incentives to researchers, particularly the younger generation. Researchers are poorly paid, in spite of their high skill level. The average annual wage in the scientific and technological establishments in 1994 was Y 6,162 ($725) (*China Statistical Yearbook 1995*, p. 117), and the lure of commerce has triggered a brain drain to the private sector. In 1993, the NSFC changed its regulations to enable a researcher to use 20 percent of his or her grant money to pay bonuses and stipends. Since 1992, several awards were established to support and acknowledge scientists in the hope to retain the most committed of the scientists. (See the following Table for the types of awards.)

AWARDS FOR YOUNG SCIENTISTS

Award/Grant	Sponsor	Amount (Y)	Age	No. Issued
Young Scientist	NSFC	81,300	35	600/year
Distinguished Scholar	State Council	600,000	45	50-80/year
100 Outstanding Project Leaders	CAS	2,000,000	40	100 over 5 years
Transcentury	SEdC	2,000,000		Not available.

Source: Science, November 1995, p. 1143.

The second development is the Internet, which is connecting Chinese scientists into the global network. In April 1994, China got its first direct Internet link. Within two years, users grew from 1,000 to 10,000. The Institute of High Energy Physics in Beijing set up its own local-area network in 1988 with dial-up links overseas, and enabled file transfers and Web browsing. It was soon followed by others. CAS's CAnet links its research institutes with the US National Science Foundation's NSFnet; the Ministry of Post and Telecommunications's ChinaNet is in the process of connecting with all provinces; the direct Internet link was connected in 1994. CERNET (China Education and Research Network) was launched in the same year with funding from SEdC. It linked all 100 key universities by the end of 1995, and the goal is to connect the rest of China's 1,000 regular universities and 200,000 primary and secondary schools by 2000. Whether this ambitious goal can be met depends on the resources of the educational institutions. While SEdC provides the seed money, institutions have to fund the purchase of computers, the campus network, and link to the regional CERNET node. To the extent that faculty members and researchers in universities with more resources will have access to the Internet's full power, China's scientific elite would be a step closer to fulfilling their mission of breaking into and staying on top of the global research front (*Science*, Nov. 1995, p. 1141).[1]

The Importance of Technical Progress in Economic Growth

The importance of technological progress to economic growth cannot be overstated. Research has found that economic growth of a nation can be attributed to four factors: growth in

---

[1] In the ongoing (1991-97) Key Studies Development Project (Cr. 2210-CHA), the World Bank is supporting: (a) research and graduate training in 133 key laboratories and special laboratories affiliated with universities and with the Chinese Academy of Sciences; (b) a pilot program to assist seven of the project laboratories to improve management efficiency and the quality of research and training of graduate science students; and (c) development of a demonstration computer network that would link Qinghua and Beijing universities and institutes of CAS in the Zhongguancun area of Beijing, and establishment of an enhanced computing facility.

capital, growth in labor, growth in human capital, and technical progress (including increases in efficiency). In spite of the rapid economic growth of East Asia, "Asian growth, like that of the Soviet Union in its high-growth era, seems to be driven by extraordinary growth in inputs like labor and capital, rather than by gains in efficiency." (Krugman, 1994: 70). A study by Kim and Lau (1995) which compared the sources of economic growth of four East Asian Newly Industrialized Countries (NICs: Hong Kong, Singapore, South Korea, and Taiwan) with those of five advanced industrial countries (G-5: France, West Germany, Japan, United Kingdom, and the United States) confirmed that technical progress remains the most important source of economic growth for the G-5 countries (except for Japan), followed by capital (except for the United States). By contrast, the most important source of economic growth of the NICs is capital accumulation, accounting for more than 60 percent of their economic growth, followed by labor, with human capital in third place. Human capital accounts for approximately 5 percent of the economic growth of the G-5 countries, and less than 15 percent of economic growth of East Asian NICs. Even allowing for growth of human capital, the gap in the level of productive efficiency between the G-5 countries and the East Asian NICs continues to widen over time.

These empirical findings have important policy implications for the NICs. "As their physical capital stocks continue to grow, their physical capital elasticities will continue to decline, and increase in the physical capital input alone will soon not be sufficient for the NICs to maintain their current rate of economic growth. It will be necessary for the NICs to devote greater resources to investment in human capital and in research and development. Otherwise it is unlikely that they will be able to catch up with the industrialized countries in terms of productive efficiency." (Kim and Lau, 1995: 20).

Kim and Lau extended their study to China and came to the same conclusion that the extraordinary growth of the Chinese economy has been driven by the accumulation of capital rather by technical progress. The above-mentioned (para. 7) policy implications thus apply to China as well. Given the gap in education levels between the four East Asia NICs and China, if the NICs have to devote greater resources to investment in human capital and research and development in order to catch up with the industrialized countries in terms of productive efficiency, it is all the more critical for China to do the same in order to maintain its current rate of economic growth. This unique role of sustaining China's development in the future will be played by higher education and the research and development community.

Overseas Training and International Cooperation

How can China improve its science and technology capacity? Overseas training and international cooperation can help China to break into the frontier of scientific knowledge, thereby opening the way to new research possibilities, and to promote cost-sharing of expensive facilities. All of these can help China to improve its industrial competitiveness. These potentials have long been recognized and valued by China. This is evidenced by the increasing number of faculty members and students who attended advanced study programs abroad, from 4,703 in 1987 to 19,000 in 1994 (State Statistical Bureau, 1995).

The benefits of cross-country exchanges are already reflected in the tremendous increase in published articles in international journals (by 106 percent between 1981-87 and 1988-93), and in international coauthorship (from 23 to 26 percent of all articles). The number of US patents granted to Chinese inventors has also increased from zero in most fields in the period 1980-83 to a handful in the period 1984-93. Although the number of patents granted to Chinese inventors is still very small in comparison to those of other countries, China has exhibited the same pattern as the Republic of Korea and Taiwan (China) in the exponential growth of the patents. This trend once again illustrates that overseas training provides unprecedented opportunities not only to acquire new knowledge, but also to become familiarized with the research and development infrastructure of industrialized countries and to make an imprint on it. Interestingly, the post-Cold War science and technology establishment in the US is also encouraged by the US National Science Board to seek international cooperation "to take advantage of valuable world resources, both material and human, in order to investigate global research questions and to share costs" (National Science Foundation, 1996).

INTERNATIONALLY COAUTHORED ARTICLES, 1981-87 AND 1988-93

	1981-87		1988-93		% Change between 1981-87 & 1988-93
	No. of Articles	% internationally-coauthored	No. of Articles	% internationally-coauthored	
China	14,734	24%	30,437	27%	107%
India	73,982	7%	52,336	11%	-29%
Asian NIEs	10,109	25%	29,846	23%	195%
Japan	199,707	7%	219,280	11%	10%
Britain	237,442	15%	210,685	22%	-11%
USA	987,214	9%	908,125	14%	-8%
World	2,266,532	7%	2,827,380	10%	25%

Source: United States National Science Board, 1996, p. 221.

US PATENTS GRANTED TO FOREIGN INVENTORS, 1980-83 AND 1984-93

	China		Taiwan (China)		Republic of Korea		Japan		USA	
	1980-83	1984-93	1980-83	1984-93	1980-83	1984-93	1980-83	1984-93	1980-83	1984-93
Computers	0.0	6.3	4.2	92.6	1.0	143.7	1,510.8	12,713.6	3,500.0	15,593.5
Industrial Machines	0.0	21.9	20.0	311.9	1.2	128.5	1,509.0	7,722.6	7,141.6	21,180.1
Radio & Television	0.0	2.2	4.0	19.1	0.0	159.2	814.5	4,298.0	1,260.2	3,965.6
Electrical & Commun. Equip.	0.5	24.5	26.7	646.8	4.5	776.2	4,081.4	32,047.0	14,052.2	69,926.0
Motor Vehicles & Equipment	0.8	10.4	7.0	107.4	1.3	34.8	991.4	5,916.5	2,496.0	7,453.2
Aircraft & Parts	0.0	5.0	2.9	35.0	0.3	13.0	537.1	2,714.5	1,317.4	4,217.0

Source: United States National Science Board, 1996, pp. 281-286.

ANNEX 5: NUMBER OF INSTITUTIONS, ENROLLMENT, AND STUDENTS-TO-TEACHER RATIOS IN REGULAR HIGHER EDUCATIONAL INSTITUTIONS, 1994

	Institutions		Undergraduate Students ('000 Students)			Undergraduate Students (Percentage)			Student Teacher Ratio	Student Total Staff Ratio
	(Number)	(Percentage)	Enrollment	Entrants	Graduates	Enrollment	Entrants	Graduates		
Comprehensive Universities	70	6	380	116	83	14	13	13	6.9	2.6
Natural Sci. & Tech. Colleges	297	28	1,017	315	209	36	35	33	7.2	2.5
Agriculture Colleges	59	5	151	50	33	5	6	5	6.4	2.3
Forestry Colleges	11	1	23	8	6	1	1	1	5.8	2.2
Medicine & Pharmacy Colleges	132	12	242	65	46	9	7	7	5.4	2.1
Teacher Training Colleges	241	22	587	210	170	21	23	27	8.1	3.6
Language & Literature Colleges	15	1	20	7	4	1	1	1	4.2	1.8
Finance & Economics Colleges	83	8	180	59	42	6	7	7	9.0	3.7
Political Science & Law Colleges	27	3	39	13	8	1	1	1	7.8	2.6
Physical Culture Colleges	15	1	17	6	4	1	1	1	5.7	2.4
Art Colleges	31	3	17	5	4	1	1	1	3.0	1.4
Nationalities Colleges	12	1	31	10	7	1	1	1	7.7	3.1
Short-cycle Vocational Colleges	87	8	94	36	22	3	4	3	8.8	4.2
Total	**1,080**	**100**	**2,798**	**900**	**637**	**100**	**100**	**100**	**7.1**	**2.7**
of which: Female			964	319	215	34	35	34	7.6	2.5

Note: The percentages are rounded.

Source: Educational Statistics Yearbook of China 1994, p. 18-19.

ANNEX 6: TEACHERS, STAFF, AND WORKERS IN REGULAR HIGHER EDUCATION INSTITUTIONS, 1994

('000 Persons)

	Teachers, Staff, and Workers in the University Proper						Personnel in Affiliated Organizations				Total Staff
	Teaching Staff	Support Staff	Administrative Personnel	Workers	Non-teaching Staff Subtotal	University Staff Subtotal	Research Organizations	University Factories	Subsidiary Units	Subtotal	
Comprehensive Universities	55	17	23	20	60	115	10	8	12	29	144
Natural Sci. & Tech. Colleges	142	50	62	55	167	309	26	36	36	97	406
Agriculture Colleges	24	6	10	11	26	50	2	10	5	17	67
Forestry Colleges	4	2	2	1	5	9	0	1	1	2	11
Medicine & Pharmacy Colleges	45	16	19	17	52	96	4	4	14	22	118
Teacher Training Colleges	73	18	30	26	74	146	3	6	8	17	163
Language & Literature Colleges	5	1	2	2	5	10	0	0	2	2	11
Finance & Economics Colleges	20	5	11	9	24	44	1	2	2	5	49
Political Science & Law Colleges	5	2	4	3	8	13	0	1	1	1	15
Physical Culture Colleges	3	1	1	1	3	6	0	0	1	1	7
Art Colleges	6	1	3	2	6	11	0	0	0	1	12
Nationalities Colleges	4	1	2	2	5	9	0	0	1	1	10
Short-cycle Vocational Colleges	11	3	5	3	10	21	0	1	0	2	22
Total	**396**	**122**	**173**	**150**	**445**	**841**	**48**	**69**	**81**	**197**	**1,040**
of which: Female	127	60	65	59	184	311	13	24	45	82	393

Source: *Educational Statistics Yearbook of China 1994*, p. 18-19.

ANNEX 7A: ADULT POST SECONDARY EDUCATION INSTITUTIONS, 1994

Type of Schools	Number of Institutions	Enrollment	Graduates	Full-time Teachers	Non-teaching Staff	Total Staff	Part-time Teachers	Student: Full-time Teacher	Student: Part-time Teacher	Student: Total Staff
		('000 persons)						Ratio		
Radio & TV Universities	46	536	100	20	25	44	16	28	35	12
Schools for Staff, Workers & Peasants	707	308	83	38	44	82	12	8	25	4
Colleges for Management Cadres	170	135	29	14	23	37	2	10	66	4
Pedagogical Colleges	245	231	62	23	23	46	1	10	167	5
Independent Correspondence Colleges	4	14	3	1	1	1	0	17	42	10
Corres. or Evening Courses of Reg. Universities		1,128	178							
Total	**1,172**	**2,352**	**455**	**95**	**115**	**210**	**31**	**25**	**75**	**11**

Source: *China Statistical Yearbook 1995.*

ANNEX 7B: ACADEMIC POSTSECONDARY QUALIFICATIONS OF FULL-TIME TEACHERS IN ADULT POSTSECONDARY EDUCATION INSTITUTIONS, 1994

	Doctorate Degrees	Master's Degrees	Bachelor's Degrees /a	Others /b	Total	Total (No. of Persons)
			---(Percent)---			
Professors	1.1	5.6	36.0	57.3	100.0	1,133
Associate Professors	0.2	2.8	30.5	66.5	100.0	19,071
Lecturers	0.0	5.4	51.2	43.4	100.0	44,676
Assistant	0.0	1.9	62.6	35.5	100.0	24,512
Instructors	0.1	3.3	55.3	41.3	100.0	5,557
Total	**0.1**	**3.9**	**50.0**	**46.0**	**100.0**	**94,949**
of which female teachers	0.0	3.1	56.0	40.9	100.0	35,167

/a   Bachelor's degrees include those who held it and those who have completed postgraduate studies without obtaining postgraduate degrees, but exclude those who have undergraduate courses without bachelor's degrees.

/b   The "Others" category includes those who had completed undergraduate courses without obtaining the bachelor's degree, and those who have completed or attended short-cycle courses.

Source: Educational Statistics Yearbook of China 1994, p. 100-101.

ANNEX 8: RESEARCH AND DEVELOPMENT PERSONNEL BY FIELD OF STUDY, 1994

Field of Study	Devoted 10% + Work Time on R&D			Devoted 90% of Work Time on R&D		
	Total R&D Personnel	Of Which Scientists & Engineers	Other Technical	Total R&D Personnel	Of Which Scientists & Engineers	Other Technical
	----Number of Persons (Thousands)----					
Natural Science	26.8	25.6	1.3	4.4	4.2	0.2
Engineering	67.6	63.2	4.4	15.3	14.1	1.2
Medicine	33.6	30.9	2.7	3.5	3.2	0.3
Agriculture	11.0	10.2	0.8	5.7	5.3	0.4
Humanities & Social Sciences	69.9	59.5	1.5	NA	NA	NA
Total R&D Personnel	**209.1**	**189.4**	**10.7**	**28.9**	**26.8**	**2.1**
Total Teaching Staff	**396.0**			**396.0**		
	----Percentage----					
Natural Science	12.8	13.5	11.8	15.3	15.7	10.2
Engineering	32.3	33.4	41.4	52.8	52.6	56.5
Medicine	16.1	16.3	25.6	12.1	11.9	14.8
Agriculture	5.3	5.4	7.4	19.8	19.8	18.5
Humanities & Social Sciences	33.5	31.4	13.8	0.0	0.0	0.0
Total	**100.0**	**100.0**	**100.0**	**100.0**	**100.0**	**100.0**
% of Teaching Staff involved in R&D	52.8			7.3		

Source: China Statistical Yearbook 1995, p. 627.

ANNEX 9: AN INTERNATIONAL BIBLIOMETRIC-BASED ASSESSMENT OF RESEARCH ACTIVITY IN CHINESE HIGHER EDUCATION AND RESEARCH INSTITUTIONS

Part A: Ranking of Higher Education Institutions
Based on 1988-90 Research Front Publication Counts

No. of Publications	Institutions
3130	Chinese Academy of Science (Beijing)
788	CCAST (Beijing)
484	Beijing University (Beijing)
420	University of Science and Technology of China (Hefei)
395	Fudan University (Shanghai)
379	Nanjing University (Nanjing, Jiangsu)
247	Qinghua University (Beijing)
177	Lanzhou University (Lanzhou, Gansu)
173	Chinese Academy of Medical Science
171	Nankai University (Tianjin)

Part B: 1988-89 Leading Academic Centers in Three Scientific Fields

Physics

100	University of Science and Technology of China (Hefei)
96	Fudan University (Shanghai)
82	Beijing University (Beijing)
71	Nanjing University (Jiangsu)
56	Shanghai Jiaotong University (Shanghai)
55	Northwest University (Xian, Shaanxi)

Solid State Physics and Materials Science

231	Beijing University
212	Fudan University (Shanghai)
211	University of Science and Technology of China (Hefei)
143	Qinghua University (Beijing)
79	Shanghai Jiaotong University (Shanghai)
71	Shandong University (Jinan)
51	University of Science and Technology in Beijing

Mathematics and Computer Science

60	Beijing University (Beijing)
44	Fudan University (Shanghai)
32	Qinghua University (Beijing)
31	Nankai University (Tianjin)
31	Zhejiang University (Hangzhou)
27	East China Normal University (Shanghai)
26	Xian Jiaotong University (Xian)
24	Shanghai Jiaotong University (Shanghai)
23	Wuhan University (Hubei)

Source: Coward and Fresne, *A Bibliometric-Based Assessment of Research Activity in the People's Republic of China,* November 1922, p. 19.

ANNEX 10: UTILIZATION OF BUILDINGS IN REGULAR HIGHER EDUCATION INSTITUTIONS, 1994

	Total		Newly Added		Under Construction	
	Sq. Meters (million)	% of Total	Sq. Meters (million)	% of Total	Sq. Meters (million)	% of Total
China (1994)						
Instructional use	40.3	33	1.5	28	2.4	38
Administrative use	6.4	5	0.1	2	0.2	3
Residential use	76.8	62	3.7	70	3.8	59
Staff residences	38.4	31	1.9	35	2.6	40
Students' dormitories	18.7	15	1.1	20	0.5	8
Others	19.7	16	0.7	13	0.7	11
Total Floor Space	**123.5**	**100**	**5.3**	**100**	**6.4**	**100**
Instructional floor space per student (m^2)	14					
Students' dorm. floor space per student (m^2)	7					
Other Floor Space per Student (m^2)	23					
Total Floor Space per Student (m^2)	**44**					
Comparative Data						
Republic of Korea (1985) (m^2)	8					
Republic of Korea (1991) (m^2)	10					

Source: Educational Statistics Yearbook of China 1994, p. 30-31; Education Indicators in Korea, 1991, p. 40.

ANNEX 11: INSTITUTIONS OF HIGHER EDUCATION BY PROVINCE AND MUNICIPALITY, 1994

Provinces and Municipalities	Total Institutions	Comprehensive Universities	Science & Engineering	Agriculture & Forestry	Medicine	Teacher Training	Economics & Finance	Politics & Law	Others
National	1,080	70	297	70	132	241	83	27	160
North									
Beijing	67	3	22	3	6	3	7	5	18
Tianjin	22	1	6	1	3	3	3	0	5
Hebei	52	1	16	4	7	13	4	0	7
Shanxi	26	4	5	1	4	7	3	1	1
Inner Mongolia	19	1	2	3	3	6	1	1	2
Northeast									
Liaoning	61	4	21	3	6	13	4	2	8
Jilin	43	3	14	4	5	8	4	1	4
Heilongjiang	43	2	14	3	6	9	4	0	5
East									
Shanghai	46	2	20	2	5	4	6	2	5
Jiangsu	67	5	24	3	8	9	4	1	13
Zhejiang	37	2	7	3	4	10	3	1	7
Anhui	35	1	8	1	4	13	4	0	4
Fujian	33	2	5	3	2	9	2	1	9
Jiangxi	31	3	8	2	6	8	2	1	1
Shandong	49	3	14	2	8	14	3	1	4
Interior and South									
Henan	50	2	14	4	5	13	3	1	8
Hubei	60	2	18	2	9	9	4	2	14
Hunan	47	3	17	2	5	12	4	1	3
Guangdong	46	9	9	5	5	6	3	1	8
Guangxi	27	1	4	1	5	8	2	0	6
Hainan	5	2	0	1	1	1	0	0	0
Southwest									
Sichuan	63	4	20	5	5	16	3	1	9
Guizhou	22	1	1	1	4	10	2	0	3
Yunnan	26	1	3	2	3	11	1	2	3
Tibet	4	1	0	1	1	0	0	0	1
Northwest									
Shaanxi	47	3	18	2	4	9	4	1	6
Gansu	17	1	3	1	2	6	1	1	2
Qinghai	7	1	0	1	1	3	0	0	1
Ningxia	7	1	1	1	1	2	0	0	1
Xinjiang	21	1	3	3	4	6	2	0	2

Note: Others include institutions of linguistics and languages, physical culture, art, and others.

Source: China Statistical Yearbook 1995. Table 18.26, pg. 599.

ANNEX 12: PROVINCIAL AND MUNICIPAL POPULATION, GDP, GDP PER CAPITA, AND HIGHER EDUCATION TEACHERS AND STAFF, 1994

Provinces and Municipalities	Population (million persons)	Provincial & Municipal GDP (billion Yuan)	Provincial & Municipal GDP Per Capita	Total Staff ('000 persons)	Full-time Teachers ('000 persons)	Teacher in 10,000 Population
National	1,199	45,006	3,754	1,040	396	3.1
North						
Beijing	11	1,084	9,593	105	36	4.8
Tianjin	9	725	7,714	28	10	1.4
Hebei	64	2,148	3,366	38	15	3.5
Shanxi	31	854	2,799	23	9	2.2
Inner Mongolia	23	682	3,017	15	7	1.6
Northeast						
Liaoning	41	2,584	6,349	59	24	5.8
Jilin	26	969	3,770	40	15	3.7
Heilongjiang	37	1,619	4,410	43	16	3.9
East						
Shanghai	14	1,972	14,499	68	22	7.0
Jiangsu	70	4,057	5,780	71	27	6.7
Zhejiang	43	2,667	6,217	28	11	2.7
Anhui	60	1,489	2,497	27	12	2.9
Fujian	32	1,685	5,300	20	8	2.1
Jiangxi	40	1,032	2,567	27	9	2.1
Shandong	87	3,872	4,466	50	20	3.8
Interior and South						
Henan	90	2,199	2,435	39	16	3.0
Hubei	57	1,879	3,284	66	25	6.1
Hunan	64	1,694	2,664	39	15	3.8
Guangdong	67	4,241	6,339	41	16	3.7
Guangxi	45	1,242	2,766	17	7	1.9
Hainan	7	331	4,662	3	1	0.3
Southwest						
Sichuan	112	2,778	2,477	68	25	4.6
Guizhou	35	521	1,506	13	6	1.3
Yunnan	39	974	2,472	17	7	1.8
Tibet	2	46	1,908	2	1	3.7
Northwest						
Shaanxi	35	847	2433	52	20	5.0
Gansu	24	452	1898	16	6	1.5
Qinghai	5	138	2940	3	1	0.3
Ningxia	5	134	2680	4	2	0.4
Xinjiang	16	674	4128	19	8	1.8

Note: Others include institutions of linguistics and languages, physical culture, art, and others.

Source: China Statistical Yearbook 1994, Table 3.3, p. 60 for population by region in 1993; *China Statistical Yearbook 1995* Table 2.11, p. 33 for GDP by region, Table 18.26, p. 599 for institutions of higher education by region, and Table 18.27 p. 601 for staff by region.,

ANNEX 13A: PUBLIC FINANCE IN CHINA, 1978-94

Year	Implicit Price Deflator (1994=100)	Gross Domestic Product	Total Govt. Revenue	Total Govt. Expenditure	Total Govt. Expenditure on Education	Total Govt. Expenditure on Higher Education	Total Own-Generated Income
In Current Prices, Billion Yuan							
1978		358.8	123.3	122.5	7.6	1.5	0.1
1979		399.8	126.3	146.9	8.8	2.3	0.1
1980		447.0	131.6	146.2	11.3	2.8	0.1
1981		477.5	138.6	144.4	12.3	3.2	N.A.
1982		518.2	141.2	148.3	13.7	3.4	0.1
1983		578.7	159.4	169.0	15.3	4.3	0.1
1984		692.8	183.5	193.9	17.9	5.2	0.1
1985		852.7	228.3	232.4	22.4	6.1	0.6
1986		968.8	244.6	263.3	26.5	7.2	N.A.
1987		1,130.7	256.9	280.0	27.7	7.5	0.7
1988		1,407.4	280.3	313.7	32.4	8.2	0.9
1989		1,599.8	326.4	363.8	49.0	8.8	1.0
1990		1,856.4	355.0	391.7	53.3	8.9	1.3
1991		2,166.5	367.2	415.2	58.1	9.9	1.5
1992		2,665.6	392.8	453.9	68.2	11.8	2.2
1993		3,413.4	481.0	546.0	75.4	13.9	2.5
1994		4,500.6	521.8	579.3	97.9	18.6	4.2
In Constant 1994 Prices, Billion Yuan							
1978	35.7	1,006.3	345.8	343.6	21.4	4.2	0.2
1979	36.9	1,082.3	341.9	397.7	23.8	6.3	0.2
1980	38.2	1,169.3	344.3	382.4	29.6	7.4	0.2
1981	39.1	1,221.0	354.4	369.2	31.3	8.2	0.0
1982	39.1	1,325.1	361.1	379.2	34.9	8.8	0.2
1983	39.6	1,459.6	402.0	426.2	38.6	10.8	0.3
1984	41.5	1,670.4	442.4	467.5	43.2	12.6	0.3
1985	45.2	1,886.7	505.1	514.2	49.7	13.5	1.2
1986	47.3	2,048.5	517.2	556.7	56.0	15.1	0.0
1987	49.7	2,273.7	516.6	563.0	55.7	15.2	1.4
1988	55.6	2,530.6	504.0	564.0	58.2	14.7	1.7
1989	60.6	2,641.9	539.0	600.8	80.9	14.4	1.6
1990	67.7	2,743.8	524.7	578.9	78.8	13.2	1.9
1991	73.1	2,962.2	502.1	567.7	79.4	13.5	2.0
1992	79.2	3,367.3	496.2	573.4	86.1	14.9	2.7
1993	89.4	3,816.2	537.8	610.4	84.3	15.5	2.8
1994	100.0	4,500.6	521.8	579.3	97.9	18.6	4.2

Note: Government expenditure includes all levels of government allocation.

Sources: GDP in current prices, the implicit price deflator, and the total consolidated government revenue and expenditure from 1978 to 1993 were taken from *China: Macroeconomic Stability in a Decentralized Economy* (World Bank, August 1995), Statistical Annex Tables 1.1, 1.3 and 7.6; those figures for 1994 were taken from *China Statistical Yearbook, 1995* (State Statistical Bureau, 1995) pp. 32 and 215. The price deflator was rebased, using 1994 prices as constant. Educational expenditure data were drawn from SEdC and State Statistical Bureau sources.

ANNEX 13B: INDICATORS OF LEVELS OF PUBLIC EXPENDITURE ON EDUCATION, 1976-94

Year	Govt. Revenue as % of GDP	Govt. Expend. as % of GDP	Govt. Expend. as % of Revenue	Govt. Educ. Expend. as % of GDP	Govt. Educ. Expend. as % of Total Govt. Expend.	Govt. Expend. on Higher Educ. as % of Total Govt. Expend.	Govt. Expend. on Higher Educ. as % of Total Govt. Educ. Expend.
1978	34.4	34.1	99.4	2.1	6.2	1.2	19.7
1979	31.6	36.7	116.3	2.2	6.0	1.6	26.3
1980	29.4	32.7	111.1	2.5	7.7	1.9	24.8
1981	29.0	30.2	104.2	2.6	8.5	2.2	26.2
1982	27.2	28.6	105.0	2.6	9.2	2.3	25.2
1983	27.5	29.2	106.0	2.6	9.0	2.5	28.1
1984	26.5	28.0	105.7	2.6	9.2	2.7	29.2
1985	26.8	27.3	101.8	2.6	9.7	2.6	27.1
1986	25.2	27.2	107.6	2.7	10.1	2.7	27.0
1987	22.7	24.8	109.0	2.4	9.9	2.7	27.2
1988	19.9	22.3	111.9	2.3	10.3	2.6	25.2
1989	20.4	22.7	111.5	3.1	13.5	2.4	17.9
1990	19.1	21.1	110.3	2.9	13.6	2.3	16.8
1991	16.9	19.2	113.1	2.7	14.0	2.4	17.1
1992	14.7	17.0	115.6	2.6	15.0	2.6	17.3
1993	14.1	16.0	113.5	2.2	13.8	2.5	18.4
1994	11.6	12.9	111.0	2.2	16.9	3.2	19.0

Source: Constructed from Annex 13A.

ANNEX 14: COMPOSITION OF REVENUE AND EXPENDITURE OF 14 SELECTED INSTITUTIONS OF HIGHER EDUCATION, 1993

(Percentage)

	Beijing		Anhui Province		Sichuan Province							Guangdong Province		
	1	2	3	4	5	6	7	8	9	10	11	12	13	14
	Municipal	Ministry	Provincial	Provincial	Provincial	SEdC	SEdC	SEdC	Ministry	Nongovt.	Provincial	Municipal &Prov.	Municipal & Prov.	Municipal & Prov.
Revenue														
Government Allocation:	73.0	80.9	62.6	49.4	79.7	62.3	43.4	46.2	62.3	33.7	83.7	73.0	73.3	80.0
Recurrent	63.8	56.7	60.6	39.7	55.1	50.1	29.0	36.0	44.7	27.2	20.6	61.3	41.4	21.7
Capital	9.2	24.0	1.9	9.7	24.7	12.3	14.3	10.3	17.6	6.5	31.8	11.7	31.9	58.3
University Generated Revenue:	27.0	19.1	28.9	50.6	20.3	37.8	56.6	53.8	37.7	66.3	16.3	27.0	26.7	20.0
1. University-funded Activities	24.5	6.0	9.1	25.6	13.5	-	-	9.8	16.9	17.8	-	2.5	12.2	8.8
University Enterprises	10.5	0.0	2.8	0.0	1.9	-	-	2.3	4.9	9.5	-	0.0	0.0	0.1
Commissioned Training	2.2	6.8	3.2	11.2	8.5	-	-	0.9	4.0	1.1	-	0.0	8.6	4.3
Educational Services	0.0	0.1	0.0	13.2	0.0	-	-	0.5	0.0	1.5	-	0.0	0.0	0.5
Research & Consultancy	0.0	0.0	0.7	0.0	0.0	-	-	1.2	0.0	1.1	-	0.0	0.0	0.2
Logistical Services	0.0	1.4		1.3	0.1	-	-	0.7	0.0	1.3	-	0.0	0.0	0.0
Other Income	11.8	0.1	2.4	0.0	3.0	-	-	4.4	7.1	3.4	-	0.0	3.6	3.8
2. Other sources (includ.Donation)	0.0	6.6	19.8	21.1	0.0	17.4	8.4	41.2	16.9	45.1	1.5	0.0	12.4	8.7
3. Student Tuition Fees	2.5	2.3	8.6	3.9	6.8	0.6	2.8	2.7	3.9	3.3	2.1	2.5	2.1	2.5
Total (Percentage)	100.0	100.0	100.0	100.0	100.0	100.0	100.0	100.0	100.0	100.0	100.0	100.0	100.0	100.0
Total Revenue (Mil. Yuan)	40.0	24.5	20.9	34.7	18.5	45.6	208.2	88.5	39.8	136.8	67.1	16.3	28.6	29.7
Expenditure														
Personnel	24.3	28.0	43.3	32.4	41.8	33.8	17.4	24.4	31.0	17.8	12.7	49.8	20.9	18.3
Student Financial Aid	3.3	4.9	5.7	2.8	4.9	9.0	1.8	2.0	2.9	1.6	0.9	10.3	2.5	1.9
Administrative	23.0	5.3	4.0	4.3	1.3	12.2	4.1	7.9	5.2	4.2	3.4	11.0	2.7	4.0
Instructional	8.4	13.8	11.4	13.7	6.1	11.3	6.8	7.5	12.3	6.3	4.5	6.9	5.9	7.7
Equipment	2.4	4.0	4.8	11.3	18.2	7.6	3.7	4.5	3.3	5.5	26.2	9.3	3.7	11.5
Repair and Maintenance	2.3	1.5	4.0	2.8	6.1	4.4	3.4	3.8	4.4	4.1	1.5	2.7	11.3	2.1
Logistical Services	12.0	7.9	3.8	6.7	7.3	3.1	5.1	0.0	0.0	5.6	2.1	0.0	4.3	0.0
Others	0.0	6.2	5.8	1.2	3.4	0.0	1.0	1.2	3.5	0.8	4.8	0.4	7.4	1.3
Capital Expenditure	18.4	18.9	11.0	16.4	6.5	14.4	15.4	17.0	31.2	37.0	38.0	8.1	41.0	52.9
Research (nonregular)	8.5	7.5	6.3	8.5	5.0	4.4	40.3	31.7	6.4	17.0	5.8	1.5	0.4	0.4
Total (Percentage)	100.0	100.0	100.0	100.0	100.0	100.0	100.0	100.0	100.0	100.0	100.0	100.0	100.0	100.0
Total Expenditure (Mil. Yuan)	38.4	31.4	20.2	17.7	16.6	39.0	194.2	73.4	36.5	120.5	63.6	16.6	29.2	32.7

Note: The percentages were rounded.

Source: Based on institutional data collected during the mission.

ANNEX 15: EXPENDITURES IN SELECTED INSTITUTIONS, 1980 AND 1993

(Million Yuan)

	Beijing		Anhui Province		Sichuan Province						Guangdong Province			
	Muni-pal	Min-istry	Provin-cial	Provin-cial	Provin-cial	SEdC	SEdC	SEdC	Min-istry	Non-Govt.	Provin-cial	Mun. & Prov.	Mun. & Prov.	Mun. & Prov.
Expenditure in 1980 (current prices)														
Personnel	2.13	1.40	1.54	1.00	0.72	1.68	5.24	2.52	2.30	4.55	1.61	0.70	0.72	0.12
Student Financial Aid	0.19	0.35	0.44	0.28	0.23	0.75	0.92	0.71	0.45	1.45	0.21	0.23	0.21	0.11
Administrative	1.07	0.19	0.30	0.14	0.05	0.51	1.24	0.47	0.35	1.27	0.38	0.15	0.10	0.04
Instructional	1.16	0.43	0.37	0.36	0.15	0.49	1.81	1.39	0.69	1.30	0.43	0.16	0.22	0.02
Equipment	0.00	0.66	0.92	0.62	0.20	1.23	3.40	1.45	0.89	3.87	1.49	0.58	0.25	0.12
Repair and Maintenance	0.33	0.24	0.28	0.24	0.04	0.37	0.99	0.86	0.62	0.76	0.28	0.20	0.27	0.02
Logistical Services	0.17	0.28	0.43	0.15	0.12	0.16	0.00	0.00	0.00	0.43	0.00	0.00	0.15	0.02
Others	0.15	0.66	0.11	0.07	0.18	0.00	0.71	0.90	0.06	0.09	0.00	0.00	0.27	0.00
Capital Expenditure	1.77	3.10	1.20	1.51	1.24	2.47	6.16	4.62	2.29	5.82	1.90	0.10	0.42	0.32
Research (nonregular)	0.97	0.20	0.09	0.05	0.01	0.22	5.52	2.43	0.30	3.58	0.08	0.00	0.06	0.76
Total	7.94	7.51	5.69	4.42	2.93	7.87	25.98	15.35	7.95	23.12	6.38	2.12	2.67	1.51
Expenditure in 1993 (Current Prices)														
Personnel	9.10	8.80	8.75	5.74	4.20	13.16	33.73	17.92	11.29	21.49	8.07	8.28	6.09	5.97
Student Financial Aid	1.22	1.53	1.15	0.50	0.49	3.49	3.66	1.49	1.03	1.95	0.60	1.72	0.72	0.63
Administrative	8.65	1.65	0.80	0.76	0.13	4.76	7.90	5.76	1.88	5.08	0.22	1.83	0.78	1.31
Instructional	7.15	4.95	2.30	2.41	0.62	4.40	13.23	5.52	4.48	7.58	2.88	1.14	1.71	2.52
Equipment	0.00	1.27	0.97	2.00	1.83	2.96	7.21	3.30	1.19	6.68	16.69	1.55	1.09	3.75
Repair and Maintenance	0.79	0.48	0.81	0.50	1.62	1.70	6.56	2.79	1.62	4.89	0.97	0.45	3.29	0.69
Logistical Services	0.86	2.48	0.76	1.18	0.73	1.21	0.00	0.00	0.00	6.73	1.35	0.00	1.25	0.00
Others	0.54	1.95	1.17	0.21	0.34	0.00	13.84	0.86	1.27	0.94	3.08	0.07	2.16	0.41
Capital Expenditure	6.91	5.94	2.24	2.90	6.55	5.60	29.85	12.51	11.38	44.62	24.15	1.35	11.96	17.30
Research (nonregular)	3.18	2.34	1.26	1.50	0.10	1.70	78.25	23.29	2.23	20.53	3.66	0.25	0.13	0.12
Total	38.40	31.39	20.20	17.70	16.61	38.98	194.24	73.44	36.38	120.49	61.67	16.64	29.16	32.70
Expenditure in 1980 (In Constant 1990 Prices)														
Personnel	3.77	2.48	2.73	1.77	1.28	2.97	9.27	4.46	4.06	8.05	2.85	1.24	1.27	0.21
Student Financial Aid	0.34	0.62	0.77	0.50	0.40	1.32	1.63	1.26	0.80	2.57	0.37	0.41	0.38	0.19
Administrative	1.89	0.34	0.53	0.25	0.08	0.91	2.19	0.83	0.62	2.25	0.67	0.27	0.17	0.07
Instructional	2.05	0.76	0.66	0.64	0.26	0.86	3.20	2.46	1.23	2.30	0.76	0.29	0.39	0.04
Equipment	0.00	1.17	1.62	1.10	0.35	2.18	6.01	2.57	1.58	6.85	2.64	1.03	0.45	0.21
Repair and Maintenance	0.58	0.42	0.50	0.42	0.08	0.65	1.75	1.52	1.10	1.35	0.50	0.35	0.48	0.04
Logistical Services	0.30	0.50	0.77	0.27	0.21	0.29	0.00	0.00	0.00	0.76	0.00	0.00	0.26	0.00
Others	0.27	1.17	0.19	0.12	0.31	0.00	1.25	1.59	0.10	0.16	0.00	0.00	0.48	0.57
Capital Expenditure	3.13	5.49	2.13	2.67	2.19	4.37	10.90	8.18	4.05	10.30	3.36	0.17	0.73	1.35
Research (nonregular)	1.72	0.35	0.16	0.08	0.02	0.39	9.77	4.29	0.53	6.34	0.14	0.00	0.11	0.00
Total	14.05	13.29	10.06	7.82	5.19	13.93	45.98	27.17	14.07	40.92	11.29	3.75	4.72	2.67
Expenditure in 1993 (In Constant 1990 Prices)														
Personnel	7.93	7.67	7.62	5.00	3.66	11.46	29.40	15.62	9.84	18.73	7.03	7.22	5.30	5.20
Student Financial Aid	1.06	1.33	1.00	0.44	0.42	3.04	3.19	1.30	0.90	1.70	0.52	1.49	0.62	0.55
Administrative	7.54	1.44	0.70	0.66	0.12	4.15	6.88	5.02	1.64	4.43	0.19	1.60	0.68	1.14
Instructional	6.23	4.31	2.00	2.10	0.54	3.84	11.53	4.81	3.91	6.61	2.51	1.00	1.49	2.20
Equipment	0.00	1.11	0.84	1.74	1.59	2.58	6.28	2.88	1.04	5.82	14.54	1.35	0.95	3.27
Repair and Maintenance	0.69	0.42	0.71	0.44	1.42	1.48	5.72	2.43	1.41	4.26	0.85	0.39	2.86	0.60
Logistical Services	0.75	2.16	0.66	1.03	0.64	1.06	0.00	0.00	0.00	5.86	1.18	0.00	1.09	0.00
Others	0.47	1.70	1.02	0.18	0.30	0.00	12.06	0.75	1.11	0.82	2.68	0.06	1.88	0.36
Capital Expenditure	6.02	5.18	1.95	2.53	5.71	4.88	26.01	10.90	9.92	38.88	21.05	1.17	10.42	15.08
Research (nonregular)	2.77	2.04	1.10	1.31	0.08	1.48	68.20	20.30	1.94	17.89	3.19	0.22	0.11	0.10
Total	33.46	27.36	17.60	15.43	14.48	33.97	169.27	64.00	31.70	105.00	53.74	14.50	25.41	28.50

Source: Based on institutional data collected during field visits.

ANNEX 16: AVERAGE ANNUAL GROWTH RATES OF DIFFERENT COMPONENTS IN EXPENDITURE IN SELECTED INSTITUTIONS, 1980-93

	Beijing		Anhui Province		Sichuan Province						Guangdong Province				Average of All Institutions
	Muni-cipal	Min-istry	Provin-cial	Provin-cial	Provin-cial	SEdC	SEdC	SEdC	Min-Istry	Non-Govt.	Provin-cial	Mun. & Prov.	Mun. & Prov.	Mun. & Prov.	
Personnel	5.90	9.10	8.20	8.30	8.40	11.00	9.30	10.00	7.00	6.70	11.30	14.50	11.60	28.00	10.66
Student Financial Aid	9.30	6.10	2.00	0.01	0.40	6.70	5.30	0.20	0.90	0.00	4.30	10.50	4.00	8.30	4.14
Administrative	11.20	11.20	2.00	7.80	2.70	12.40	9.20	19.00	7.80	5.30	0.00	15.00	11.00	23.80	9.89
Instructional	8.90	14.30	8.90	9.60	5.70	12.10	10.40	5.30	9.30	8.40	16.10	10.00	10.80	37.40	11.94
Equipment	0.00	0.01	0.05	3.60	8.90	10.60	0.00	0.00	0.00	17.00	23.00	0.00	11.60	23.40	7.01
Repair and Maintenance	1.30	0.01	2.70	0.02	25.20	6.50	9.50	3.70	1.90	9.30	4.20	1.00	14.80	24.30	7.46
Logistical Services	7.30	12.00	0.01	10.40	8.90	10.60	0.00	0.00	0.00	17.00	0.00	0.00	11.60	0.00	5.56
Others	4.50	2.90	13.80	3.10	0.01	0.00	19.10	0.00	20.50	13.40	0.00	0.00	5.50	0.00	5.92
Capital Expenditure	5.10	0.01	0.01	0.01	7.60	1.00	6.90	2.20	7.10	10.70	25.80	0.00	22.60	20.43	7.82
Research (nonregular)	3.70	14.40	15.80	23.40	10.90	10.90	16.10	12.70	10.40	8.30	47.60	0.00	0.20	0.00	12.46
Average Annual Growth Rate	8.00	5.70	4.40	5.40	8.20	7.10	10.50	6.80	6.40	7.50	21.50	10.90	13.80	19.90	9.72

Note: The percentages are rounded.

Source: Based on institutional data collected during field visits.

ANNEX 17: PER STUDENT SPENDING IN 14 SELECTED INSTITUTIONS IN 1993

	Enrollment (# of Students)	Government Allocation	Per Capita Government Allocation	University Generated Revenue	Per Capita University Generated Revenue	Total Per Capita Allocation
				(Yuan)		
Beijing Ministry	4,231	19,845,000	4,690	4,693,000	1,109	5,799
Anhui Provincial	5,412	13,050,000	2,411	7,813,000	1,444	3,855
Shanghai Municipal	1,297	6,010,000	4,634	6,090,741	4,696	9,330
Sichuan Ministry	4,175	17,130,000	4,103	17,530,000	4,199	8,302
Sichuan SEdC	-	40,896,000	-	47,576,000	-	-
Sichuan SEdC	6,785	28,468,000	4,196	17,205,000	2,536	6,732
Guangdong SEdC	19,284	90,286,000	4,682	117,887,000	6,113	10,795
Guangdong SEdC	7,380	20,973,558	2,842	-	-	-
Guangdong Ministry	2,815	24,821,000	8,817	15,026,000	5,338	14,155
Guangdong Municipal and Provincial	3,546	20,973,558	5,915	7,625,859	2,151	8,066
Guangdong Municipal and Provincial	3,512	11,904,000	3,390	4,400,000	1,253	4,643
Guangdong Provincial	4,963	56,130,000	11,310	10,960,000	2,208	13,518
Guangdong	2,590	23,750,000	9,170	5,950,000	2,297	11,467
Guangdong nongovernment	11,805	46,140,000	3,909	90,640,000	7,678	11,587

Source: Based on institutional data collected during field visits.

ANNEX 18: STUDENT FINANCIAL AID AND TUITION REVENUE, 1980-93

(Yuan)

	1980			1990			1991			1992			1993		
	Fin. Aid	Tuit. Rev.	Ratio	Fin. Aid	Tuit. Rev.	Ratio	Fin. Aid	Tuit. Rev.	Ratio	Fin. Aid	Tuit. Rev.	Ratio	Fin. Aid	Tuit. Rev.	Ratio
Beijing Ministry	348,000	-	-	974,000	106,000	9.19	1,234,000	313,000	3.94	1,194,000	108,000	11.6	1,534,000	563,000	2.72
Anhui Provincial	435,000	-	-	838,000	121,500	6.90	921,000	269,000	3.42	1,148,000	1,786,600	0.64	-	-	-
Sichuan Ministry	280,000	-	-	260,000	150,000	1.73	330,000	320,000	1.03	540,000	570,000	0.95	500,000	1,360,000	0.37
Sichuan SEdC	713,000	-	-	1,633,000	576,000	2.84	1,365,000	976,000	1.41	1,540,000	1,774,000	0.87	1,489,000	2,425,000	0.61
Sichuan Provincial	227,566	-	-	297,224	77,864	3.82	368,147	170,005	2.17	455,463	594,920	0.77	496,637	1,262,370	0.39
Sichuan SEdC	745,000	-	-	1,653,000	-	-	1,963,000	-	-	3,013,000	216,000	13.95	3,494,000	271,000	12.89
Sichuan SEdC	921,000	-	-	3,082,000	556,000	5.51	3,017,000	2,117,000	1.43	3,363,000	3,246,000	1.04	3,684,000	5,735,000	0.64
Guangdong Ministry	452,000	-	-	1,119,000	229,000	4.89	969,000	329,000	2.95	882,000	427,000	2.07	1,034,000	1,658,000	0.66
Guangdong Municipal and Provincial		-	-	585,291	183,996	3.18	589,940	322,717	1.83	584,881	410,176	1.43	715,911	597,555	1.20
Guangdong Municipal and Provincial	229,920	-	-	1,074,010	-	-	1,419,510	-	-	1,631,660	692,000	2.36	1,714,490	4,000,000	0.43
Guangdong Municipal and Provincial		-	-	550,000	860,000	0.64	590,000	890,000	0.66	590,000	1,300,000	0.45	600,000	1,410,000	0.43
Guangdong Municipal and Provincial	110,000	-	-	390,000	70,000	5.57	410,000	230,000	1.78	560,000	440,000	1.27	630,000	750,000	0.84
Guangdong Non-governmental	1,450,000	-	-	2,720,000	1,010,000	2.69	1,890,000	1,630,000	1.16	1,970,000	2,990,000	0.66	1,950,000	4,570,000	0.43

Source: Based on institutional data collected during field visits.

ANNEX 19: STUDENT FAMILY BACKGROUND, 1980-93

(Percentage)

	1980		1986		1989		1993	
	Male	Female	Male	Female	Male	Female	Male	Female
Guangdong Ministry Undergraduate Students:								
Intellectual managers in industries								
and Govt. cadres	47	56	34	42	43	48	40	50
Workers and peasants	44	17	59	43	51	43	53	39
Other	9	28	7	15	6	8	8	11
Total	**100**	**100**	**100**	**100**	**100**	**100**	**100**	**100**
Number of Students	1,291	675	1,744	841	1,649	992	1,385	866
Guangdong Ministry Graduate Students:								
Intellectual	24	11	22	15	19	27	8	14
Managers in industries	-	-	-	-	-	-	-	-
Govt. cadres	26	26	49	51	37	52	36	61
Workers	18	2	12	5	17	8	11	11
Peasants	22	0	13	2	26	3	44	14
Other	10	60	5	27	1	11	1	0
Total	**100**	**100**	**100**	**100**	**100**	**100**	**100**	**100**
Number of Students	82	53	190	123	446	113	423	131
Guangdong Municipal & Provincial:								
Intellectual	12	8	8	8	8	7	7	7
Managers in industries	-	-	-	-	-	-	-	-
Govt. cadres	15	15	15	15	15	15	16	18
Workers	30	30	30	30	30	30	30	30
Peasants	40	40	40	40	40	40	40	40
Other	3	8	7	7	7	7	7	5
Total	**100**	**100**	**100**	**100**	**100**	**100**	**100**	**100**
Number of Students	730	224	995	459	2,472	470	2,324	1,222
Guangdong Municipal & Provincial:								
Intellectual	26	16	17	16	18	17	18	18
Managers in industries	4	3	3	4	3	4	3	4
Govt. cadres	13	13	12	12	13	13	12	13
Workers	22	21	24	27	27	24	25	25
Peasants	28	28	29	29	30	26	32	30
Other	8	18	14	13	8	16	10	9
Total	**100**	**100**	**100**	**100**	**100**	**100**	**100**	**100**
Number of Students	450	662	1,429	1,637	1,417	1,878	1,577	1,935
Guangdong Municipal & Provincial:								
Intellectual	17	27	13	18	15	23	22	23
Managers in industries	-	-	-	-	-	-	-	-
Govt. cadres	3	14	4	3	11	12	18	10
Workers	20	20	22	20	27	34	32	38
Peasants	60	39	61	59	46	30	28	29
Other	-	-	-	-	-	-	-	-
Total	**100**	**100**	**100**	**100**	**100**	**100**	**100**	**100**
Number of Students	504	132	840	540	1,821	1,107	1,540	1,050

ANNEX 19 (cont'd)

	1980		1986		1989		1993	
	Male	Female	Male	Female	Male	Female	Male	Female
Sichuan SEdC:								
Intellectual	18	19	19	23	16	15	21	21
Managers in industries	0	0	0	0	0	0	0	0
Govt. cadres	9	9	9	8	8	13	8	24
Workers	25	16	19	20	25	22	21	18
Peasants	44	51	50	47	48	47	49	32
Other	3	5	3	2	3	2	2	5
Total	**100**	**100**	**100**	**100**	**100**	**100**	**100**	**100**
Number of Students	5,144	2,452	9,208	4,021	10,606	4,610	13,184	5,310
Sichuan Ministry:								
Intellectual	-	-	10	8	11	15	12	13
Managers in industries	-	-	-	-	0	0	1	1
Govt. cadres	-	-	15	14	13	13	10	7
Workers	-	-	31	31	26	26	30	32
Peasants	-	-	43	45	45	40	45	44
Other	-	-	2	2	4	6	2	2
Total	**-**	**-**	**100**	**100**	**100**	**100**	**100**	**100**
Number of Students	-	-	1,577	1,129	1,594	1,351	2,484	1,691
Sichuan SEdC:								
Intellectual	32	31	24	33	17	14	20	11
Managers in industries	-	-	-	-	-	-	-	-
Govt. cadres	25	27	19	24	26	30	23	33
Workers	18	17	26	12	20	13	21	21
Peasants	17	16	28	21	31	38	27	30
Other	8	8	3	10	6	5	9	6
Total	**100**	**100**	**100**	**100**	**100**	**100**	**100**	**100**
Number of Students	3,664	989	6,896	1,082	7,196	1,761	7,886	2,065
Sichuan Ministry								
Intellectual	6	7	6	7	6	6	6	6
Managers in industries	3	3	3	3	3	3	3	3
Govt. cadres	5	6	5	4	5	5	5	5
Workers	10	12	9	10	10	10	9	9
Peasants	75	69	75	74	74	75	75	75
Other	1	2	2	2	2	2	2	2
Total	**100**	**100**	**100**	**100**	**100**	**100**	**100**	**100**
Number of Students	2,028	413	2,592	712	2,336	662	3,096	1,135

Note: Percentages are rounded.

ANNEX 20: EXPLANATION OF PROJECTION

Enrollment Projection

Enrollment expansion is affected by the growth rate of the relevant age cohort, as much as it is by public policy of whether to set enrollment quotas to restrict growth or to let enrollment be driven by demand and the private ability to pay. The population of the 18-to-22-year-olds in China is projected by the World Bank to decline gradually from 1994 to 2001, when the generation born after the implementation of the one-child policy in 1979 comes of age (Annexes 21A and 21B). The size of the 18-to-22 age cohort is projected to fluctuate between 88 million at the lowest point in 2001 and 117 million at the highest 2009. The projected enrollment is based on two different enrollment growth rates (Table 4.8 and Annex 23):

(a)   **Gradual growth.** If enrollment is to follow **the historical average annual enrollment growth rate of 7.6 percent up to 2020**, China would reach an enrollment ratio of 5 percent by 2000, nearly 8 percent by 2010, and nearly 19 percent by 2020. This growth rate, however, lags behind the historical GDP growth rates.

(b)   **Fast growth.** If enrollment growth is to catch up with the **historical average annual GDP growth rate of 9.8 percent**, the enrollment ratio would reach 5.5 percent by 2000, nearly 11 percent in 2010, and 25 percent in 2020. Although the ratio of 25 percent by 2020 would be similar to those in middle-income countries nowadays, the enrollment ratio in 2000 is still only 5 percent, half of the current enrollment ratio of Indonesia (see Table 1.2 for comparison).

Projection of GDP

To estimate the amount of public resources available in the future, projection is made of three scenarios of average annual GDP growth rates between 1995 and 2020 at 7 percent; 8 percent; and 9 percent, respectively (Annex 22). The reason for choosing these average annual growth rates is as follows—7 and 8 percent fall within the government's own target, and 9 percent is close to the historical growth rate of 9.8 percent between 1978 and 1994. The projected GDP then forms the basis for the projection of the government expenditure on higher education (Annex 22).

Projection of Government Expenditure on Higher Education

The projection of government expenditure on higher education assumes that future government expenditure remains at 12.9 percent of GDP (the ratio in 1994), and the government expenditure on higher education is about 2.6 percent of total government spending (the ratio of 1992) (Annex 27). The reason for choosing the 1992 ratio instead of the 1994 ratio is because government expenditure on higher education in 1994 increased considerably over the previous years, and that this level might conflict with the overall objective of deficit reduction. The projection is based on the pessimistic assumptions that the future growth of revenue remains unchanged and that the future growth of public spending on higher education will be constrained by the need to reduce the consolidated government deficit (Annexes 13A and 13B). Using these ratios for projection, total government expenditure on higher education would increase from about Y 19 billion to Y 79 billion (in constant 1994 prices), if the GDP grows at 7 percent per year between 1994 and 2020; it would grow to Y 100 billion if the GDP grows at 8 percent and to Y 128 billion if the GDP grows at 9 percent (Annex 26). However, if the government's tax reform succeeds in increasing revenue and in reducing deficits, public spending in education could be higher irrespective of the GDP growth rate.

If public subsidy per student remains at the level of 1994 (Y 6,667) for the next 25 years, and GDP grows at 7 percent per year, the system that relies on public subsidy alone would be able to accommodate 3 million students in 2000, 6 million in 2010, and 12 million in 2020 (Annex 26). However, if GDP grows at 8 percent and public subsidy per student remains at the 1994 level, the system that relies on public subsidy alone would be able to accommodate 3.2 million in 2000, 7 million in 2021, and 15 million in 2020. If GDP grows at 9 percent, while every thing remains constant, then the system can enroll 3.4 million students in 2000, 8 million in 2010, and 19 million in 2020. Only at the last scenario of fast GDP growth would the increase in enrollment be close to the growth rate at the historical level of 7.6 percent (Annex 23). Therefore, to finance more rapid enrollment expansion and qualitative improvement, it is necessary to increase cost recovery and institution-generated income.

Projection on Cost Recovery and Institution-generated Revenue

The Chinese government's current policy on cost recovery targets 20 percent of the cost to be recovered by 1997. To meet this objective, fees have to be raised at 20 percent per year between 1995 and 1997; it can then increase at 3 percent per year in real terms (Annex 28A). However, allowance is made for flexible implementation at institutional level. How much revenue can be generated from tuition depends very much on how fast the economy and enrollment grow. Needless to say, household income will increase as the economy grows, which enables a larger share of household financing. At the same time, if the economy grows fast, public expenditure on higher education will also increase. Faster enrollment increase would mean that tuition income will rise and that the money needed for student loan and the variable cost will also increase.

It is not easy to estimate the potential of institution-generated revenue, given available data for only two years (1990-1992), which is too short a time span to provide reliable trends (Table 4.4). The growth rates of various university activities were very high and might not be sustainable, given the current government policy of tightening credit. Therefore, assumptions have been made about a lower growth rate of each source of university-generated revenue than the two-year trend.

If the GDP grows fast, revenue from enterprises is projected to grow at an annual average of 5 percent, that from training at 5 percent, that from educational services at the historical rate of 10.5 percent (because it is the principal service of higher education institutions), that from research and consultancy at the historical rate of 14 percent, that from logistical services at 0.1 percent, that from donation at 1 percent, and that from other sources at the historical rate of 8.5 percent. The projected total revenue generated from institutions may rise from Y 4 billion to Y 31 billion between 1994 and 2020. If the economy grows slowly, the annual growth rates of revenue from all of these activities may half, yielding revenue of 12 billion by 2020.

The total projected revenue (which includes government allocation, student fees, and institution-generated revenue) could grow from Y 25 billion in 1994 to Y 172-226 billion by 2020, if GDP grows at 7-9 percent and enrollment grows at 7.6 percent. It would reach Y 191-245 billion if enrollment grows at 9.8 percent (Annex 28A). Part of the revenue growth may come from improved efficiency in terms of higher student-to-staff ratios and better use of buildings. The respective share from each of these sources will change between 1994 and 2020—public expenditure may fall from 74 to 51-73 percent of the total revenue for higher education, student tuition fees may grow from 9 to 24-31 percent, and institution-generated income will increase from 14 to 18 percent if enrollment grows at 7.6 percent (Annex 28A). However, if enrollment grows at 9.8 percent, by 2020 public spending on higher education may be between 46 and 58 percent, student fees may account for 30 to 38 percent, and institution-generated income may constitute 13 to 16 percent.

ANNEX 21A: POPULATION PROJECTION, 1990-2020

China (Excluding Taiwan)—Population Projection ('000) with NRR=1 by 2030

Age Group	1990	1995	2000	2005	2010	2015	2020
Total M+F	1,133,683	1,193,991	1,249,742	1,296,218	1,342,033	1,385,864	1,426,566
Males:							
0-4	60,242	52,857	51,979	48,720	49,734	50,707	51,241
5-9	47,467	59,714	52,479	51,676	48,484	49,514	50,504
10-14	49,530	47,233	59,494	52,317	51,541	48,369	49,410
15-19	63,348	49,232	46,996	59,249	52,131	51,372	48,224
20-24	65,727	62,779	48,841	46,676	58,904	51,844	51,107
25-29	55,048	65,023	62,202	48,443	46,352	58,518	51,519
30-34	43,876	54,417	64,402	61,683	48,093	46,034	58,140
35-39	44,901	43,295	53,805	63,768	61,148	47,696	45,675
40-44	33,403	44,159	42,643	53,080	62,994	60,440	47,170
45-49	26,191	32,604	43,177	41,762	52,071	61,857	59,406
50-54	24,345	25,235	31,468	41,759	40,481	50,547	60,133
55-59	22,138	22,969	23,850	29,814	39,693	38,576	48,289
60-64	17,908	20,212	210,10	21,881	27,482	36,752	35,876
65-69	13,518	15,533	17,572	18,338	19,245	24,346	32,791
70-74	9,089	10,807	12,454	14,161	14,949	15,870	20,307
75+	8,465	10,272	12,361	14,597	17,158	19,313	21,429
Total	**585,194**	**616,341**	**644,734**	**667,923**	**690,459**	**711,752**	**731,221**
Females:							
0-4	57,945	48,517	47,681	44,651	45,539	46,398	46,856
5-9	44,152	57,549	48,255	47,483	44,507	45,404	46,273
10-14	46,249	43,974	57,393	48,152	47,407	44,442	45,345
15-19	59,404	46,016	43,806	57,235	48,051	47,316	44,365
20-24	61,411	58,952	45,729	43,600	57,042	47,900	47,181
25-29	50,757	60,822	58,504	45,448	43,399	56,805	47,716
30-34	40,380	50,205	60,300	58,095	45,196	43,176	56,540
35-39	41,906	39,874	49,686	59,783	57,686	44,899	42,914
40-44	30,218	41,285	39,344	49,116	59,198	57,159	44,518
45-49	23,083	29,614	40,527	38,692	48,396	58,387	56,430
50-54	21,391	22,416	28,809	39,520	37,827	47,381	57,244
55-59	19,929	20,490	21,515	27,733	38,178	36,623	45,975
60-64	16,619	18,662	19,235	20,274	26,265	36,288	34,937
65-69	13,521	14,943	16,837	17,444	18,528	24,154	33,583
70-74	9,973	11,324	12,572	14,264	14,947	16,052	21,157
75+	11,553	13,007	14,816	16,805	19,411	21,727	23,312
Total	**548,489**	**577,649**	**605,008**	**628,296**	**651,574**	**674,112**	**695,345**
Birth rate		18.1	16.9	15.1	14.8	14.5	14.2
Death rate		7.3	7.6	7.7	7.8	8.1	8.4
Rate of national increase		1.07	.93	.74	.70	.65	.58
Net migration rate		-.3	-.2	-.1	-.0	-.0	-.0
Growth rate		1.04	.91	.73	.69	.64	.58
Total fertility		1.900	1.900	1.900	1.948	1.994	2.040
NRR		.860	.864	.870	.897	.921	.944
e(0) - Both sexes		68.99	69.63	70.57	71.71	72.49	73.28
e(15) - Both sexes		57.07	57.41	57.97	58.75	59.37	60.02
IMR - Both sexes		31.2	28.3	24.1	20.1	18.4	16.8
q(5) - Both sexes		.0378	.0340	.0289	.0241	.0222	.0203
Dep. ratio	48.8	47.7	47.7	42.8	41.2	41.5	45.1

Source: Statistical Yearbook of China; Study Team projections.

ANNEX 21B: PROJECTION OF THE 18-22 AGE GROUP, 1990-2050

China (Excluding Taiwan)—Projection ('000) with NRR=1 by 2050

Population By Special Age Groups For Selected Years; Units = 1,000s

Age Group	199	199	199	199	199	199	199	199	199	1999
Males: 18-22	66,70	66,13	64,92	63,02	60,46	57,48	54,39	51,48	49,01	47,248
Total	585,19	592,34	599,03	605,26	611,03	616,34	621,71	627,24	632,92	638,757
Females: 18-22	62,48	62,01	60,91	59,15	56,75	53,94	51,02	48,23	45,85	44,118
Total	548,48	555,11	561,35	567,18	572,61	577,64	583,59	589,20	594,59	599,837
Both Sexes: 18-22	129,18	128,14	125,83	122,18	117,21	111,42	105,41	99,71	94,87	91,366
Total	1,133,68	1,147,45	1,160,38	1,172,45	1,183,65	1,193,99	1,205,31	1,216,45	1,227,52	1,238,594

	200	200	200	200	200	200	200	200	200	2009
Males: 18-22	46,17	45,77	45,99	46,81	48,19	40,11	52,57	55,57	59,05	59,706
Total	644,73	650,43	655,61	660,25	664,35	667,92	672,15	676,52	681,03	685,676
Females: 18-22	43,03	42,61	42,83	43,69	45,16	47,25	49,95	53,25	57,12	57,467
Total	605,00	611,49	616,96	621,54	625,29	628,29	633,62	638,49	643,04	647,369
Both Sexes: 18-22	89,20	88,38	88,83	90,50	93,36	97,36	102,52	108,83	116,18	117,173
Total	1,249,74	1,261,92	1,272,58	1,281,79	1,289,65	1,296,21	1,305,77	1,315,01	1,324,07	1,333,045

	201	201	201	201	201	201	201	201	201	2019
Males: 18-22	59,41	58,09	55,62	51,97	50,61	49,85	49,70	50,16	51,22	51,945
Total	690,45	695,12	699,58	703,84	707,90	711,75	715,82	719,80	723,70	727,514
Females: 18-22	56,83	55,11	52,18	47,96	46,70	46,00	45,85	46,27	47,24	47,893
Total	651,57	657,30	662,33	666,74	670,65	674,11	679,52	684,28	688,46	692,135
Both Sexes: 18-22	116,25	113,21	107,81	99,93	97,32	95,86	95,56	96,43	98,46	99,838
Total	1,342,03	1,352,43	1,362,91	1,370,59	1,378,55	1,385,86	1,395,35	1,404,09	1,412,17	1,419,649

	202	202	203	203	204	204	205
Males: 18-22	51,98	46,49	50,55	50,00	51,08	50,51	50,42
Total	731,22	747,89	760,85	769,85	776,43	780,48	782,56
Females: 18-22	47,92	42,80	46,48	45,93	46,87	46,29	46,16
Total	695,34	714,28	729,78	741,21	750,32	756,64	760,22
Both Sexes: 18-22	99,91	89,29	97,04	95,94	97,96	96,80	96,59
Total	1,426,56	1,462,17	1,490,64	1,511,06	1,526,75	1,537,12	1,542,78

Source: *Statistical Yearbook of China;* Study Team projections.

ANNEX 22: PROJECTED POPULATION, GDP, GDP PER CAPITA AND TOTAL GOVERNMENT EXPENDITURES, 1995-2020

(In Constant 1994 Prices)

Year	Projected Total Population (Bi. Persons)	Slow Growth Scenario Projected GDP (r=7% p.a.) (Bi. Yuan)	Projected GDP Per Capita (Yuan)	Medium Growth Scenario Projected GDP (r=8% p.a.) (Bi. Yuan)	Projected GDP Per Capita (Yuan)	Fast Growth Scenario Projected GDP (r=9% p.a.) (Bi. Yuan)	Projected GDP Per Capita (Yuan)	Projected Total Government Expenditures (12.9% of GDP) Assume GDP growth r=7% (Bi. Yuan)	Assume GDP growth r=8% (Bi. Yuan)	Assume GDP growth r=9% (Bi. Yuan)
1994	1.18	4,501	3,802	4,501	3,802	4,501	3,802	579	579	579
1995	1.19	4,816	4,033	4,861	4,071	4,906	4,109	621	627	633
1996	1.21	5,153	4,275	5,249	4,355	5,347	4,436	665	677	690
1997	1.22	5,513	4,532	5,669	4,661	5,828	4,791	711	731	752
1998	1.23	5,899	4,806	6,123	4,988	6,353	5,175	761	790	820
1999	1.24	6,312	5,096	6,613	5,339	6,925	5,591	814	853	893
2000	1.25	6,754	5,404	7,142	5,715	7,548	6,040	871	921	974
2001	1.26	7,227	5,727	7,713	6,112	8,227	6,520	932	995	1,061
2002	1.27	7,733	6,076	8,330	6,546	8,968	7,047	998	1,075	1,157
2003	1.28	8,274	6,455	8,997	7,019	9,775	7,626	1,067	1,161	1,261
2004	1.29	8,853	6,865	9,716	7,534	10,655	8,262	1,142	1,253	1,374
2005	1.30	9,473	7,308	10,494	8,096	11,613	8,959	1,222	1,354	1,498
2006	1.31	10,136	7,763	11,333	8,679	12,659	9,694	1,308	1,462	1,633
2007	1.32	10,846	8,248	12,240	9,308	13,798	10,493	1,399	1,579	1,780
2008	1.32	11,605	8,765	13,219	9,984	15,040	11,359	1,497	1,705	1,940
2009	1.33	12,417	9,315	14,277	10,710	16,393	12,298	1,602	1,842	2,115
2010	1.34	13,286	9,900	15,419	11,489	17,869	13,315	1,714	1,989	2,305
2011	1.35	14,217	10,512	16,652	12,313	19,477	14,401	1,834	2,148	2,513
2012	1.36	15,212	11,169	17,984	13,205	21,230	15,588	1,962	2,320	2,739
2013	1.37	16,276	11,875	19,423	14,171	23,140	16,884	2,100	2,506	2,985
2014	1.38	17,416	12,633	20,977	15,217	25,223	18,297	2,247	2,706	3,254
2015	1.40	18,635	13,350	22,655	16,230	27,493	19,696	2,404	2,923	3,547
2016	1.40	19,939	14,290	24,468	17,535	29,968	21,477	2,572	3,156	3,866
2017	1.40	21,335	15,195	26,425	18,820	32,665	23,264	2,752	3,409	4,214
2018	1.41	22,829	16,166	28,539	20,209	35,604	25,213	2,945	3,682	4,593
2019	1.42	24,427	17,206	30,822	21,711	38,809	27,337	3,151	3,976	5,006
2020	1.43	26,136	18,321	33,288	23,334	42,302	29,653	3,372	4,294	5,457

Source: Study Team projections.

ANNEX 23: ENROLLMENT PROJECTION, 1994-2020

Year	Projected 18-22 Age Group (Mln persons)	Projected Enrollment (r=7.6% p.a., 1994-2020) (Mln persons)	Projected Enrollment (r=7.6% p.a., 1994-2020) (% of Age Group)	Projected Enrollment (r=9.8% p.a., 1994-2020) (Mln persons)	Projected Enrollment (r=9.8% p.a., 1994-2020) (% of Age Group)
1994	117.2	2.8	2.4	2.8	2.4
1995	111.4	3.0	2.7	3.1	2.7
1996	105.4	3.2	3.1	3.4	3.2
1997	99.7	3.5	3.5	3.7	3.7
1998	94.9	3.7	3.9	4.1	4.3
1999	91.4	4.0	4.4	4.5	4.9
2000	89.2	4.3	4.9	4.9	5.5
2001	88.4	4.7	5.3	5.4	6.1
2002	88.8	5.0	5.6	5.9	6.6
2003	90.5	5.4	6.0	6.5	7.2
2004	93.4	5.8	6.2	7.1	7.6
2005	97.4	6.2	6.4	7.8	8.0
2006	102.5	6.7	6.6	8.6	8.4
2007	108.8	7.2	6.6	9.4	8.6
2008	116.2	7.8	6.7	10.3	8.9
2009	117.2	8.4	7.1	11.3	9.7
2010	116.3	9.0	7.7	12.5	10.7
2011	113.2	9.7	8.6	13.7	12.1
2012	107.8	10.4	9.7	15.0	13.9
2013	99.9	11.2	11.2	16.5	16.5
2014	97.3	12.1	12.4	18.1	18.6
2015	95.9	13.0	13.6	19.9	20.7
2016	95.6	14.0	14.6	20.9	21.8
2017	96.4	15.0	15.6	21.9	22.7
2018	98.5	16.2	16.4	23.0	23.4
2019	99.8	17.4	17.4	24.2	24.2
2020	99.9	18.7	18.8	25.4	25.4

Source: Study Team projections.

ANNEX 24: PROJECTED STUDENT-TO-STAFF RATIOS BY DIFFERENT ENROLLMENT GROWTH RATES, 1994-2020

	Scenario at Historical Staff Growth Rate of 4.45% p.a., 1994-2020			Scenario at Reduced Staff Growth Rate to 1.0% p.a., 1994-2020		
	Total Staff	Student-to-Staff Ratios		Total Staff	Student-to-Staff Ratios	
Year	in Higher Educ. (Mln persons)	(Enrollment growth r=7.6%)	(Enrollment growth r=9.8%)	in Higher Educ. (Mln persons)	(Enrollment growth r=7.6%)	(Enrollment growth r=9.8%)
1994	1.0	2.7	2.7	1.0	2.7	2.7
1995	1.1	2.8	2.8	1.1	2.9	2.9
1996	1.1	2.8	3.0	1.1	3.0	3.2
1997	1.2	2.9	3.1	1.1	3.2	3.4
1998	1.2	3.0	3.3	1.1	3.5	3.7
1999	1.3	3.1	3.4	1.1	3.7	4.1
2000	1.4	3.2	3.6	1.1	3.9	4.4
2001	1.4	3.3	3.8	1.1	4.2	4.8
2002	1.5	3.4	4.0	1.1	4.5	5.2
2003	1.5	3.5	4.2	1.1	4.7	5.7
2004	1.6	3.6	4.4	1.1	5.1	6.2
2005	1.7	3.7	4.6	1.2	5.4	6.7
2006	1.8	3.8	4.9	1.2	5.7	7.3
2007	1.8	3.9	5.1	1.2	6.1	7.9
2008	1.9	4.1	5.4	1.2	6.5	8.6
2009	2.0	4.2	5.7	1.2	6.9	9.4
2010	2.1	4.3	6.0	1.2	7.4	10.2
2011	2.2	4.4	6.3	1.2	7.9	11.1
2012	2.3	4.6	6.6	1.2	8.4	12.1
2013	2.4	4.7	6.9	1.3	8.9	13.1
2014	2.5	4.9	7.3	1.3	9.5	14.3
2015	2.6	5.0	7.7	1.3	10.1	15.5
2016	2.7	5.2	7.7	1.3	10.8	16.1
2017	2.8	5.3	7.7	1.3	11.5	16.8
2018	3.0	5.5	7.8	1.3	12.3	17.4
2019	3.1	5.6	7.8	1.3	13.1	18.1
2020	3.2	5.8	7.9	1.3	13.9	18.8

Source: Study Team projections.

ANNEX 25: PROJECTED PERSONNEL COSTS, 1994-2020

(In Constant 1994 Prices)

	At Historical Staff Growth Rate of 4.45% p.a. Estimated Personnel Cost as % of Total				At Reduced Staff Growth Rate of 1.0% p.a. Estimated Personnel Cost as % of Total				At Reduced Staff Growth Rate of 1.0% p.a. Estimated Personnel Cost as % of Total			
	Total Wages (r=8.9%)	Wages as % of Expenditure on Higher Education			Total Wages (r=8.9%)	Wages as % of Expenditure on Higher Education			Total Wages (r=11% p.a.)	Wages as % of Expenditure on Higher Education		
Year	Bln Yuan	(GDPr=7%)	(GDPr=8%)	(GDPr=9%)	Bln Yuan	(GDPr=7%)	(GDPr=8%)	(GDPr=9%)	Bln Yuan	(GDPr=7%)	(GDPr=8%)	(GDPr=9%)
1994	6.2	41.4	41.4	41.4	6.2	41.4	41.4	41.4	6.2	41.4	41.4	41.4
1995	7.1	44	43.6	43.2	6.9	42.5	42.1	41.7	7.0	43.3	42.9	42.5
1996	8.1	46.9	46	45.2	7.5	43.7	42.9	42.1	7.8	45.4	44.5	43.7
1997	9.3	50.1	48.8	47.4	8.3	44.9	43.7	42.5	8.8	47.6	46.2	45.0
1998	10.6	53.7	51.8	49.9	9.1	46.2	44.5	42.9	9.9	49.9	48.0	46.3
1999	12.2	57.7	55.1	52.0	10.1	47.5	45.4	43.3	11.1	52.3	49.9	47.7
2000	14.1	62.1	58.7	6.0	11.1	48.9	46.2	43.8	12.4	54.8	51.9	49.1
2001	16.2	67	62.8	55.6	12.2	50.3	47.1	44.2	13.9	57.5	53.9	50.5
2002	18.8	72.5	67.3	58.9	13.4	51.8	48.1	44.6	15.6	60.3	56.0	52.0
2003	21.8	78.6	72.3	62.5	14.8	53.3	49.0	45.1	17.6	63.3	58.2	53.6
2004	25.4	85.5	77.9	66.5	16.3	54.9	50.0	45.6	19.7	66.4	60.5	55.2
2005	29.6	93.2	84.1	71.0	17.9	56.5	51.0	46.1	22.1	69.7	62.9	56.8
2006	34.7	101.9	91.2	76.0	19.8	58.1	52.0	46.6	24.9	73.1	65.4	58.5
2007	40.7	111.9	99.1	81.6	21.8	59.9	53.0	47.1	27.9	76.7	68.0	60.3
2008	47.9	123.1	108.1	87.9	24.0	61.6	54.1	47.6	31.4	80.5	70.7	62.2
2009	56.6	136.0	118.3	95.0	26.4	63.5	55.2	48.1	35.2	84.6	73.5	64.1
2010	67.2	150.7	129.9	112.0	29.1	65.4	56.4	48.6	39.6	88.8	76.5	66.0
2011	79.9	167.6	143.1	122.3	32.1	67.4	57.5	49.2	44.5	93.2	79.6	68.0
2012	95.5	187.1	158.3	134.1	35.4	69.4	58.7	49.7	49.9	97.9	82.8	70.1
2013	114.5	209.8	175.8	147.5	39.0	71.5	59.9	50.3	56.1	102.8	86.2	72.3
2014	137.9	236.1	196.0	163.0	43.1	73.7	61.2	50.9	63.1	108.0	89.7	74.6
2015	166.8	266.8	219.5	180.9	47.5	76.0	62.5	51.5	70.9	113.5	93.3	76.9
2016	202.6	302.9	246.9	201.6	52.4	78.3	63.8	52.1	79.7	119.2	97.2	79.3
2017	247.2	345.5	279	225.7	57.8	80.7	65.2	52.7	89.6	125.3	101.1	81.8
2018	303.2	395.9	316.7	253.9	63.7	83.2	66.6	53.4	100.8	131.7	105.3	84.4
2019	373.6	456.0	361.4	287.0	70.3	85.8	68.0	54.0	113.4	138.4	109.7	87.1
2020	462.7	527.9	414.5	326.1	77.6	88.5	69.5	54.7	127.5	145.5	114.2	89.9

Source: Study Team estimates.

ANNEX 26: PROJECTED PUBLIC EXPENDITURE ON HIGHER EDUCATION AND ENROLLMENT IF PUBLIC SPENDING PER STUDENT REMAINS AT THE 1994 LEVEL, 1994-2020

(In Constant 1994 Prices)

Year	Projected Govt. Expend on Higher Educ. (GDP r=7%) (Billion Y)	Projected Govt. Expend on Higher Educ. (GDP r=8%)	Projected Govt. Expend on Higher Educ. (GDP r=9%)	Enrollment if Public Spending per Student Remains at Y 6,645 & GDP r=7%	Enrollment if Public Spending per Student Remains at Y 6,645 & GDP r=8% (Million Persons)	Enrollment if Public Spending per Student Remains at Y 6,645 & GDP r=9%
1994	18.6	18.6	18.6	2.8	2.8	2.8
1995	16.2	16.3	16.5	2.3	2.3	2.3
1996	17.3	17.6	17.9	2.3	2.4	2.4
1997	18.5	19.0	19.5	2.5	2.6	2.6
1998	19.8	20.5	21.3	2.7	2.8	2.9
1999	21.2	22.2	23.2	2.9	3.0	3.1
2000	22.7	24.0	25.3	3.1	3.2	3.4
2001	24.2	25.9	27.6	3.3	3.5	3.7
2002	25.9	27.9	30.1	3.5	3.8	4.1
2003	27.8	30.2	32.8	3.8	4.1	4.4
2004	29.7	32.6	35.7	4.0	4.4	4.8
2005	31.8	35.2	39.0	4.3	4.8	5.3
2006	34.0	38.0	42.5	4.6	5.1	5.7
2007	36.4	41.1	46.3	4.9	5.6	6.3
2008	38.9	44.3	50.4	5.3	6.0	6.8
2009	41.6	47.9	55.0	5.6	6.5	7.4
2010	44.6	51.7	59.9	6.0	7.0	8.1
2011	47.7	55.9	65.3	6.5	7.6	8.8
2012	51.0	60.3	71.2	6.9	8.2	9.6
2013	54.6	65.1	77.6	7.4	8.8	10.5
2014	58.4	70.4	84.6	7.9	9.5	11.4
2015	52.6	76.0	92.2	8.5	10.3	12.5
2016	55.9	82.1	100.5	9.0	11.1	13.6
2017	71.6	88.6	109.6	9.7	12.0	14.8
2018	76.6	95.7	119.4	10.4	13.0	16.2
2019	81.9	103.4	130.2	11.1	14.0	17.6
2020	87.7	111.6	141.9	11.9	15.1	19.2

Source: Study Team estimates.

ANNEX 27: PROJECTED UNIVERSITY-GENERATED REVENUE, 1994-2020

(Billion Yuan, in Constant 1994 Prices)

Projected University-Generated Revenue if GDP Grows Fast *(Billion Yuan)*

Year	Enterprises (r=5%)	Training (r=5%)	Educational Services (r=10.5%)	Research & Consultancy (r=14%)	Logistical Services (r=.1%)	Other Sources (r=5%)	Donation (r=1%)	Total University-Generated Revenue
1994	1.2	0.7	0.3	0.4	0.2	1.2	0.3	4.2
1995	1.2	0.8	0.4	0.5	0.2	1.2	0.3	4.5
1996	1.3	0.8	0.4	0.5	0.2	1.3	0.3	4.8
1997	1.3	0.8	0.5	0.6	0.2	1.3	0.3	5.1
1998	1.4	0.9	0.5	0.7	0.2	1.4	0.4	5.5
1999	1.5	0.9	0.6	0.8	0.2	1.5	0.4	5.8
2000	1.5	1.0	0.6	0.9	0.2	1.5	0.4	6.2
2001	1.6	1.0	0.7	1.0	0.2	1.6	0.5	6.7
2002	1.7	1.1	0.8	1.2	0.2	1.7	0.5	7.2
2003	1.8	1.1	0.9	1.3	0.2	1.8	0.6	7.7
2004	1.9	1.2	0.9	1.5	0.2	1.9	0.6	8.2
2005	2.0	1.2	1.0	1.7	0.2	2.0	0.7	8.9
2006	2.1	1.3	1.1	2.0	0.2	2.1	0.8	9.5
2007	2.2	1.3	1.2	2.2	0.2	2.2	0.9	10.3
2008	2.3	1.4	1.4	2.5	0.2	2.3	1.0	11.1
2009	2.4	1.5	1.5	2.9	0.3	2.4	1.0	12.0
2010	2.5	1.6	1.7	3.3	0.3	2.5	1.1	13.0
2011	2.6	1.6	1.9	3.8	0.3	2.6	1.3	14.1
2012	2.8	1.7	2.0	4.3	0.3	2.8	1.4	15.3
2013	2.9	1.8	2.3	4.9	0.3	2.9	1.5	16.6
2014	3.1	1.9	2.5	5.6	0.3	3.1	1.7	18.1
2015	3.2	2.0	2.8	6.4	0.3	3.2	1.9	19.7
2016	3.4	2.1	3.1	7.3	0.3	3.4	2.0	21.5
2017	3.5	2.2	3.4	8.3	0.3	3.5	2.2	23.5
2018	3.7	2.3	3.7	9.4	0.3	3.7	2.5	25.7
2019	3.9	2.4	4.1	10.8	0.3	3.9	2.7	28.1
2020	4.1	2.5	4.5	12.3	0.3	4.1	3.0	30.8

Projected University-Generated Revenue if GDP Grows Slow

Year	Enterprises (r=2.5%)	Training (r=4%)	Educational Services (r=8%)	Research & Consultancy (r=7%)	Logistical Services (r=.1%)	Other Sources (r=2%)	Donation (r=.01%)	Total University-Generated Revenue
1994	1.2	0.7	0.3	0.4	0.2	1.2	0.3	4.2
1995	1.2	0.7	0.4	0.4	0.2	1.2	0.3	4.4
1996	1.2	0.8	0.4	0.5	0.2	1.2	0.3	4.5
1997	1.2	0.8	0.4	0.5	0.2	1.2	0.3	4.7
1998	1.3	0.8	0.5	0.5	0.2	1.3	0.3	4.8
1999	1.3	0.9	0.5	0.6	0.2	1.3	0.3	5.0
2000	1.3	0.9	0.5	0.6	0.2	1.3	0.3	5.2
2001	1.4	1.0	0.6	0.7	0.2	1.4	0.3	5.3
2002	1.4	1.0	0.6	0.7	0.2	1.4	0.3	5.5
2003	1.4	1.1	0.7	0.8	0.2	1.4	0.3	5.7
2004	1.5	1.1	0.7	0.9	0.2	1.5	0.3	5.9
2005	1.5	1.2	0.8	0.9	0.2	1.5	0.3	6.2
2006	1.6	1.2	0.9	1.0	0.2	1.5	0.3	6.4
2007	1.6	1.3	0.9	1.0	0.2	1.6	0.3	6.7
2008	1.7	1.3	1.0	1.1	0.2	1.6	0.3	6.9
2009	1.7	1.4	1.1	1.2	0.2	1.6	0.3	7.2
2010	1.8	1.5	1.2	1.3	0.2	1.7	0.3	7.5
2011	1.8	1.5	1.3	1.4	0.2	1.7	0.3	7.8
2012	1.9	1.6	1.4	1.5	0.2	1.8	0.3	8.1
2013	1.9	1.6	1.5	1.6	0.2	1.8	0.3	8.4
2014	2.0	1.7	1.6	1.7	0.2	1.8	0.3	8.8
2015	2.1	1.8	1.7	1.8	0.2	1.9	0.3	9.2
2016	2.1	1.8	1.8	1.9	0.2	1.9	0.3	9.6
2017	2.2	1.9	2.0	2.1	0.2	1.9	0.3	10.0
2018	2.1	1.9	2.2	2.2	0.2	1.9	0.3	10.5
2019	2.1	1.9	2.3	2.2	0.2	1.9	0.3	11.0
2020	2.2	2.0	2.5	2.4	0.2	1.9	0.3	11.5

Source: Study Team estimates.

ANNEX 28A: PROJECTED TOTAL PUBLIC AND PRIVATE RESOURCES AT DIFFERENT ENROLLMENT AND GDP GROWTH RATES, 1994-2020

(In Constant 1994 Prices)

	Projected Government Expenditure on Higher Education if GDP Growth Differs			Tuition Fees Per Student (r=20% to 1997; r=3% afterwards)	Projected Tuition Fees if Enrollment Growth Differs		Projected Own-Generated Revenue /a	Total Public and Private Resources					
	(GDP r=7%)	(GDP r=8%)	(GDP r=9%)		Growth Differs			If GDP r=7%, Enrollment r=7.6%	If GDP r=8%, Enrollment r=7.6%	If GDP r=9%, Enrollment r=7.6%	If GDP r=7%, Enrollment r=9.8%	If GDP r=8%, Enrollment r=9.8%	If GDP r=7%, Enrollment r=9.8%
					(r=7.6%)	(r=9.8%)							
	(1)	(2)	(3)	Y	(4)	(5)	(6)	(1+4+6)	(2+4+6)	(3+4+6)	(1+5+6)	(2+5+6)	(3+5+6)
	——Billion Y——				——Billion Y——			——Billion Y——					
1994	18.6	18.6	18.6	840.0	2.3	2.3	4.2	25.2	25.2	25.2	25.2	25.2	25.2
1995	16.2	16.3	16.5	1,008.0	3.0	3.1	4.5	23.7	23.8	24.0	23.7	23.9	24.0
1996	17.3	17.6	17.9	1,209.6	3.9	4.1	4.8	26.0	26.3	26.6	26.2	26.5	26.8
1997	18.5	19.0	19.5	1,451.5	5.0	5.4	5.1	28.7	29.2	29.7	29.0	29.5	30.0
1998	19.8	20.5	21.3	1,495.1	5.6	6.1	5.5	30.8	31.6	32.4	31.3	32.1	32.8
1999	21.2	22.2	23.2	1,539.9	6.2	6.9	5.8	33.2	34.2	35.3	33.9	34.9	35.9
2000	22.7	24.0	25.3	1,586.1	6.9	7.8	6.2	35.8	37.1	38.4	36.6	37.9	39.3
2001	24.2	25.9	27.6	1,633.7	7.6	8.8	6.7	38.5	40.2	41.9	39.7	41.3	43.0
2002	25.9	27.9	30.1	1,682.7	8.4	9.9	7.2	41.5	43.5	45.7	43.0	45.0	47.1
2003	27.8	30.2	32.8	1,733.2	9.3	11.2	7.7	44.8	47.2	49.8	46.6	49.1	51.7
2004	29.7	32.6	35.7	1,785.2	10.4	12.7	8.2	48.3	51.2	54.3	50.6	53.5	56.7
2005	31.8	35.2	39.0	1,838.7	11.5	14.3	8.9	52.1	55.5	59.3	55.0	58.4	62.2
2006	34.0	38.0	42.5	1,893.9	12.7	16.2	9.5	56.3	60.3	64.7	59.8	63.8	68.2
2007	36.4	41.1	46.3	1,950.7	14.1	18.3	10.3	60.8	65.4	70.7	65.0	69.7	74.9
2008	38.9	44.3	50.4	2,009.2	15.6	20.8	11.1	65.7	71.1	77.2	70.8	76.2	82.3
2009	41.6	47.9	55.0	2,069.5	17.3	23.5	12.0	71.0	77.2	84.3	77.1	83.4	90.5
2010	44.6	51.7	59.9	2,131.6	19.2	26.5	13.0	76.8	83.9	92.1	84.1	91.2	99.5
2011	47.7	55.9	65.3	2,195.6	21.3	30.0	14.1	83.0	91.2	100.7	91.8	99.9	109.4
2012	51.0	60.3	71.2	2,261.4	23.6	33.9	15.3	89.9	99.2	110.1	100.2	109.5	120.4
2013	54.6	65.1	77.6	2,329.3	26.1	38.4	16.6	97.3	107.9	120.3	109.6	120.1	132.6
2014	58.4	70.4	84.6	2,399.1	29.0	43.4	18.1	105.4	117.4	131.6	119.9	131.8	146.1
2015	62.5	76.0	92.2	2,471.1	32.1	49.1	19.7	114.3	127.8	144.0	131.3	144.8	161.0
2016	66.9	82.1	100.5	2,545.2	35.6	53.1	21.5	123.9	139.1	157.6	141.5	156.6	175.1
2017	71.6	88.6	109.6	2,621.6	39.4	57.4	23.5	134.4	151.5	172.4	152.5	169.5	190.5
2018	76.6	95.7	119.4	2,700.3	43.7	62.1	25.7	145.9	165.1	188.8	164.3	183.5	207.2
2019	81.9	103.4	130.2	2,781.3	48.4	67.2	28.1	158.5	179.9	206.7	177.2	198.7	225.5
2020	87.7	111.6	141.9	2,864.7	53.7	72.7	30.8	172.2	196.2	226.4	191.2	215.1	245.4

/a Due to the many possible combinations depending on the scenarios of GDP and enrollment growth, this table only takes the fast growth scenario for institution-generated revenue (Column 6) to illustrate this point.

Note: The estimates for the average tuition fees have taken into account fee exemptions of certain categories of students. This means that the fee level for popular and lucrative subject specialties must be much higher in order to cross-subsidize others.

Source: Study Team estimates.

ANNEX 28B: PUBLIC AND PRIVATE RESOURCES AS A PERCENTAGE OF TOTAL RESOURCES AT VARIOUS GROWTH RATES OF GDP AND ENROLLMENT, 1994-2020

Year	Projected Govt. Expenditures as % of Total Resources if Enrollment r=7.6%			Projected Govt. Expenditures as % of Total Resources if Enrollment r=9.8%			Projected Tuition Fee Revenue as % of Total Resources if Enrollment r=7.6%			Projected Tuition Fee Revenue as % of Total Resources if Enrollment r=9.8%			Projected Institution-Generated Income as % of Total Resources if Enrollment r=7.6%			Projected Institution-Generated Income as % of Total Resources if Enrollment r=9.8%		
	(GDP r=7%)	(GDP r=8%)	(GDP r=9%)	(GDP r=7%)	(GDP r=8%)	(GDP r=9%)	(GDP r=7%)	(GDP r=8%)	(GDP r=9%)	(GDP r=7%)	(GDP r=8%)	(GDP r=9%)	(GDP r=7%)	(GDP r=8%)	(GDP r=9%)	(GDP r=7%)	(GDP r=8%)	(GDP r=9%)
1994	73.9	73.9	73.9	73.9	73.9	73.9	9.3	9.3	9.3	9.3	9.3	9.3	16.8	16.8	16.8	16.8	16.8	16.8
1995	68.2	68.4	68.6	68.0	68.2	68.4	12.8	12.7	12.6	13.0	12.9	12.8	19.0	18.9	18.8	19.0	18.9	18.7
1996	66.5	66.9	67.3	66.1	66.5	66.9	15.0	14.8	14.7	15.6	15.4	15.2	18.5	18.2	18.0	18.4	18.1	17.9
1997	64.5	65.2	65.8	63.8	64.5	65.1	17.6	17.3	17.0	18.5	18.2	17.9	17.9	17.5	17.2	17.7	17.3	17.0
1998	64.2	65.0	65.8	63.2	64.1	64.9	18.1	17.7	17.3	19.4	18.9	18.5	17.7	17.3	16.9	17.4	17.0	16.6
1999	63.8	64.8	65.9	62.5	63.6	64.7	18.7	18.1	17.6	20.3	19.7	19.1	17.6	17.0	16.5	17.2	16.7	16.2
2000	63.4	64.6	65.9	61.8	63.1	64.4	19.2	18.5	17.9	21.2	20.4	19.7	17.4	16.8	16.2	17.0	16.4	15.9
2001	62.9	64.4	65.9	61.1	62.6	64.1	19.8	19.0	18.2	22.1	21.2	20.4	17.3	16.6	15.9	16.8	16.2	15.5
2002	62.5	64.2	65.9	60.3	62.1	63.8	20.3	19.4	18.5	23.1	22.0	21.0	17.2	16.4	15.7	16.6	15.9	15.2
2003	62.0	63.9	65.8	59.5	61.5	63.4	20.9	19.8	18.8	24.0	22.9	21.7	17.1	16.3	15.4	16.5	15.6	14.8
2004	61.5	63.7	65.8	58.7	60.9	63.1	21.5	20.2	19.1	25.1	23.7	22.4	17.1	16.1	15.2	16.3	15.4	14.5
2005	61.0	63.4	65.7	57.8	60.3	62.7	22.0	20.7	19.4	26.1	24.6	23.1	17.0	16.0	14.9	16.1	15.2	14.3
2006	60.4	63.1	65.6	56.9	59.6	62.2	22.6	21.1	19.7	27.1	25.4	23.8	17.0	15.8	14.7	16.0	15.0	14.0
2007	59.9	62.7	65.5	56.0	58.9	61.8	23.2	21.6	20.0	28.2	26.3	24.5	16.9	15.7	14.6	15.8	14.8	13.7
2008	59.3	62.4	65.4	55.0	58.2	61.3	23.8	22.0	20.3	29.3	27.2	25.2	16.9	15.6	14.4	15.7	14.6	13.5
2009	58.7	62.0	65.2	54.0	57.4	60.8	24.4	22.4	20.5	30.4	28.2	25.9	16.9	15.5	14.2	15.6	14.4	13.3
2010	58.1	61.6	65.1	53.0	56.7	60.3	25.0	22.9	20.8	31.6	29.1	26.7	16.9	15.5	14.1	15.4	14.2	13.1
2011	57.4	61.2	64.9	52.0	55.9	59.7	25.6	23.3	21.1	32.7	30.0	27.4	17.0	15.4	14.0	15.3	14.1	12.9
2012	56.8	60.8	64.7	50.9	55.1	59.1	26.2	23.8	21.4	33.9	31.0	28.2	17.0	15.4	13.9	15.2	13.9	12.7
2013	56.1	60.4	64.5	49.8	54.2	58.5	26.9	24.2	21.7	35.0	32.0	29.0	17.1	15.4	13.8	15.1	13.8	12.5
2014	55.4	59.9	64.3	48.7	53.4	57.9	27.5	24.7	22.0	36.2	32.9	29.7	17.1	15.4	13.7	15.1	13.7	12.4
2015	54.7	59.5	64.0	47.6	52.5	57.3	28.1	25.1	22.3	37.4	33.9	30.5	17.2	15.4	13.7	15.0	13.6	12.2
2016	54.0	59.0	63.8	47.3	52.4	57.4	28.7	25.6	22.6	37.5	33.9	30.3	17.3	15.4	13.6	15.2	13.7	12.3
2017	53.2	58.5	63.5	46.9	52.3	57.5	29.3	26.0	22.9	37.7	33.9	30.2	17.4	15.5	13.6	15.4	13.8	12.3
2018	52.5	58.0	63.3	46.6	52.2	57.6	29.9	26.5	23.1	37.8	33.9	30.0	17.6	15.5	13.6	15.6	14.0	12.4
2019	51.7	57.5	63.0	46.2	52.0	57.7	30.6	26.9	23.4	37.9	33.8	29.8	17.7	15.6	13.6	15.9	14.2	12.5
2020	50.9	56.9	62.7	45.9	51.9	57.8	31.2	27.4	23.7	38.0	33.8	29.6	17.9	15.7	13.6	16.1	14.3	12.6

Note: This table presents the estimates of the share of various sources of revenue as a percentage of total revenue. It should be noted that while revenue from tuition fees increases with enrollment expansion, the variable cost will also go up, and so will the resources required to provide student loans and grants in order to safeguard equity.

Source: Study team estimates.

ANNEX 29: HISTORY AND FUTURE PERSPECTIVES OF TELEVISION UNIVERSITIES[1]

In 1978, the Ministry of Education and the Ministry of Radio and Television jointly founded the Chinese television universities with the objective of addressing the constraints on human resources. In 1979, the Central Radio and Television University (CRTVU) was established in Beijing and 28 Provincial Radio and Television Universities (PTVUs) were set up in the provinces and the municipalities. Now there are 46 PTVUs with thousands of local stations (See Annex 7A for source).

The CRTVU registered no students, but controlled most of the undergraduate curriculum through courses it made and the national examinations it set. PTVUs were responsible for enrolling students, and for supporting these courses with printed teaching materials and broadcasting basic and specialized courses. Initially, these TVUs enrolled professional staff, industrial and commercial workers, scientific and technological technicians, secondary school teachers, and the members of the military who passed an entrance examination. In the early days, most students were released on basic pay to study 36 hours a week in local classes during the day, often at their place of work or in a special study center. The World Bank supported the development of this system with a loan of $85 million in 1982. A flexible self-study examination system was introduced in 1983 to enable spare-time students to use TVU materials for independent study. Enrollment grew rapidly, peaking in 1985 with 673,000 students. Between 1979 and 1991, 1.3 million students graduated with credentials from TVUs, and another 3 million studied courses without obtaining credits.

A series of measures introduced in 1986 and 1987 changed the original direction of TVUs. In 1986, short-cycle TVU courses covering science, engineering, economics, and teacher training, were introduced. In 1987, to raise the quality of TVU's intake, applicants for undergraduate programs were required to pass the national university entrance examination; independent study classes were closed down; post-university courses (mostly on engineering, economics, and finance) were introduced for in-service, skill-upgrading; and teacher training was introduced. The last emphasis was derived from the 1985 reform which called for nine years of basic education for all by 2000. To reach this target required training 70 percent of junior secondary school teachers and 20 percent of primary school teachers who were unqualified. With the introduction of satellite borne transmission in 1986, the capacity of TV broadcasting was expanded dramatically. About half of the satellite transmission time was used for in-service training of primary and secondary school teachers. The State Education Commission encouraged joint running of schools and merging of various TVUs with other adult education institutions, such as correspondence universities, workers' colleges, evening universities, and conventional universities. Courses studied under the TVUs could be recognized by local institutions, which could award certificates jointly

---

[1] The content of this annex draws heavily from the article by Ma, Weixiang and David Hawkridge, "China's Changing Policy and Practice in Television Education, 1978-1993," *International Journal of Educational Development*, Vol. 15, No. 1, 1995, pp. 27-36.

with the TVUs to successful candidates. In part because of the expansion of correspondence courses and evening schools in regular universities which accounted for 48 percent of enrollment in the adult higher education system, in part because of the dull quality of TV courses, and in part because of the requirement of passing university entrance examinations, enrollment in TVUs gradually declined to over half a million students by 1994 or 23 percent of total enrollment in the adult system (Annex 7A).

The potential of television education is recognized by the government. The 1993 Reform document called for China to develop vigorously television education and for completion by 2000 all the TV ground stations for the satellite broadcasting network. In the meanwhile, the objectives of training sufficient technicians, teachers, and for upgrading post-secondary qualifications of workers are continued to be met by the use of TV and distance learning. The potential of combining television with computer network has yet to be realized in the 21st century.

ANNEX 30A: EXISTING STUDENT LOAN PROGRAMS

Country (Loan Organization)	Repayment Mechanism	Administering Institution	Purpose of Support	Average Loan Value	Year Begun	% of Students with Loans	Data Year
Latin America & Caribbean							
Argentina (INCE)	Mortgage Loan	Autonomous Body	Living				
Barbados (SRLF)	Mortgage Loan	Autonomous Body	Tuition & Living	$11,000	1976	12	1989
Bolivia (CIDEP)	Mortgage Loan		Living				
Brazil (CEP)	Mortgage Loan	Commercial Banks	Tuition	$400	1974	25	1989
Chile	Graduated	Universities	Tuition		1981		1988
Colombia (ICETEX)	Mortgage Loan	Autonomous Body	Tuition & Living	$280	1953	6	1985
Costa Rica (CONAPE)	Mortgage Loan	Commercial Banks	Tuition & Living		1977		1983
Dominican Republic (FCE)	Mortgage Loan	Autonomous Body	Living				
Ecuador (IECE)	Mortgage Loan	Autonomous Body	Living			3	
El Salvador (Educredito)	Mortgage Loan	Autonomous Body					
Honduras (Educredito)	Mortgage Loan	Autonomous Body	Tuition & Living	$2,700	1976	1	1991
Jamaica (SLB)	Mortgage Loan	Autonomous Body	Tuition & Living	$405	1970	20	1985
Mexico	Mortgage Loan	Commercial Banks					
Nicaragua (Educredito)	Mortgage Loan	Autonomous Body					
Panama (IFARHU)	Mortgage Loan	Autonomous Body			1966	6	
Peru (INABEC)	Mortgage Loan	Autonomous Body					
Trinidad & Tobago (SRLF)	Mortgage Loan	Autonomous Body	Tuition & Living		1972		
Venezuela (Educredito)	Mortgage Loan	Other	Tuition & Living	$400	1967	1	1991
(FGMA)	Mortgage Loan	Universities	Tuition & Living	$2,200	1975	1	1991
(BANAP)	Mortgage Loan	Commercial Banks	Tuition & Living	$700		1	1991
Asia							
China	Mortgage Loan	Universities	Tuition & Living		1987	30	1989
India	Mortgage Loan	Other	Tuition & Living	$85	1963	1	1989
Indonesia /a	Mortgage Loan	Universities & Commercial Banks	Tuition & Living	$550	1982	3	1986
Republic of Korea	Mortgage Loan	Commercial Banks	Tuition & Living		1975		
Malaysia	Mortgage Loan	Commercial Banks	Living	$1,300	1985		
Philippines	Mortgage Loan		Tuition		1976	1	
Pakistan	Mortgage Loan	Commercial Banks	Tuition & Living		1974		
Sri Lanka	Mortgage Loan	Commercial Banks			1964		
Middle East, North Africa							
Egypt	Mortgage Loan	Autonomous Body				5	1980
		Commercial Banks				2	1980
Israel /a	Mortgage Loan	Commercial Banks	Tuition & Living			12	1983
Jordan	Mortgage Loan						
Morocco	Mortgage Loan	Commercial Banks	Tuition			<1	1990
Sub-Saharan Africa							
Ghana	Income Contingent	Government Dept.	Living	$200	1989	68	1990
Kenya	Mortgage Loan	Commercial Banks	Living	$845	1973	100	1990
Nigeria /a	Mortgage Loan	Autonomous Body	Living				
Rwanda							
Burundi /a							
Malawi	Mortgage Loan		Living	$80	1988	50	1989
Tanzania /a	Mortgage Loan		Living				

(cont'd)

Country (Loan Organization)	Repayment Mechanism	Administering Institution	Purpose of Support	Average Loan Value	Year Begun	% of Students with Loans	Data Year
Industrial Countries							
Australia	Income Contingent	Government Dept.	Tuition	$1,750	1989	81	1990
Canada (Quebec)	Mortgage Loan	Commercial Banks	Tuition & Living	$2,800	1963	59	1990
Denmark	Mortgage Loan	Commercial Banks	Living	$3,700	1975		1985
Finland	Mortgage Loan		Living	$2,200	1986		1987
France	Mortgage Loan	Government Dept.	Living			1	
Germany	Mortgage Loan		Living	$1,500	1974	30	1987
Hong Kong	Mortgage Loan	Government Dept.	Tuition & Living	$1,050	1969	26	1989
Netherlands	Mortgage Loan		Living	$200			1989
Norway	Mortgage Loan	Autonomous Body	Living	$4,000		80	1986
Japan	Mortgage Loan	Autonomous Body	Tuition & Living	$2,500		19	1987
Singapore	Mortgage Loan	Government Dept. Commercial Banks	Tuition & Living			39	1990
Sweden	Income Contingent	Autonomous Body	Living	$5,828			
United Kingdom	Mortgage Loan	Autonomous Body	Living	$750	1990	7	1990
USA	Mortgage Loan	Commercial Banks	Tuition & Living	$2,176	1964	28	1987

/a Programs in Indonesia, Israel, Nigeria, Tanzania and Burundi have been abandoned.

Note: Blanks imply information was not available.

Source: Douglas Albrecht and Adrian Ziderman, "Deferred Cost Recovery for Higher Education: Student Loan Programs in Developing Countries." World Bank Discussion Paper No. 137, 1991.

ANNEX 30B: CHECKLIST OF POLICY OPTIONS FOR DEFERRED COST RECOVERY

Structure/Policy		Options	Description
Lending Institution	a.	Autonomous Public Body	The most common institutional structure is to create a publicly administered and financed loan organization to distribute and collect loans.
	b.	Public Banks	Another common institutional structure utilities publicly owned commercial banks to administer loans.
	c.	Private Commercial Banks	In countries with more developed banking systems private banks may be used to allocate loans (US, Indonesia, Denmark).
	d.	Higher Education Institutions	Governments may transfer funds to higher education institutions for the purpose of administering loans (China, Chile).
	e.	Directly from Government Accounts	Money is disbursed directly from government ministries or trust fund, and collected by treasury (Australia, Ghana).
Repayment Mechanism	a.	Mortgage Type Loan	The most common approach by which the capitalized loan is broken into equal monthly payments.
	b.	Income Contingent Loan	Payments are a fixed portion of monthly or annual income, thus putting a limit on the debt burden to a graduate (Sweden).
	c.	Graduated Payments	Payments fixed in advance, but increase with time.
	d.	Income Contingent Loan (Tax)	Same as 'b' except payment may be collected through the taxation system (Australia).
	e.	Deferral of Social Benefits	Repayment is through an already existing payroll tax in which pension benefits do not begin to accrue until the loan is repaid (Ghana).
	f.	Graduate Tax/Equity Finance	Students contribute through a lifetime increase in their tax contribution. (Offered briefly at Yale University, proposed in US and UK).
	g.	Employer Contribution Through Tax or Loan	In countries where graduates are scarce, employers contribute to loan or tax repayments as a form of "scarcity" tax. Loan repayments are shared between employers and employees in Ghana and China.
	h.	National Service	Repayment through labor that is socially valuable to and in demand by the society.
Targeting	a.	Means Testing	Selection of credit recipients on the basis of family or individual (Sweden, Norway) income. Or more complex socioeconomic status indicators (Chile).
	b.	Ability Criteria	Selection of students on the basis of performance at secondary school, on national exams or within universities (Indonesia).
	c.	Priority Areas	Priority support for students who study in fields of national manpower priority—e.g. engineering, teacher training, health (Colombia, Barbados).
	d.	Restricted Length	Limitation on availability of funds to a fixed period of study—as the official duration of a given course (Brazil, Denmark).
Interest Rates & Subsidies	a.	Fixed Real or Floating	Interest rates can be fixed in relation to inflation at either negative, zero percent or positive real rates, or they can float at an index of commercial rates.

(cont'd)

Structure/Policy		Options	Description
	b.	Differential Interest Rates	Students charged different rates of interest based on their economic situation, thus targeting more subsidized support to need (US, Japan).
	c.	Repayment Length	The length of the repayment period can be varied to achieve a balance between debt burden and financial efficiency.
	d.	Graduated Annuities	Payments can be calculated so they are smaller in the first years and larger later on.
	e.	Upfront Discount on Tuition	Allow students who are eligible for a subsidized loan to have their fees reduced by a fixed percentage if they forego the loan (Australia, Israel).
Default Minimization	a.	Grace Period	Allow students a specified time after graduation before repayment begins, with the assumption that they need time to find employment.
	b.	Income Threshold	Allow graduates to defer payment during any time in which their income falls below a specified level (Sweden, Kenya, UK).
	c.	Incentives for Financial Agent	Where the government is the guarantor on the loans, the government discounts the value of that guarantee sufficiently so that institutions prefer to collect from the student.
	d.	Require Guarantor	Requiring an income earning cosigner on a loan who agrees to pay in the event that the graduate does not (Ghana, Barbados, Brazil).
	e.	Payroll Deductions	Requiring employees to withhold a portion of salary of graduates for the purpose of payment the loan (Jamaica).
	f.	Income Tax to Locate Defaulters	Governments to locate individuals that might be in default, through taxation institutions (Canada).
	g.	Moral Pressure	Publish lists of defaulters (Jamaica).
	h.	Required Insurance	Require student to pay an up-front fee to insure against losses that result from death or debilitating illness or accidents (Brazil).
	i.	Bar Further Credit	Bar access to further credit if in default (Brazil).
	j.	Collection Agencies	Utilize private collection agencies to locate students and secure payment (Honduras, Colombia).

Source: Douglas Albrecht and Adrian Ziderman, "Deferred Cost Recovery for Higher Education: Student Loan Programs in Developing Countries," World Bank Discussion Paper No. 137, 1991.

ANNEX 30C: HIDDEN SUBSIDIES AND GOVERNMENT LOSSES ON SELECTED STUDENT LOAN PROGRAMS

Country	Nominal Interest Rate (%)	Real Interest Rate (%)	Maximum or Projected Repayment Period	Hidden Grant to Students Percent of Loan (%)	Govt. Loss with Default (%)	Govt. Loss with Default & Adminis- trative (%)	Year	Estimates
(1)	(2)	(3)	(4)	(5)	(6)	(7)	(8)	
MORTGAGE LOANS								
Colombia I	11.0 a	-10.6	8	73	76 c	87	1978	Administrative 2%
Colombia II	24.0	3.0 b	5	29	38 c	47	1985	Administrative 2%
Sweden	4.3	-3.0	20	61	62	70	1988	Administrative 1%
Indonesia	6.0	-2.3 b	10	57	61	71	1985	Default 10%, Admin. 2%
USA (GSL)	8.0 a	3.8 b	10	29	41	53	1986	Administrative 2%
Hong Kong	0.0	-6.3	5	43	43	47	1985	Administrative 2%
UK	6.0	0.0	7	26	30	41	1989	Default 5%, Admin. 1%
Norway	11.5 a	5.6	20	33	33	48	1986	Administrative 1%
Denmark	8.0 a	1.6	10	52	56	62	1986	Administrative 1%
Finland	6.5 a	-0.6	10	45	46	52	1986	Default 2%, Admin. 1%
Brazil I	15.0	-35.0 b	5	91	94	98	1983	Default 30%, Admin. 2%
Brazil II	318.0	-14.9	8	62	65	71	1989	Default 10%, Admin. 2%
Jamaica I	6.0	-10.7	9	74	84 c	92	1987	Administrative 2%
Jamaica II	12.0	-5.6	9	56	62 c	70	1988	Default 20%, Admin. 2%
Barbados	8.0	4.1	12	13	18	33	1988	Default 5%, Admin. 2%
Kenya	2.0	-6.9	10	70	94 c	103	1989	Administrative 2%
Quebec	10.0 a	5.2	10	31	31	37	1989	Administrative 1%
Chile	varies	1.0 b	10	48	69 c	82	1989	Administrative 2%
Japan	0.0	-1.4	20	50	51	60	1987	Administrative 1%
Venezuela	4.0	-23	20	93	98	108	1991	Administrative 3%
Honduras	12.0	3	8	51	53	73	1991	Administrative 5%
INCOME CONTINGENT LOANS								
Australia	varies	0.0	17	48	52	57	1990	Evasion 3%, Admin. 0.5%
Sweden	varies	1.0	10	28	30	33	1990	Evasion 3%, Admin. 0.5%

General Notes: All subsidy calculations use a real opportunity cost of capital according to the government rate of borrowing or estimates used by the World Bank. Loans are assumed to be paid in equal installments over a four-year period, adjusted in size each year to keep up with inflation. Given the availability of relevant data, Swedish income contingent calculation is based on Australia's age earning profile information.

(1) Countries with I and II refer to situations where the loan program underwent reform.
(2) Nominal interest rate refers only to the rate during repayment. 'a' refers to loans that use a different rate during the disbursement and grace period. 'b' denotes those programs with interest rates which are indexed.
(3) Real interest rates use Purchasing Power Parity formula, where inflation is based on the average of the 1980-88 period as reported in the World Development Report, except in instances noted where a five-year average of inflation was calculated from the data date.
(4) The payment length is the maximum prescribed in the loan, except for the two income contingent loans where it is the repayment length that is implied by the average income profile of a graduate. This does *not* include grace periods.
(5) The hidden grant percentage is calculated as a discounted cash flow of the student's account, and therefore excludes default and administrative costs.
(6) The government loss due to default subtracts the percent of default from each year of the repayment stream. 'c' denotes where these figures have been estimated. For Colombia, Jamaica, Chile and Kenya the figure used is loans in arrears.
(7) The loss with default and administrative costs subtracts an annual administrative cost related to outstanding debt each year.
(8) Year is date from which loan information was collected, and from which inflation calculations were made.

Source: Douglas Albrecht and Adrian Ziderman, "Deferred Cost Recovery for Higher Education: Student Loan Programs in Developing Countries," World Bank Discussion Paper No. 137, 1991.

METHODOLOGICAL NOTE FOR CALCULATING SUBSIDIES ON MORTGAGE LOAN PROGRAMS

1. Students receive equal real value loans over a four-year disbursement period in lump sums at the beginning of each year.

2. Administrative costs are spread out evenly during the life of the loan.

3. Default is the frequency of loans that fail to repay. It is expressed as a probability for each year of repayment.

4. Grace periods have been rounded to the nearest year.

5. Repayments are in equal nominal amounts in yearly installments, at the beginning of each payment period.

6. Inflation is constant throughout the life of the loan.

7. Defaulted loans carry an administrative cost equal to good loans.

(1)   Calculating the Student Subsidy

PV = present value
D   = disbursement value
i   = initial interest rate (during lending period)
I   = Interest rate during repayment period
g   = grace period in years
n   = repayment length
r   = opportunity cost of capital, from time of lending onward
L   = disbursement length

Amortization value $= A = D\sum_{l=1}^{l=L}(1+i)^{g+(l-1)}$

The annual payment $= P = \dfrac{A*I}{1-(1+i)-n}$

The cash flow is as follows:

4 years of loan disbursements of equal real values (adjusted for inflation each year)
0 during the period of grace, and
P during the repayment length (n)

$$\text{PV disbursement} = \sum_{l=1}^{l=L} \frac{Dl}{(1+r)^{l-1}}$$

$$\text{PV repayments} = \underset{-}{P} \sum_{n=1}^{n=N} \frac{1}{(1+r)^{g+L-1+n}}$$

$ Subsidy to student = PV_{disb} - PV_{repay}

% Subsidy to student = $(PV_{disb} - PV_{repay})/PV_{disb}$

(2) Calculating loss with default

The calculations are the same, except that payment amounts are reduced to include the probability that they are not made. Thus, the cash stream uses the following repayments:

$P_{def} = P*(1-d)$ where d is the probability of default.

Thus, the cash stream is only adjusted during the years of repayment.

(3) Calculating the total loss to the government

Each year of each stream is adjusted to reflect the cost of administering the loans. This is calculated by using the annual percent cost of servicing outstanding debt.

od = outstanding debt on loan
ac = administrative cost of servicing loan, as percent of outstanding debt each year
t = year in the loan life
cf = previous cash flow, including deductions for likelihood of default
CF = adjustment cash flow, including deductions for both default and administrative costs

Thus, in each year the cash flow is adjusted:

$CF_t = cf_t - (od_t * ac)$

and the PV and subsidies are calculated as in section 1.

Source: Douglas Albrecht and Adrian Ziderman, "Deferred Cost Recovery for Higher Education: Study Loan Programs in Developing Countries." World Bank Discussion Paper No. 137, 1991.

REFERENCES

Albrecht, Douglas & Ziderman, Adrian (1991). *Deferred Cost Recovery for Higher Education: Student Loan Programs in Development Countries*. World Bank Discussion Paper 137. Washington, DC.

————— (1992). *Funding Mechanisms for Higher Education: Financing for Stability, Efficiency, and Responsiveness*. World Bank Discussion Paper 153. Washington, DC.

Altbach, Philip (1979). *The Academic Profession: Perceptions on an International Crisis*. Occasional Papers Series, Buffalo, New York: State University of New York at Buffalo.

Bai, Zhou (1993). "A Survey Concerning the Contemporary Situation of the Faculty Contingent in Higher Education Institutions." *China's Higher Education*, No. 12, pp. 21-22.

Becher, Tony (1990). *Academic Tribes and Territories: Intellectual Inquiry and the Culture of Disciplines*. Milton Keynes: The Society for Research into Higher Education and the Open University Press.

Beijing Normal University (1994). "On the Situation of Scholars Studying Abroad and Their Intention of Returning to China." *Educational Research*, May.

Birdsall, Nancy (1995). "Public Spending on Higher Education in Developing Countries: Too Much or Too Little?" (mimeograph). Washington, DC: World Bank.

Blackburn, McKinley L. (1990). "What can Explain the Increase in Earnings Inequality Among Males." *Industrial Relations*, Vol. 29, No. 3, pp. 441-456.

—————, David E. Bloom, and Richard Freeman (1990). "The Declining Economic Position of Less Skilled American Men." In Gary Burtless, ed. *A Future of Lousy Jobs?* Washington, DC: The Brookings Institution, pp. 31-76.

—————, David E. Bloom, and Richard Freeman (1991). "Changes in Earnings Differentials in the 1980s: Concordance, Convergence, Causes, and Consequences." National Bureau of Economic Research Working Paper Series, No. 3901, Cambridge, MA.

Bound, John, and Richard Freeman (1992). "What Went Wrong? The Erosion of Relative Earnings and Employment Among Young Black Men in the 1980s." *Quarterly Journal of Economics*, Vol. 107, No. 426, pp. 201-232.

Cao, Xiaonan (1996). "The Strategic Role of Faculty Development and Management During the Reform of Higher Education in China." Paper presented at the Annual Conference of the Comparative and International Education Society, March 6–10, Williamsburg, VA.

Chen, Liankun (1994). "An Analysis on the Current Situation and Future Scenarios of Higher Education Funding Sources." *Jiaoyu Yanjiu* (*Educational Research*), April, Beijing, China.

Cheng, Kai Ming (1987). *The Concept of Legitimacy in Educational Policy Making: Alternative Explanations of Two Policy Episodes in Hong Kong.* Doctorate thesis, University of London Institute of Education.

Chung Yue-Ping (1990). "Changes of Rates of Return to Education Over Time: The Case Study of Hong Kong." Paper presented in the 1990 Annual Conference of the Comparative and International Education Society, March 22–25, Anaheim, CA.

————— (1991). "An Economic Evaluation of Overseas University Education from the Perspective of the Sending Country" (mimeograph).

—————, and Richard Yue-chim Wong (Ed.) (1992). *The Economics and Financing of Hong Kong Education.* Hong Kong: The Chinese University Press.

Clark, Burton (1987). *The Academic Life: Small Worlds, Different Worlds.* Princeton, NJ: The Carnegie Foundation for the Advancement of Teaching.

Coward, H. Roberts (1994). *Bibliometric Indicators of Research Activity and Infrastructure*, p. 18 & 22.

—————, and Fresne, Ronald R. (1992). *A Bibliometric-Based Assessment of Research Activity in the People's Republic of China.*

————— (1990). *Research Activity in the Pacific Rim Nations: Survey of a 1988 Bibliometric Database.* p. 4.

CPC (Communist Party of China) Central Committee (1985). *Decision on Education Reform.* Beijing, China: Foreign Languages Press.

CPC Central Committee and State Council of China (1993). *Program for Reform and Development of Chinese Education.* Beijing, China.

Davis, S. J. (1992). "Cross-Country Patterns of Change in Relative Wages." *National Bureau of Economic Research Macroeconomics Annual.* Cambridge, MA: The MIT Press.

Department of Education of the Republic of China (1993). *Education Statistics of the Republic of China.* Taipei: Department of Education.

Editorial Board of China Education Yearbook (1984). *China Education Yearbook (1949-81).* Beijing, China: China Encyclopedia Publishing House.

————— (1985). *China Education Yearbook (1982-84).* Beijing, China: People's Education Press.

————— (1988). *China Education Yearbook (1985-86).* Beijing, China: People's Education Press.

————— (1990). *China Education Yearbook.* Beijing, China: People's Education Press.

————— (1993). *China Education Yearbook.* Beijing, China: People' Education Press.

FBIS, No. 191, October 2, 1991.

Fields, Gary S. (1984). "Employment, Income Distribution and Economic Growth in Seven Small Open Economies." *The Economic Journal.* Vol. 94, pp. 74-83.

_____ (1994). "Changing Labor Market Conditions and Economic Development in Hong Kong, the Republic of Korea, Singapore, and Taiwan, China." *The World Bank Economic Review.* Vol. 8, No. 3, pp. 395-414.

Fwu, Bih-jen (1993). *Long-term Changes in Rates of Return to Education, Occupational Attainment, and Married Female Labor Force Participation: A Case Study of Taiwan (1976-1990).* Doctorate Dissertation, University of California, Los Angeles.

_____ (1982). *A Perspective on Education in Hong Kong: Report by a Visiting Panel.*

Guo, Fei (1993). "On Salaries of University Teachers." *China's Education Daily*, July 7.

Hao, K. & and Zhang, L. (1987). "On the Reform in the Structure of Chinese Higher Education." *Jiaoyu Yanjiu (Educational Research)*, December, Beijing, China.

Hao, K. & Wang, Y. (1987). *Research on the Structure of Chinese Higher Education.* Beijing, China: People's Education Press.

Hao, Keming (1993). "A Significant Outline for Education Development in China." *Jiaoyu Yanjiu (Educational Research)*, May, Beijing, China.

Hayhoe, Ruth (1996). *China's Universities—1895-1995: A Century of Cultural Conflict.* New York: Garland Publishing, Inc.

He, Jin (1994). "The Dean's Dilemma." Mission Note. Washington, DC: World Bank.

_____ (1994). "Student Views on Curriculum Reform." Mission Note. Washington, DC: World Bank.

He, Xiaoxin et al. (1995). "Investigation and Analysis into the Changing Psychology of Teachers in University." *Nanjing Academic Journal*, no. 1.

Hu, Zhongtao (1994). "Ideas and Policies for Strengthening the Building of a Contingent of Young Faculty." *Beijing Normal University Academic Journal*, March.

International Advisory Panel, Chinese Review Committee (1991). *Evaluation Report, Chinese University Development Project II (CUDP II).* Washington, DC: World Bank.

Jiangsu Education Accounting Association (1989). *Papers on Financial Reform in Education.* Nanjing, China.

Jiao, J. (1988). "Establishing a New Mechanism for Resolving the Problems of Education Funds in China." *Zhongguo Jiaoyu Bao (China Education Daily)*, August 18, Beijing, China.

Johnston, Todd (1991). "Wages, Benefits and the Promotion Process for Chinese University Faculty." *China Quarterly*, No. 125, March, pp. 137-155.

Katz, Lawrence F., and Murphy, Kevin M. (1992). "Changes in Relative Wages, 1963-1987: Supply and Demand Factors." *Quarterly Journal of Economic Review.* Vol. 107, No. 426, pp. 35-78.

Kim, Gwang-Jo (1994). "The Relationship between Education Expansion and Wage Differentials in Korea Between 1980 and 1990." Dissertation, Harvard University, Cambridge, MA.

Kim, Jong-Li, and Lawrence Lau (1995). "The Role of Human Capital in the Economic Growth of the East Asian Newly Industrialized Countries." *Asia-Pacific Economic Review*, Vol. 1, No. 3, December.

Knight, John B., and Richard H. Sabot (1990). *Education, Productivity, and Inequality: The East African Natural Experiment.* New York: Oxford Press.

Kong, Fanbai (1988). *Issues in Financial Reform of Higher Education Institutions.* Shenyang, China: Liaoning University Press.

Kristof, Kathy M. (1996). "Grads Should do Homework Before Picking Loan-Payback Plan." *Los Angeles Times*, June 16.

Krugman, Paul (1994). "The Myth of Asia's Miracle." *Foreign Affairs*, November/December.

Levy, Frank, and Richard Murnane (1992). "U.S. Earnings Level and Earnings Inequality: A Review of Recent Trends and Proposed Explanation." *Journal of Economic Literature.* Vol. 30, September, pp. 1333-13381.

Luo, L. (1990). "University Faculty Salaries: Current Situation, Causes and Impact, and Strategies." *Journal of Higher Education,* March. Wuhan, China.

Mansfield, Edwin (1994). *Economic Returns from Investments in Research and Training.* Washington, DC: World Bank.

Mervis, Jeffrey (1995). "The Long March to Topnotch Science." *Science*, Vol. 270, November.

Min, W. (1990). "Chinese Higher Education: Mode of Expansion and Economies of Scale." *Jiaoyu Yanjiu (Educational Research)*, October. Beijing, China.

Mincer, Jacob (1974). *Schooling, Experience, and Earnings.* New York: Colombia University Press.

_____ (1989). "Human Capital and the Labor Market: A Review of Current Research." *Educational Researcher.* pp. 27-34.

_____ (1991). "Human Capital, Technology, and the Wage Structure: What Do Time Series Show?" Cambridge, MA: National Bureau of Economic Research, Working Paper 3581.

Ministry of Education of China (1984). *Achievement of Education in China (1949-83).* Beijing, China: People's Education Press.

Ministry of Education of the Republic of Korea (1991-94). *Educational Indicators in Korea.* Seoul: Ministry of Education.

_____ (1994). *Statistical Yearbook of Education.* Seoul: Ministry of Education.

Mukherjee, Hena, and Jasbir Sarjit Singh (1993). *Staff Development Approaches in Higher Education: Learning from Experience.* World Bank Commissioned Study, Commonwealth Secretariat: London, U.K.

OECD (Organization for Economic Cooperation and Development) (1993). *Employee Outlooks.* Paris: OECD.

_____ (1995). *Education at a Glance: OECD Indicators.* Paris: OECD.

Office of the Academic Degrees Committee of the State Council (1990). *Directory of Disciplines and Specialties for Doctor's, Master's and Graduate Students.* Beijing, China.

Orleans, Leo A. (1988). *Chinese Students in America: Policies, Issues and Numbers.* Washington, DC: National Academy Press.

Paik, Sung-Joon (1995). *Educational Finance in Korea.* Seoul: Korean Educational Development Institute.

Psacharopoulos, George (1973). *Returns to Education: An International Comparison.* San Francisco: Jossey-Bass.

_____ (1981). "Returns to Education: An Updated International Comparison." *Comparative Education.* Vol. 17, No. 3.

_____ (1985). "Returns to Education: A Further International Update and Implications." *Journal of Human Resources.* Vol. 20, No. 4.

_____, Jee-Peng Tan, and Emmanuel Jimenez (1986). *Financing Education in Developing Countries: An Exploration of Policy Options.* Washington, DC: World Bank.

_____ (1993). "Returns to Investment in Education: A Global Update." Policy Research Working Paper 1067, Washington, DC: World Bank.

_____, and Maureen Woodhall (1985). *Education for Development: An Analysis for Investment Choice.* Washington, DC: World Bank.

Sappington, David E. M. (1994). *Principles of Regulatory Policy Design.* Background paper for the World Bank's *World Development Report.*

Schultz, Theodore W. (1961). "Investment in Human Capital." *American Economic Review.* Vol. 51, No. 1, pp. 1-17.

_____ (1971), *Investment in Human Capital: The Role of Education and of Research.* New York: The Free Press.

_____ (1975). "The Value of the Ability to Deal with Disequilibria." *Journal of Economic Literature.* Vol. 13, pp. 827-846.

_____ (1981). *Investing in People.* Berkeley, CA: University of California Press.

Science, Special Issue, November 1995.

Spenner, Kenneth (1985). "Upgrading and Downgrading of Occupations: Issues, Evidence, and Implications for Education." *Review of Educational Research.* Vol. 55, No. 2, pp. 125-154.

_____ (1988). "Technological Change, Skill Requirements, and Education: The Case for Uncertainty." In R. Cyert and D. Mowery, eds. *The Impact of Technological Change on Employment and Economic Growth.* Cambridge, MA: Ballinger Publishing Company.

State Education Commission of China (1988). *Education Finance and Teachers' Salaries.* Beijing, China: Educational Science Press.

——————— (1989). *The Development and Reform of Education in China, 1986-88.* Beijing, China.

——————— (1993). *Educational Statistics Yearbook of China for 1992.* Beijing, China: People's Education Press.

——————— (1991). *Education Statistics Yearbook of China, 1990.* Beijing, China: People's Education Press.

State Statistical Bureau of China (1993). *Statistical Yearbook of China 1993.* Beijing, China: China Statistical Publishing House.

——————— (1994). *Statistical Yearbook of China 1994.* Beijing, China: China Statistical Publishing House.

——————— (1995). *Statistical Yearbook of China 1995.* Beijing, China: China Statistical Publishing House.

Statistical Bureau of the Republic of China (1993). *Taiwan Statistical Data Book.* Taipei: Statistical Bureau.

Tan, Jee-Peng & Alain Mingat (1989). *Education Development in Asia: A Comparative Analysis on Cost and Financial Issues.* Washington, DC: World Bank.

——————— (1992). *Education in Asia: A Comparative Study of Cost and Financing.* Washington, DC: World Bank.

UNESCO (United Nations Educational, Scientific, and Cultural Organization) (1995). *Statistical Yearbook.* Paris: UNESCO.

——————— (1993). *World Education Report.* Paris: UNESCO.

UNDP (United Nations Development Programme). (Various Years). *Human Development Report.* New York: UNDP.

United States National Science Foundation (1993). *Human Resources for Science and Technology: the Asia Region.* Washington, DC: National Science Foundation.

——————— (1996). *Science and Engineering Indicators 1996.* Washington, DC: National Science Foundation.

Van Vucht, Frans A. (1991). *Autonomy and Accountability in Government/University Relationships.* Paper prepared for the World Bank seminar in Kuala Lumpur, Malaysia. June.

Wang, Shanmai (1988). *Education Investment and Financial Reform.* Beijing, China: Beijing Institute of Economics Press.

Welch, F. (1970). "Education in Production." *Journal of Political Economy.* Vol. 78, pp. 35-59.

World Bank (1985). *China: Issues and Prospects in Education.* Washington, DC: World Bank.

——————— (1985). *China: Long-Term Development Issues and Options.* Washington, DC: World Bank.

_____ (1986). *China: Management and Finance of Higher Education*. Washington, DC: World Bank.

_____ (1993). *The East Asian Miracle: Economic Growth and Public Policy*. New York: Oxford University Press.

_____ (1994). *China: Country Economic Memorandum*. Washington, DC: World Bank.

_____ (1994). *Higher Education: The Lessons of Experience*. Washington, DC: World Bank.

_____ (1994). *University Research for Graduate Education Project*. Washington, DC: World Bank.

_____ (1995a). *World Development Report 1995: Workers in an Integrating World.* New York: Oxford University Press.

_____ (1995b). *The Employment Crisis in Industrial Countries: Is International Integration to Blame?* Regional Perspectives on World Development Report 1995. Washington, DC: World Bank.

_____ (1995c). *Involving Workers in East Asian Growth.* Regional Perspectives on World Development Report 1995. Washington, DC: World Bank.

_____ (1995d). *Labor and Economic Reform in Latin America and the Caribbean.* Regional Perspectives on World Development Report 1995. Washington, DC: World Bank.

_____ (1995e). *China: Macroeconomic Stability in a Decentralized Economy.* A World Bank Country Study. Washington, DC: World Bank.

_____ (1995f). *Finance and Development.* A Quarterly Publication of the International Monetary Fund and the World Bank. Washington, DC: World Bank.

_____ (1995g). *Technology Development Project*. Washington, DC: World Bank.

_____ (1996). *The Chinese Economy: Fighting Inflation, Deepening Reform.* Washington, DC: World Bank.

Wu, Kin Bing (1995). *The Changing Worth of A University Education: A Case Study of Hong Kong During a Period of Rapid Economic and Social Change, 1976 to 1986.* Doctoral Dissertation, Harvard University.

Xinhua (*New China*), September 30, 1991.

Yuan, L. (1988). "The Shortage of Education Funds in China." *Jiaoyu Yanjiu* (*Educational Research*), July. Beijing, China.

Zhongguo Gaodeng Jiaoyu (*Chinese Higher Education*), No. 12, 1993.

Zhongguo Jiaoyu Bao (*China Education Daily*), February 3, 1990.

Distributors of World Bank Publications

Prices and credit terms vary from country to country. Consult your local distributor before placing an order.

ARGENTINA
Oficina del Libro Internacional
Av. Cordoba 1877
1120 Buenos Aires
Tel: (54 1) 815-8354
Fax: (54 1) 815-8156

AUSTRALIA, FIJI, PAPUA NEW GUINEA, SOLOMON ISLANDS, VANUATU, AND WESTERN SAMOA
D.A. Information Services
648 Whitehorse Road
Mitcham 3132
Victoria
Tel: (61) 3 9210 7777
Fax: (61) 3 9210 7788
E-mail: service@dadirect.com.au
URL: http://www.dadirect.com.au

AUSTRIA
Gerold and Co.
Weihburggasse 26
A-1011 Wien
Tel: (43 1) 512-47-31-0
Fax: (43 1) 512-47-31-29
URL: http://www.gerold.co/at.online

BANGLADESH
Micro Industries Development
Assistance Society (MIDAS)
House 5, Road 16
Dhanmondi R/Area
Dhaka 1209
Tel: (880 2) 326427
Fax: (880 2) 811188

BELGIUM
Jean De Lannoy
Av. du Roi 202
1060 Brussels
Tel: (32 2) 538-5169
Fax: (32 2) 538-0841

BRAZIL
Publicações Tecnicas Internacionais Ltda.
Rua Peixoto Gomide, 209
01409 Sao Paulo, SP.
Tel: (55 11) 259-6644
Fax: (55 11) 258-6990
E-mail: postmaster@pti.uol.br
URL: http://www.uol.br

CANADA
Renouf Publishing Co. Ltd.
5369 Canotek Road
Ottawa, Ontario K1J 9J3
Tel: (613) 745-2665
Fax: (613) 745-7660
E-mail: order.dept@renoufbooks.com
URL: http:// www.renoufbooks.com

CHINA
China Financial & Economic
Publishing House
8, Da Fo Si Dong Jie
Beijing
Tel: (86 10) 6333-8257
Fax: (86 10) 6401-7365

COLOMBIA
Infoenlace Ltda.
Carrera 6 No. 51-21
Apartado Aereo 34270
Santafé de Bogotá, D.C.
Tel: (57 1) 285-2798
Fax: (57 1) 285-2798

COTE D'IVOIRE
Center d'Edition et de Diffusion Africaines
(CEDA)
04 B.P. 541
Abidjan 04
Tel: (225) 24 6510;24 6511
Fax: (225) 25 0567

CYPRUS
Center for Applied Research
Cyprus College
6, Diogenes Street, Engomi
P.O. Box 2006
Nicosia
Tel: (357 2) 44-1730
Fax: (357 2) 46-2051

CZECH REPUBLIC
National Information Center
prodejna, Konviktska 5
CS – 113 57 Prague 1
Tel: (42 2) 2422-9433
Fax: (42 2) 2422-1484
URL: http://www.nis.cz/

DENMARK
SamfundsLitteratur
Rosenoerns Allé 11
DK-1970 Frederiksberg C
Tel: (45 31) 351942
Fax: (45 31) 357822

ECUADOR
Libri Mundi
Libreria Internacional
P.O. Box 17-01-3029
Juan Leon Mera 851
Quito
Tel: (593 2) 521-606; (593 2) 544-185
Fax: (593 2) 504-209
E-mail: librimu1@librimundi.com.ec
E-mail: librimu2@librimundi.com.ec

EGYPT, ARAB REPUBLIC OF
Al Ahram Distribution Agency
Al Galaa Street
Cairo
Tel: (20 2) 578-6083
Fax: (20 2) 578-6833

The Middle East Observer
41, Sherif Street
Cairo
Tel: (20 2) 393-9732
Fax: (20 2) 393-9732

FINLAND
Akateeminen Kirjakauppa
P.O. Box 128
FIN-00101 Helsinki
Tel: (358 0) 121 4418
Fax: (358 0) 121-4435
E-mail: akatilaus@stockmann.fi
URL: http://www.akateeminen.com/

FRANCE
World Bank Publications
66, avenue d'léna
75116 Paris
Tel: (33 1) 40-69-30-56/57
Fax: (33 1) 40-69-30-68

GERMANY
UNO-Verlag
Poppelsdorfer Allee 55
53115 Bonn
Tel: (49 228) 212940
Fax: (49 228) 217492

GREECE
Papasotiriou S.A.
35, Stournara Str.
106 82 Athens
Tel: (30 1) 364-1826
Fax: (30 1) 364-8254

HAITI
Culture Diffusion
5, Rue Capois
C.P. 257
Port-au-Prince
Tel: (509) 23 9260
Fax: (509) 23 4858

HONG KONG, MACAO
Asia 2000 Ltd.
Sales & Circulation Department
Seabird House, unit 1101-02
22-28 Wyndham Street, Central
Hong Kong
Tel: (852) 2530-1409
Fax: (852) 2526-1107
E-mail: sales@asia2000.com.hk
URL: http://www.asia2000.com.hk

HUNGARY
Euro Info Service
Margitszgeti Europa Haz
H-1138 Budapest
Tel: (36 1) 111 6061
Fax: (36 1) 302 5035
E-mail: euroinfo@mail.matav.hu

INDIA
Allied Publishers Ltd.
751 Mount Road
Madras - 600 002
Tel: (91 44) 852-3938
Fax: (91 44) 852-0649

INDONESIA
Pt. Indira Limited
Jalan Borobudur 20
P.O. Box 181
Jakarta 10320
Tel: (62 21) 390-4290
Fax: (62 21) 390-4289

IRAN
Ketab Sara Co. Publishers
Khaled Estamboli Ave., 6th Street
Delafrooz Alley No. 8
P.O. Box 15745-733
Tehran 15117
Tel: (98 21) 8717819; 8716104
Fax: (98 21) 8712479
E-mail: ketab-sara@neda.net.ir

Kowkab Publishers
P.O. Box 19575-511
Tehran
Tel: (98 21) 258-3723
Fax: (98 21) 258-3723

IRELAND
Government Supplies Agency
Oifig an tSoláthair
4-5 Harcourt Road
Dublin 2
Tel: (353 1) 661-3111
Fax: (353 1) 475-2670

ISRAEL
Yozmot Literature Ltd.
P.O. Box 56055
3 Yohanan Hasandlar Street
Tel Aviv 61560
Tel: (972 3) 5285-397
Fax: (972 3) 5285-397

R.O.Y. International
PO Box 13056
Tel Aviv 61130
Tel: (972 3) 5461423
Fax: (972 3) 5461442
E-mail: royil@netvision.net.il

Palestinian Authority/Middle East
Index Information Services
P.O.B. 19502 Jerusalem
Tel: (972 2) 6271219
Fax: (972 2) 6271634

ITALY
Licosa Commissionaria Sansoni SPA
Via Duca Di Calabria, 1/1
Casella Postale 552
50125 Firenze
Tel: (55) 645-415
Fax: (55) 641-257
E-mail: licosa@ftbcc.it
URL: http://www.ftbcc.it/licosa

JAMAICA
Ian Randle Publishers Ltd.
206 Old Hope Road, Kingston 6
Tel: 809-927-2085
Fax: 809-977-0243
E-mail: irpl@colis.com

JAPAN
Eastern Book Service
3-13 Hongo 3-chome, Bunkyo-ku
Tokyo 113
Tel: (81 3) 3818-0861
Fax: (81 3) 3818-0864
E-mail: orders@svt-ebs.co.jp
URL: http://www.bekkoame.or.jp/~svt-ebs

KENYA
Africa Book Service (E.A.) Ltd.
Quaran House, Mfangano Street
P.O. Box 45245
Nairobi
Tel: (254 2) 223 641
Fax: (254 2) 330 272

KOREA, REPUBLIC OF
Daejon Trading Co. Ltd.
P.O. Box 34, Youida, 706 Seoun Bldg
44-6 Youido-Dong, Yeongchengo-Ku
Seoul
Tel: (82 2) 785-1631/4
Fax: (82 2) 784-0315

MALAYSIA
University of Malaya Cooperative
Bookshop, Limited
P.O. Box 1127
Jalan Pantai Baru
59700 Kuala Lumpur
Tel: (60 3) 756-5000
Fax: (60 3) 755-4424

MEXICO
INFOTEC
Av. San Fernando No. 37
Col. Toriello Guerra
14050 Mexico, D.F.
Tel: (52 5) 624-2800
Fax: (52 5) 624-2822
E-mail: infotec@rtn.net.mx
URL: http://rtn.net.mx

NEPAL
Everest Media International Services (P) Ltd.
GPO Box 5443
Kathmandu
Tel: (977 1) 472 152
Fax: (977 1) 224 431

NETHERLANDS
De Lindeboom/InOr-Publikaties
P.O. Box 202, 7480 AE Haaksbergen
Tel: (31 53) 574-0004
Fax: (31 53) 572-9296
E-mail: lindeboo@worldonline.nl
URL: http://www.worldonline.nl/~lindeboo

NEW ZEALAND
EBSCO NZ Ltd.
Private Mail Bag 99914
New Market
Auckland
Tel: (64 9) 524-8119
Fax: (64 9) 524-8067

NIGERIA
University Press Limited
Three Crowns Building Jericho
Private Mail Bag 5095
Ibadan
Tel: (234 22) 41-1356
Fax: (234 22) 41-2056

NORWAY
NIC Info A/S
Book Department, Postboks 6512 Etterstad
N-0606 Oslo
Tel: (47 22) 97-4500
Fax: (47 22) 97-4545

PAKISTAN
Mirza Book Agency
65, Shahrah-e-Quaid-e-Azam
Lahore 54000
Tel: (92 42) 735 3601
Fax: (92 42) 576 3714

Oxford University Press
5 Bangalore Town
Sharae Faisal
PO Box 13033
Karachi-75350
Tel: (92 21) 446307
Fax: (92 21) 4547640
E-mail: oup@oup.khi.erum.com.pk

Pak Book Corporation
Aziz Chambers 21, Queen's Road
Lahore
Tel: (92 42) 636 3222; 636 0885
Fax: (92 42) 636 2328
E-mail: pbc@brain.net.pk

PERU
Editorial Desarrollo SA
Apartado 3824, Lima 1
Tel: (51 14) 285380
Fax: (51 14) 286628

PHILIPPINES
International Booksource Center Inc.
1127-A Antipolo St. Barangay, Venezuela
Makati City
Tel: (63 2) 896 6501; 6505; 6507
Fax: (63 2) 896 1741

POLAND
International Publishing Service
Ul. Piekna 31/37
00-677 Warzawa
Tel: (48 2) 628-6089
Fax: (48 2) 621-7255
E-mail: books%ips@ikp.atm.com.pl
URL: http://www.ipscg.waw.pl/ips/export/

PORTUGAL
Livraria Portugal
Apartado 2681, Rua Do Carmo 70-74
1200 Lisbon
Tel: (1) 347-4982
Fax: (1) 347-0264

ROMANIA
Compani De Librari Bucuresti S.A.
Str. Lipscani no. 26, sector 3
Bucharest
Tel: (40 1) 613 9645
Fax: (40 1) 312 4000

RUSSIAN FEDERATION
Isdatelstvo <Ves Mir>
9a, Lolpachniy Pereulok
Moscow 101831
Tel: (7 095) 917 87 49
Fax: (7 095) 917 92 59

SINGAPORE, TAIWAN, MYANMAR, BRUNEI
Asahgate Publishing Asia Pacific Pte. Ltd.
41 Kallang Pudding Road #04-03
Golden Wheel Building
Singapore 349316
Tel: (65) 741-5166
Fax: (65) 742-9356
E-mail: ashgate@asianconnect.com

SLOVENIA
Gospodarski Vestnik Publishing Group
Dunajska cesta 5
1000 Ljubljana
Tel: (386 61) 133 83 47; 132 12 30
Fax: (386 61) 133 80 30
E-mail: repansekj@gvestnik.si

SOUTH AFRICA, BOTSWANA
International Subscription Service
P.O. Box 41095
Craighall
Johannesburg 2024
Tel: (27 11) 880-1448
Fax: (27 11) 880-6248
E-mail: iss@is.co.za

SPAIN
Mundi-Prensa Libros, S.A.
Castello 37
28001 Madrid
Tel: (34 1) 431-3399
Fax: (34 1) 575-3998
E-mail: libreria@mundiprensa.es
URL: http://www.mundiprensa.es/

Mundi-Prensa Barcelona
Consell de Cent, 391
08009 Barcelona
Tel: (34 3) 488-3492
Fax: (34 3) 487-7659
E-mail: barcelona@mundiprensa.es

SRI LANKA, THE MALDIVES
Lake House Bookshop
100, Sir Chittampalam Gardiner Mawatha
Colombo 2
Tel: (94 1) 32105
Fax: (94 1) 432104
E-mail: LHL@sri.lanka.net

SWEDEN
Wennergren-Williams AB
P.O. Box 1305
S-171 25 Solna
Tel: (46 8) 705-97-50
Fax: (46 8) 27-00-71
E-mail: mail@wwi.se

SWITZERLAND
Librairie Payot Service Institutionnel
Côtes-de-Montbenon 30
1002 Lausanne
Tel: (41 21) 341-3229
Fax: (41 21) 341-3235

ADECO Van Diermen EditionsTechniques
Ch. de Lacuez 41
CH1807 Blonay
Tel: (41 21) 943 2673
Fax: (41 21) 943 3605

TANZANIA
Oxford University Press
Maktaba Street, PO Box 5299
Dar es Salaam
Tel: (255 51) 29209
Fax: (255 51) 46822

THAILAND
Central Books Distribution
306 Silom Road
Bangkok 10500
Tel: (66 2) 235-5400
Fax: (66 2) 237-8321

TRINIDAD & TOBAGO, AND THE CARRIBBEAN
Systematics Studies Unit
9 Watts Street
Curepe
Trinidad, West Indies
Tel: (809) 662-5654
Fax: (809) 662-5654
E-mail: tobe@trinidad.net

UGANDA
Gustro Ltd.
PO Box 9997, Madhvani Building
Plot 16/4 Jinja Rd.
Kampala
Tel: (256 41) 254 763
Fax: (256 41) 251 468

UNITED KINGDOM
Microinfo Ltd.
P.O. Box 3, Alton, Hampshire GU34 2PG
England
Tel: (44 1420) 86848
Fax: (44 1420) 89889
E-mail: wbank@ukinfo.demon.co.uk
URL: http://www.microinfo.co.uk

VENEZUELA
Tecni-Ciencia Libros, S.A.
Centro Cuidad Comercial Tamanco
Nivel C2, Caracas
Tel: (58 2) 959 5547; 5035; 0016
Fax: (58 2) 959 5636

ZAMBIA
University Bookshop, University of Zambia
Great East Road Campus
P.O. Box 32379
Lusaka
Tel: (260 1) 252 576
Fax: (260 1) 253 952

ZIMBABWE
Longman Zimbabwe (Pvt.)Ltd.
Tourle Road, Ardbennie
P.O. Box ST125
Southerton
Harare
Tel: (263 4) 6216617
Fax: (263 4) 621670

06/1997